MODERN MONEY

The Ultimate Monetary System
or
The Ultimate System for Theft by Deception

Modern money is not this:

It's just this: $100

Electronic numbers

Modern money does not represent wealth.
it represents debt owed to the banking system

The interest on these debts has taken the great wealth produced by the working people and placed into the hands of the few people who control the banking system.

This book explains how our banking system is taking this once very productive nation into bankruptcy.

DEDICATION

This book is dedicated to my wife Judie in appreciation of both the good and the rough years that we have shared together. For her patience and understanding as she stood in the gaps as I began to understand that things were not as they seemed or as they should be. Then as I spent many years trying to get people to understand and except the truth about how our money system really functions.

To my sons Brad and Cory who from the time they could walk were the best 'business partners' and friends a man could have. They completely ran our ranch when the desire for answers became so overwhelming. This enabled me to have the time to study all the material that I found on the subject of money, rights and liberty. The hardest part of all was to separate the wheat from the chaff because of all the conflicting & false information that abounds.

To my grandchildren who hopefully will be able to live a much better life in a much better country.

To all the people who are able and willing to think clearly and not just follow blindly along.

To all the people who share my vision for a better nation and are willing to do something that will truly make a difference.

ACKNOWLEDGEMENT

This book has been a struggle to write because being a writer is not where my talent lies. This book would not exist except for the kindness of the people who stepped forth and unselfishly volunteered there time to assist me in putting my thoughts and research down on paper.

Thank you to my brother Lloyd who was the first one to suggest that I set my thoughts and research down on paper.

Thanks to my co-author Gregory K. Soderberg who was the first person to step forth and ask if I could use some help and then freely gave his help over the years.

Thank you to Leon Voit for all the time he put into creating the flow charts that were used to explain the money flows, for all the time and energy and for all the other things he has done to assist me.

Thanks go to Thomas Hedin although he did not help on the book he has done lots of work into creating the Byron Dale Channel on you tube

Thank you, Dr. Tami Andrews, Doctor of Chiropractic. Through the use of Spinal Decompression treatments Dr. Andrews successfully restored to me the use of my legs after I began to slowly lose their use due to a back injury. When Dr. Andrews learned I was working on a book she volunteered hours of her time to help direct the flow of the book.

Thanks go to my next door neighbor Jenny Nilsson, a freelance Instructional Designer, when learning of my effort to write a book volunteered her time to proof read my work.

CONTENTS

Published by Northern Lights Publishing Company
7007 Lynmar Lane, Edina, MN 55435

INTRODUCTION

The American Dream

America has always been a nation where people came looking for a better life. They have flooded to America believing that it is here, above all places, that through hard work, thrift, courage, determination and a few good ideas they could experience the thrill of self-accomplishment, freedom and the pride of owning their own property.

America was to be the county where you could own your own home, you could own your own vehicle, be free of debt and other unwanted obligations. A country where you could have the right to live, to work, earn and maintain a reasonable standard of living (with enough leisure time to fully enjoy life) doing work that you enjoy. A country where you can raise your family to become productive members of society, where children could build upon their parent's experiences, progress and achievements, and life would become richer and fuller for every person according to their own ability.

At first glance, it looks like we have achieved the American dream. In the 17th and 18th centuries North America was basically a raw empty land with few people, mostly hunters and gatherers, living off the land. Then people from many nations, mostly Europeans, began immigrating to America to escape poor living conditions in Europe, due to the wars and corruption of the kings and the landed elite. (The lords and friends of the kings who controlled most of the land)

These people saw America as a land full of natural resources free for the taking. (Totally, disregarding the rights of the people that were already living here, but that is a story for a different time.) As more people came, they moved westward across the continent. As these people from many different nations and different cultures came together, they were exposed to different ideas.

This exposure to different ideas led to many more new ideas. In this new land they were for the most part free to apply their new ideas. By combining their

ideas and physical labors with nature's raw resources and natural reproduction processes, the descendants of these people created unbelievable amounts of goods and services to enhance mankind's material standard of living.
Look around. You will see the millions of homes, skyscrapers, automobiles, airplanes, factories, trucks, agricultural products, and power equipment of every kind and description that working people have produced.

As the result of this productivity, we have millions of people, *at least on the surface*, living the American dream. They are driving nice cars and living in attractive homes filled with every gadget imaginable. Every day huge tonnages of goods flow through commerce. **All these goods were produced as wealth** by applying man's physical and mental labor to earth's raw resources.

Up until the last 30 years, Americans working in America produced most of the things Americans used. Most of these commercial goods are now manufactured by the Chinese living in China while illegal immigrants hold millions of our domestic jobs. We need to start thinking about why, as a nation, we are exporting jobs and importing people.

The American Nightmare

The American dream has turned into
The American nightmare for millions of Americans.

Most people's greatest nightmare would be to wake up in the morning to witness the stock market falling through the floor, their investments quickly becoming worthless and to discover that they are losing every thing that they had worked years to acquire, their savings, pension and maybe their business. Or, they go to work one day to learn that they have just lost their job and their income. This can cause them to lose their home, their car and many times even their pets. The only things they have left are the friendly banker and the banker's lawyer; only to find out that they are no longer friendly?

These things don't have to happen at the same time to change the American dream into the American nightmare. When people carry as much debt as most Americans do, any one of these things can trigger the slide into foreclosure. Failure to make a couple of payments on a debt often causes the creditor to raise its interest rates or tighten its credit line. As word spreads that a person's credit rating is falling, it often prompts other businesses to close their credit line to that person and start demanding payment up front. This forces more missed payments, and soon a foreclosure action commences.

The impact of foreclosure often starts a cascading series of mental and emotional stresses that destroy most people's lives in ways that are largely invisible to people around them. These emotional losses can be as great as the economic losses.

The experience of struggling under financial stress or going through a foreclosure creates tension and feelings of fear and uncertainty between husband and wife that spills over into the lives of the children. The depression that many people suffer after the loss of a job or a foreclosure often saps their energy to the point where it is hard for them to get or keep a job.

Unless your head is jammed deeply in the sand, you know that the majority of Americans have seen their standard of living decline during the last 25 years. Wages for most of the population have stagnated or fallen. The cost of going to college has become a huge financial burden and for many a monetary debt so large that it would have been unbelievable a few years ago. After they have gone far into debt to get a college degree, they often find the high paying jobs they were expecting no longer exist.

In America today, working people spend more time worrying about holding on to what they have than they do dreaming about their future. Anyone who reads a paper or listens to the news have seen the statistics showing the growing numbers of mortgage delinquencies nationwide and the country's growing financial crisis. The numbers are frightening.

In 1979, employees working in factories numbered around 20 million. Today the number is near 15 million. One of the first things factory workers who lost their jobs learned is that they couldn't find a new job that pays as well as the one they lost. (A commonly shared fact among people who have lost their jobs, to downsizing, mergers and off shoring.)

Only in America do we export high paying jobs by the millions and import lower paid legal and illegal emigrant workers by the millions, to drive down wages. While as the same time most of the media is telling us that this is a good economy.

Between 1860-70 the national hourly wage was 18.75 cents an hour. _Department of Commerce history data U. S. Colonial times to present_ No social security or income taxes were taken from your pay before you received it.

In 1870, according to the original store ledger, Martz Furniture in Leroy, Minnesota, sold a new wooden kitchen chair for 30 cents. It took 1 hour and 36 minutes of labor to purchase the new chair. In 1993, the same kind of chair cost $100.00. The national hourly wage in 1993 was $8.23, _Minnesota Dept. Economics 1995_ with social security and other federal and state taxes taken out before you got your pay check. In 1993, it took 12.2 hours of labor to buy the new chair. The average hourly wage between 1870 and 1993 increased 44 times; the price of the chair increased 333 times.

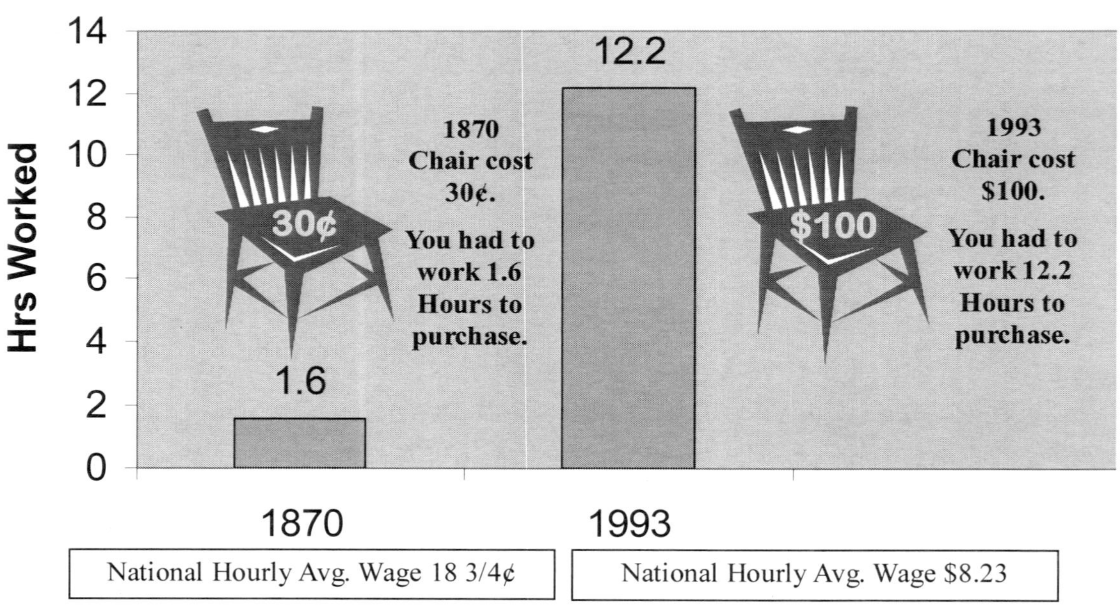

In 1870, a family could make a very comfortable living on just one income. Today many two-income families have trouble making ends meet.

When I was growing up in the 1950's, my folks lived on a cattle ranch. My mother did not work outside the home. In 1952, they built a new 45 x 35 ft 1-1/2 story house. My dad sold 12 yearlings to pay for all the lumber needed to build the house. He paid the carpenter $1.50 an hour. The carpenter owned and lived in a very nice house and his wife did not work outside the home. I don't remember having any classmates who had both parents working outside the home. At that time it was the rule, rather than the exception, that the average family had a good standard of living with a single breadwinner. By 1993, the average national hourly wage was $8.23 an hour. All families living on that wage must have at least two breadwinners to just pay the monthly living expenses.

From Reader's Digest, Feb. 1995, Condensed from The Wall Street Journal article by Jude Wanniski, we read another story similar to mine:

In the period between 1950 and 1970 it was the rule-rather then the exception-that an ordinary family, without higher education, could sustain itself decently on the income of a single breadwinner. In 1955, I was 19 and living in Brooklyn, NY. My father, who had a sixth-grade education, maintained our family of five on a wage of $82 a week as a bookbinder. The monthly rent in 1954 was under $90, gas and electricity another $7 to $10. We had a 1949 Plymouth sedan that my father bought for $1200.

My first good suit bought for my 1954 high school graduation, was $30. In the summer of 1950 I worked as an office boy on Wall Street for 75 cents an hour, with time and a half for overtime.

College fees in 1955 at U.C.L.A. were $200 a semester for an out-of-stator like me, only $50 for a Californian. Tuition at a private school like U.S.C. was reckoned at $20 per credit. Still, you could work your way through without help from parents or the government.

I worked summers as a common construction laborer in New York City for $85 a week, $83 after deductions for income tax and Social Security. A skilled Union carpenter or electrician made $125 per week in New York City, $120 after payroll deductions. The scale was lower else where in the country, but so were consumer prices.

Working as a newspaperman in 1963 in Las Vegas, Nev. I earned $125 per week. I saved $2000 and bought an upscale, brand-new three-bedroom home, with a two-car garage, on a quarter-acre a half-mile from the center of town. It cost $20,000. The monthly payment was $120, including principal and interest, taxes and insurance. I bought a new Volkswagen Beetle for $1600.

My father's bindery job in 1954 paid $82 a week, with $80 after deductions; today, at $820 per week the net would be $662. A carpenter's $125 before deductions was as good as $1200 today before payroll taxes, but the net paycheck was then $120; it's now the equivalent of $92.

A $20,000 house now costs at least $200,000 but with interest rates and property taxes being what they are, it's way out of the reach of a young person just out of college, not to mention high school.

There are many stories like the one Jerry Lobdill wrote and sent to me.

Yesterday (September 2, 1996) on National Public Radio some economist was saying that this country has been on the upswing of a business cycle for nine years now. Last week I read in the Washington Post that the Labor Department's figures show that we have an improving economy and unemployment is down. President Clinton said we have the best economic situation we've had in 28 years.

Nine years ago I was a Principal Scientist with a major corporation. I owned a very nice four-bedroom house, had two good cars, paid $540/month in child support, had excellent benefits, and lived a very good life. Today I have been unemployed for two years (thanks to down sizing) cannot find even temporary work that will pay more than 20% of my last salary. I own no real estate, have no savings, have two old decrepit cars, have been unable to pay child support for two years, have gone without dental care, and were it not for my wife's job, we'd be homeless. So, if the last nine years has been good for business, it sure hasn't been good for me. Nor has it been good for many others.

There are, nationwide, a growing number of people in my circumstances. I know plenty of them personally. Hardly a person can be found who does not know several people with similar stories. There must be, conservatively, some half million senior scientists, mathematicians, engineers, and managers scattered across the country who have been downsized" or "restructured" into long term unemployment since 1990.

Oddly these folks, with a great pool of technical know-how, broad experience, and talent "don't have the exact experience or credentials" the technical job description now asked for, and industry no longer believe that any experience or knowledge which is not specifically within certain software packages, languages, and hardware is not at all transferable from say, a defense application to a commercial application. What is not said is that if you've got 20 years experience as a top technical person you won't want to do a similar job for 50% of your former pay and fewer benefits, and your experience doesn't count for anything today. Never mind that you're used to learning new methods and using software, hardware etc. as a normal part of your professional work. How can there be such a disparity between reality and the rosy picture politicians and Wall Street economists paint? Naturally those who profit from the status quo are going to try to flim-flam the electorate into accepting the situation. Politicians want to be elected, and profiteers don't want to see their cash cows slaughtered. Today neither major political party is able to see the new underclass that is being built out of the ruins of the former

upper middle class. The reason is that the multinational corporations have decided that the cost of American labor is too high, and they are taking united action to assert their global versus US citizenship so that they can homogenize their labor costs at the lowest possible level worldwide. Teens see their fathers and mothers out of work or worried that they may be the next to be downsized. Those in there twenties find salaries and cost of living out of proportion. Many cannot afford their own apartments, and must share apartments just to have a place to live. Those in their 30s with two $20,000 cars, a couple of children and a $250,000 mortgage wondering if they'll be able to keep the American Dream alive, and those over 40 see it evaporating before their very eyes.

The labor statistics do not reflect this malaise. Why not? I have had some time to ponder this question recently and have discovered that these statistics are carefully constructed to avoid telling the truth about the economy. They are crafted to support those who are profiting from what could be the greatest socioeconomic disaster our country has ever witnessed. The US Labor Department Bureau of Labor Statistics publishes the unemployment figures used by all pundits each month. These figures give very optimistic estimates of the number of new jobs created, the percentage of the workforce who are unemployed, and the number of new applications for unemployment insurance. What is unreported is how many jobs are being created and eliminated each month within various pay rate categories.

Recently, I asked Mr. Thomas Nardone, Supervisory Economist, Division of Labor Force Statistics, Bureau of Labor Statistics, to explain why his division did not provide the following type of report each month: chart by Jerry Lobdill

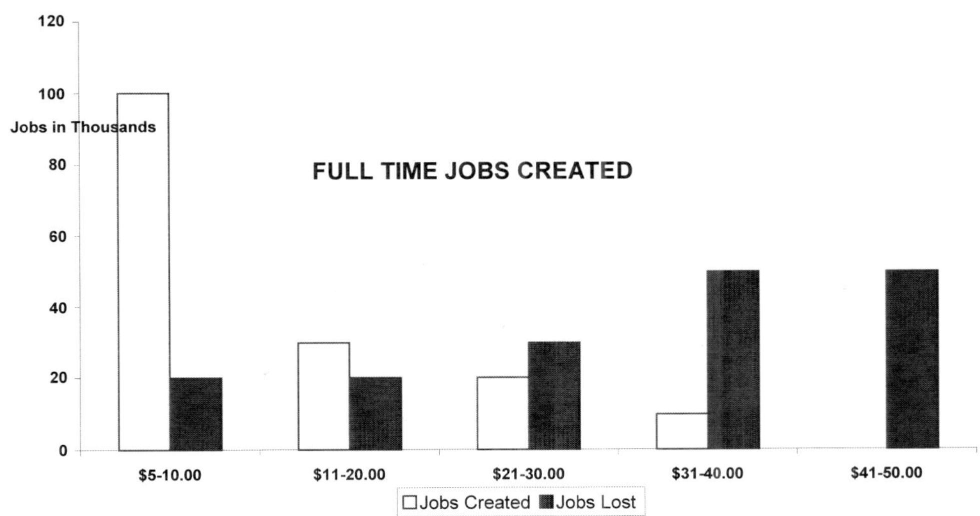

I explained that part-time (PT) jobs created could be included in the data in the following way: A PT job for twenty hour's a week at $7/hr would be 0.5 full-time (FT) jobs in the $5-$10 category above. The pay categories have been arbitrarily selected for illustrative purposes. Fringe benefits that normally are provided in full employment might be ignored when compiling the data, or the FT pay could be adjusted to reflect the added compensatory value of such benefits.

The chart tells us at a glance that most all of the jobs the economy created in this example were in the lowest pay bracket, and that there was a net loss of well-paying jobs. Mr. Nardone responded to the effect that while such a metric of the economy would be useful, his agency does not collect the data necessary to produce it due to "a combination of technical issues and resource limitations". I replied that since the data his agency does report is inaccurate and misleading in a harmful way, his explanation was unsatisfactory. I added the following comments. "It is really worse than a waste of money to report what you do. It, in fact, causes both the big winners and the big losers in the society to be ignored. Your reports create an ambiguous cover for Wall Street to hide behind to assert that the economy is doing well when in fact:

1. *The gap between have and have-nots is widening alarmingly.*
2. *Entire professions are being transformed into obsolete jobs in the US economy because they are going overseas and not being replaced with equal paying jobs.*
3. *Age discrimination in downsizing is rampant,*
4. *Older workers' jobs are "eliminated" and reinvented with the same responsibilities but with much less experience required and typically 50% of the pay the jobs previously commanded. This effect pleases politicians and Wall Street but defrauds the American citizenry."*

Business Week, in an April 18, 2005 editorial entitled: *Jobless in Detroit-And Germany*, said, *"Michigan, at 7.5% has the highest unemployment rate of any state in the U.S. The problem is sclerotic corporate healthcare, pension, and wage policies that are hugely expensive. Manufacturers are increasingly uncompetitive in the global economy. People who still have jobs and those who are retired are doing quite well, but at the expense of their children and others who can't get jobs because companies find the cost of hiring prohibitive".*

It is very interesting that in 2005, papers and magazines were carrying articles expressing concern for all the unemployed American citizens. Then in just two short years, in 2007, the papers and the airwaves are full of talk that there are not enough people for the jobs. The nation needs open borders so that people both legally and illegally can pour into the country, to insure there will be enough people to fill all the job openings. Of course the new immigrants, especially the illegal ones, work for lower wages.

There is no question that wages are a large part of the cost of production. However, lower wages will not provide the long-term solutions that business needs to be profitable. In fact, in a short time, lower wages hurt the sale of goods and services. Consumers who receive a cut in wages have less money to spend on the products and services business is offering. If consumers don't buy, business can't sell. If business doesn't sell, profits go down. If consumers are going to maintain the same spending rate they had with higher wages, their only alternative is to raise their debt level. This is a short-term fix.

Soon they will need an increase in wages to service their increased indebtedness. If they don't get the wage increase, they will be forced to work two jobs. When that no longer works, people will start missing payments which soon leads to foreclosure and loss of homes and other possessions. We are seeing that now in 2008. Cutting wages is not the long-term answer to falling profits. The answer lies where few people want to look.

Modern Money Secrets hiding in plain sight:

Banks get to acquire the currency, promissory notes and mortgages payable to them, Government bonds and other securities by simply issuing their promise to pay.

Chapter 1
Something is wrong

Millions of people are working hard to earn money, many are working two jobs. It seems that now most households need to have two incomes. Now in 2008-2009 many people are losing their jobs. America is filled with business schools, books on how to manage your business for a profit and financial "experts" who are quick to advise us on how to manage money and invest wisely. They recommend ways to shop wisely, to save and to manage one's time and resources properly. Every week somebody is pushing a new scheme to get-rich-quick. Yet, in spite of all this 'expert' advice and get-rich-quick schemes, the public and private debt grows larger with each passing year.

Most of these people try to follow the 'good advice experts' yet we are collectively getting deeper into debt.

Something is wrong when we are consistently told things are made more efficiently, faster and with better tools. Yet, our cost of living keeps going up.

Something is wrong when the prices of finished goods keep going up faster than the price of wages and raw materials. It requires more hours of labor to buy the same finished product which is made out of cheaper material.

Something is wrong when the majority of people find that the day-to-day struggle to survive is so great that it leaves them with no time for relaxation or enjoyment. All our energy goes to work, sleep and go back to work.

Something is wrong when news tells us that the economy is good and lots of jobs are created. Then in a few years it all changes and the news reports the economy is doing poorly and lots of jobs are being lost. Then in a few more years the new reports are back to telling us the economy is good. They call this the business cycle. However, if you tune out the news and go out and look at the natural cycle of life, you see a different picture. The natural world has production cycles. Every thing comes from a seed that strives mighty to grow, mature and reseed itself so that the cycles of life will continue with new wealth being created with the completion each cycle. The natural reproduction cycles create no debt.

The only reason the economy has big swings without suffering a huge natural disaster, is because of manipulations of the money supply by the banking system. The business cycle is the manipulation of the money supply not a natural occurring process. Because of our debauched money system the collective debt always goes up. This growing debt causes the people to suffer increasing stress. How can a nation and its governments get trillions of dollars in debt, when the people living in that nation have done little but produce and recycle wealth for the last 250 years? This is totally illogical.

Something is wrong when men like Alan Greenspan state, ***"One key element behind our current prosperity is the rise in the value, markets place on the capital assets of U.S. businesses. Corporations are already relying increasingly on borrowing to finance capital investment".*** How can Greenspan, or anyone, say we are prospering when the corporations and everyone else are relying increasingly on borrowing to finance capital investment or to just stay in business.

We need to stop and ask, "*What effect does an increase in market value have on your cash flow?*" You buy a house and the house doubles in value. How does that help your cash flow? The truth is an increase in value doesn't help your cash flow. It doesn't give you any more money to spend on food, clothes or to make mortgage payments, etc. The fact is it hurts your cash flow because the higher market value causes your property taxes to go up, which causes your cost of living to go up. The only way that you can gain access to any money (increase your cash flow) from the increased value of your home, is to borrow more money on your house or sell your house.

The value (price) of things goes up for one of the following reasons:

- You need to raise your selling price to maintain your profit margin,
- You simply want more profit,
- Greed,
- The bankers need the value of things to go up so they can justify making more loans,

We need to understand the value of something is only a mental concept. However the debt on something is an amount set down in writing and is enforceable by court order.

Something is wrong when we are taught that we can borrow ourselves into personal and national prosperity. Any thinking person knows that is impossible.

"You can't run business borrowing money, and I've run a business. You can't run government borrowing money. We're over $3 trillion in debt. The whole value of America, the last time I saw the figure, the value of everything in this country-the forests, farms, the gold, the copper, the people, everything was less than $4.5 trillion. We're almost there. We're going to have to get to the point where every cent of tax we collect local, state, and federal won't be able to pay the interest on our debt. That's some 'fix' to be in." *Barry Goldwater PARADE MAGAZINE Nov, 28,1993*

It should be very clear that we are trying to run everything on borrowed money. It should also be very clear that it is not working. Americans are working longer hours yet the debt just keeps growing. According to the Grandfather Economic Report found at http://mwhodges.home.att.net. The total debt as of March 2005 stood at:

- Household Sector Debt $10.3 Trillion
- Business Sector Debt $ 7.8 Trillion
- Domestic Sector Debt $12.0 Trillion
- State & Local Sector Debt $ 1.7 Trillion
- Federal Government Debt $ 7.6 Trillion

Included here is some information Gordon Hutchinson, a friend of mine, collected from several sources and sent to me.

In 1985, we had GDP of $4.2 trillion and a total debt of $7.5 trillion. In 1990, we had GDP of $5.8 trillion a total debt of $11.8 trillion. Between 1985 and 1990 for every trillion in GDP growth, debt grew $2.7 trillion.

In 1995, the GDP was $7.4 trillion and total debt was $16.4 trillion. Between 1990 and 1995, for every $1 trillion in GDP growth, debt grew $2.9 trillion.

In 2000, the GDP was $9.8 trillion and total debt was $24.6 trillion. Between 1995 and 2000, for every $1 trillion in GDP growth, debt grew $3.4 trillion. In 2005, GDP was $12.5 trillion and the total debt was $36.5 trillion. Between 2000 and 2005, for every $1 trillion in GDP growth, debt grew $4.4 trillion!

By the end of 2006, GDP was $13.2 trillion and the total debt was $44.8 trillion. At the end of 2007, total debt grew to 48.8 trillion dollars, a debt growth of $4 trillion in one year.

http://www.federalreserve.gov/RELEASES/z1/current/accessible/l1.htm

Total Credit Market Debt by decade from 1946 through 2006

Year	Total Debt	% over previous decade in billions of dollars
1946	$359.8	n.a.
1956	$611.4	4.3%
1966	$1,187.0	94.1%
1976	$2,904.9	144.7%
1986	$9,816.1	237.9%
1996	$19,744.2	101.1%
2006	$44,747.0	126.6%
2016 (est.)	$101,000.0	125.7%

Notice that, for the last four decades, our debt has more than doubled each decade. This is because our privately owned, debt-based system requires more and more debt just to pay the compounding interest on the previous debt.

It should be clear that the nation as whole can't manage or work its way into prosperity using borrowed money. It is sad that the majority of the people don't understand the sinister nature of debt money and interest. Many people understand and see the interest cost they pay directly when making house, car and installment plan payments. Very few realize the interest on their personal loans is only a small part of the total interest bill that they pay. They don't realize that most businesses have huge debts (for an example, I read in the paper that the Chicago Tribune has a 12. 8 billion dollar debt), and the interest on those debts is passed on to the consumer though higher prices and/or lower wages. They don't realize that the federal, state, county, city governments and school districts have huge debts, and that the interest on those debts is also passed on to the consumer through higher taxes and fees.

Something is wrong when rural farm papers shout from their headline that "RURAL AMERICA IS GOING BROKE" as the TRI-STATES LIVESTOCK NEWS did in Jan. 9, 1999 when the farmers were being paid the lowest prices in 60 years. At the lowest point, the cost of a ten-pound ham to the consumer was more than the farmers were being paid for the whole hog. The price of a hundred-pound sack of potatoes dipped below the cost of a large order of fries at McDonald's. The price farmers received for a bushel of wheat was about as much as a loaf of bread costs at the supermarket.

Those prices drove thousands of hard working productive families, who by

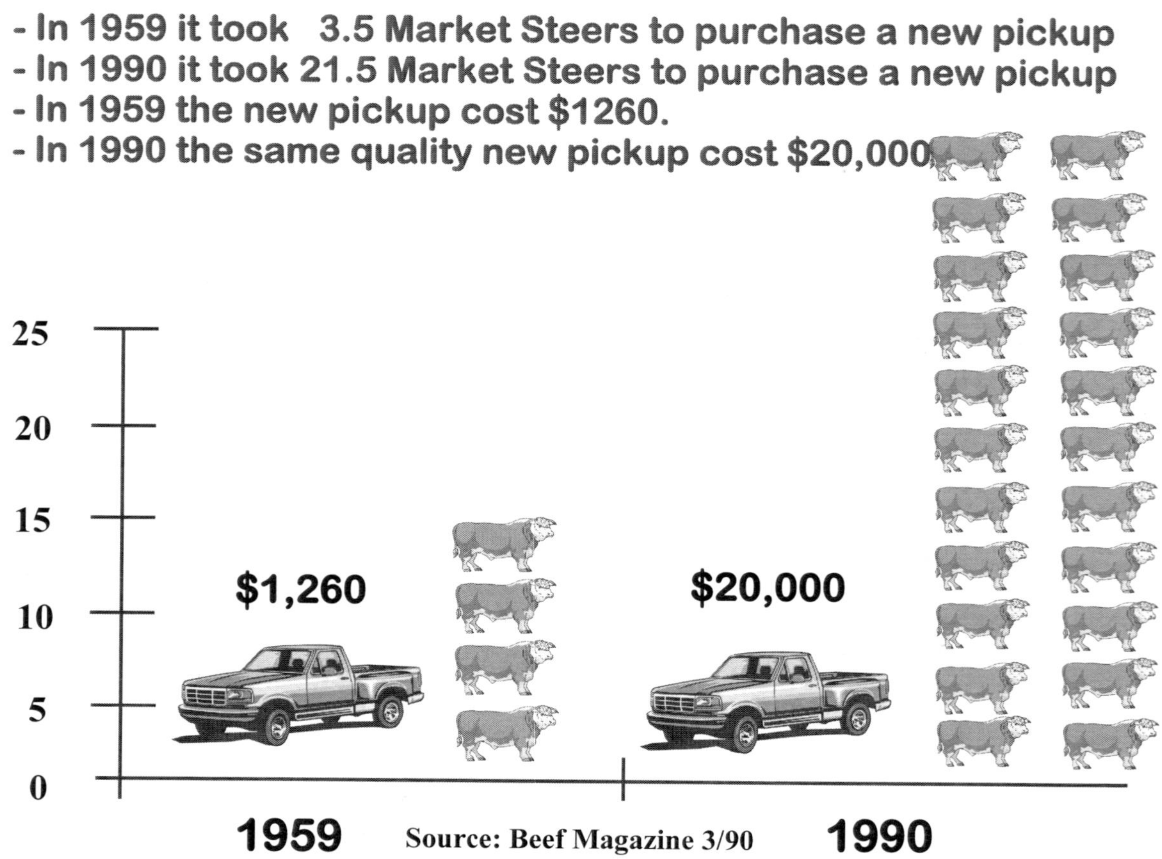

their occupation produce renewable wealth from the earth every year, from their chosen way of life. In 1998, it took forty five 1000 pound market steers to purchase a new pickup.

In 1929 it took 1500 Bushels of Wheat to purchase a new Buick Car.

In 1990 it took 10,000 Bushels of Wheat to purchase the same type of Buick car.

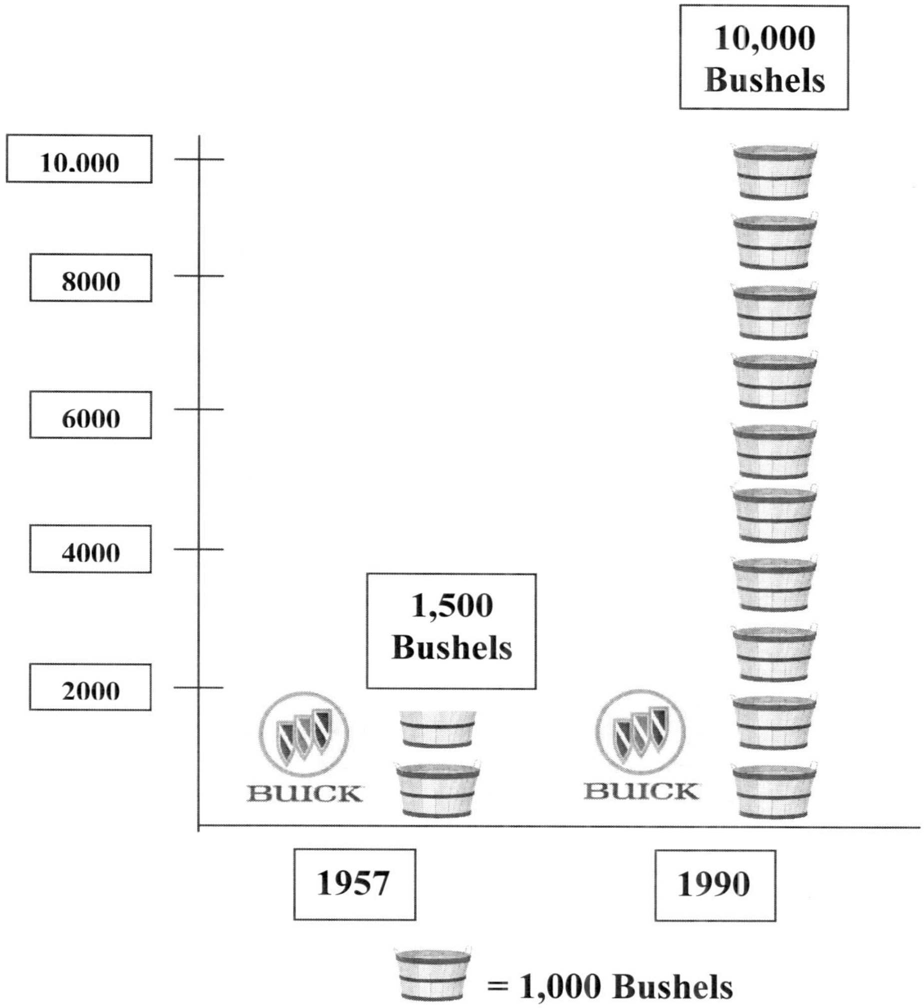

Source: Bill Pullman, who lived next to the man and his father who sold the wheat and bought the cars.

The American farmers and rancher produce more real and renewable wealth than any one else and receives the least benefit of the wealth produced. The American financial system produces no real wealth and receives the most benefits.

On the consumer side of the economy, **Lou Dobbs** and others have written books on how government and big corporations are turning the American dream into the American nightmare. Wages are being forced down, and we have the highest number ever of dual-income families trying hard to earn the money needed to buy the things for which the farmers receive such low prices.

Americans spend a lot of time talking about money, what they do to earn it, and how to get the most benefit when they spend it. Most everyone works doing something that is valuable to someone else. Yet, the total debt grows. The top 10% get richer and richer while millions of Americans live from paycheck to paycheck with help from ever-growing credit card and other debts. Often this does not show on the outside.

It's like a TV ad states: ***"I have a great looking life, I have a big house, two cars, I am a member of the country club, etc. How do I do it, I am up to my ears in debt. Someone help me!"***

Thousands of families are barely managing to make home mortgage payments, car mortgage payments and their other monthly household expenses. Each year more Americans are being forced to have a second or even a third income to maintain the same standard of living their parents had, with only one breadwinner in the family.

On Friday, March 31, 2000, The Department of Commerce reported that U.S. consumers spent more than they earned in February as personal spending increased at more than twice the rate of income. Personal consumption expenditures increased $62.4 billion while personal income increased only $32.6 billion. By March 2005, the household debt has grown to $10.3 trillion. Source http://mwhodges.home.att.net/nat-debt/debt-nat.htm.

Something is wrong when Americans are continuously told that people are in debt only because they are spending too much, that they are spending and living beyond their means and that is bad. Yet we are constantly approached, by phone or mail, by a bank or credit card company trying to get us to sign up for a new credit card, or take out a new loan and go even deeper into debt so that we can spent some more money, and that is good, because the consumer must spent to keep the economy going.

At the same time, America is producing thousands of salesmen telling them and training them to go forth and get rich using every trick in the book to convince other Americans that they have great needs that can only be filled by buying whatever it is that the high-powered salesman is selling.

Why do we never hear, "Why do we the people do all the work and produce all the wealth, but the banking system always has the money? Money we must borrow and pay interest on just to have a medium-of-exchange?"

When our money represents what we produce and only used as a tool to exchange goods and services there could be no living beyond one's 'means'.

I believe the true definition of living beyond one's means is consuming more than what has been produced. It is impossible to consume more than what has been produced. Have you ever been able to wear a shirt before it was manufactured? Have you ever been able to eat any food before it was grown? It is self-evident that it is impossible for people to collectively live beyond their capacity to produce. Clearly something else is happening.

I know of many people who get off work at one job just in time to get to their other job. Even two incomes must not be enough because the credit card debt and other consumer debt are climbing out of sight. Before the year 2000, the American household-sector had mortgages, consumer credit and other debts of $6.2 trillion. Source 1999 letter from Donald J. Winn Flow of Funds Federal Reserve Board to United States Senator Rod Grams in response to a letter from me.

According to a letter my co-author Greg received from the Federal Reserve Bank of Chicago, the total debt was much greater.

Federal Reserve Bank of Chicago

April 6, 1994

Gregory K. Soderberg
2410 Fourth Drive, SW
Austin, MN 55912

Dear Mr. Soderberg,

Thank you for your letter of April. Unfortunately, we may not be of much help. The answers to your questions are, by nature quite difficult.

1. As most of the $26 trillion dollars in debt represents market instruments, most of it accrues interest. However, how much represents market instruments is difficult to ascertain.

2. Calculating the APR would be virtually impossible, as the credit terms on each instrument that is interest bearing, as well as how the interest on that instrument is calculated, would have to be known.

3. Finally, the data on interest-bearing instruments in the various sectors (households, business, financial institutions, etc.) is scattered and not readily available in anyone place. It would have to be aggregated, and in some cases imputed, to arrive at even a rough estimate.

I am sorry we cannot provide you with better answers. Thank you for your interest in the subject and this publication.

Sincerely,

Timothy P. Schilling
Public Information Specialist

In 1994, the credit card delinquencies reached a fourteen year high. Bankruptcies were running around 1.5 million a year. The bankruptcy rate was eight times greater than it was during the Great Depression of the 1930's. By end of 2006, the debt rose to $46 trillion (not including trillions of dollars of unfunded liabilities, social security, government and private company pensions, and trillions in derivative debt). Now in 2008 the total is over $53 trillion and millions of families are losing their homes because they can't afford their house payment.

Weekly we hear news concerning the ever growing debt that is hanging over the whole world like a dark cloud. Business news reports about companies merging, downsizing, laying off workers or moving their produce lines out of the country and encouraging millions of illegal immigrants to enter the United States. All for benefit of cutting labor costs for big corporations. Leaving many Americans unemployed and underemployed this has forced some into bankruptcy. How can anyone call this a good system? The only way is with their eyes and ears closed tightly to reality. **Believe it or not this was also the news in 1994.**

How did we get into over 53 trillion dollars of interest-bearing debt when, for the last 250 years, working men and women throughout this nation have created immense wealth by combining their ideas and labor with natural raw resources of the earth? There is no inherent debt in the wealth creating process.

To illustrate let's consider the following:

- If you use the trees and minerals provided by the earth to make an axe. Then using your axe you cut down some of the trees, shape them, and build yourself a house. In time new trees grow back and you now have both the trees and the house. Would you have a money debt to anyone for your house or the trees? Of course not!
- If you planted cotton with horse power, then picked the cotton and processed it into clothes yourself, would you have a money debt for the clothes? Of course not! There is simply no inherent money debt in the wealth production process!
- If you picked up shells at the seashore and strung them into wampum beads, then used beads as a medium of exchange (money), would you have an interest-bearing money debt? Of course not!
- If you dug some gold or silver out of the ground and minted it into coins, then used the coins for your medium of exchange, would you have an interest-bearing money debt? Of course not!
- If you printed pieces of paper and put a picture and words on it, then used them as a medium of exchange would you have an interest-bearing money debt? Of course not!

So <u>where</u> does the debt come from?

The only place the interest-bearing debt could come from is the process that is used to create our money and move that money into circulation. **There is clearly something wrong with the way today's money is moved into circulation.**

Something is wrong when people living in what is called the wealthiest nation in the world don't have enough money to start new ventures, expand an existing business, buy or build a house or buy a car unless we go to the banking system and borrow.

Something is wrong when no matter how much we collectively borrow from the banking system it never runs out of money to loan. It seems very hard to save doesn't it? Statistics show people are saving less. Yet the banking system, claiming they are loaning someone's savings (*"With your saving dollars, we have been able to make agricultural loans, home loans, consumer loans, and business loans.")* Source Donald R. Halvorson President St. Ansgar State Bank are making more loans and never seem to run out of money to lend. **Strange isn't it**? It is time the people begin to really start thinking and then ask the question, **where does the banking system get the money it loans?**

Something is wrong when we are told that the problem is that the government just prints too much money, yet the government and most of the people are always short of money and have to borrow to have the things that they want and need.

Something is wrong when stores have to advertise no money down, no payments and no interest for six months to a year in order to sell their merchandise. This does not seem to me like these stores believe they are trying to sell to people who have too much money. Why are people with too much money always looking for sales and price discounts?

No Money Down!
No Payment!
No Interest!

Something is wrong when we live in a nation with so many natural resources and innovative, productive people yet our debt grows so rapidly. 1998 and 1999 we had between 90 to 95% employment, which should mean ninety to ninety five percent of all able bodied working age people have a job producing a product or providing a service and are earning a paycheck for their effort. With 90 to 95% of all able-bodied working-age people working and getting paid for producing wealth or providing services that enhance wealth, there should be no reason for that nation to get collectively deeper into debt with each passing year.

America's Total Debt Report

$ 53 Trillion -- soaring

household, business, financial and government sectors

by Michael Hodges

updated March 2008

a chapter of the Grandfather Economic Reports

America has become more debt-dependent –than ever before with total debt of $53 Trillion, $75,154 per man, woman and child

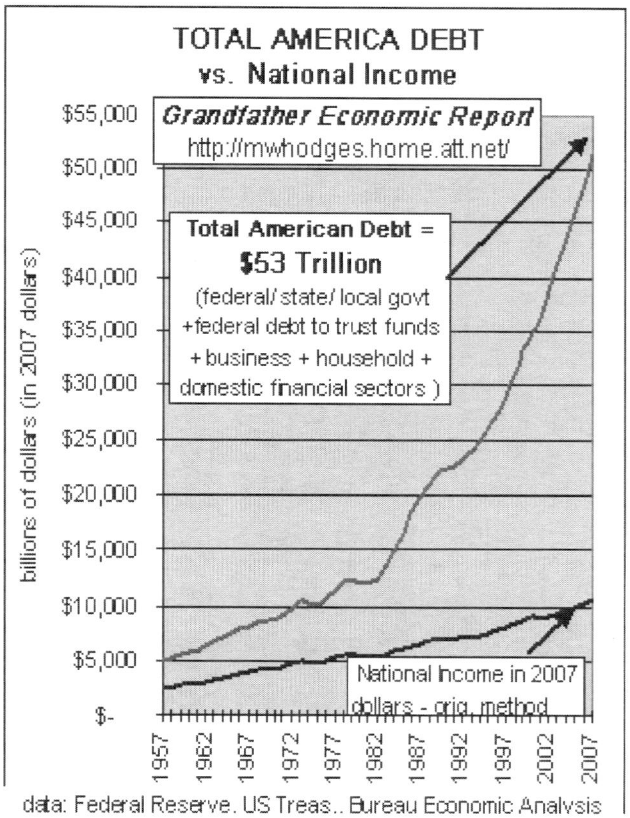

The chart shows the debt in 1957 was $693 billion (the left bar in the chart) - - or about $4,000 per capita.

Today's debt has grown above **$53 trillion** (the right bar in the chart)- - 76 times higher - - to **$175,154 per man, woman and child - or $700,616 per family of 4**.

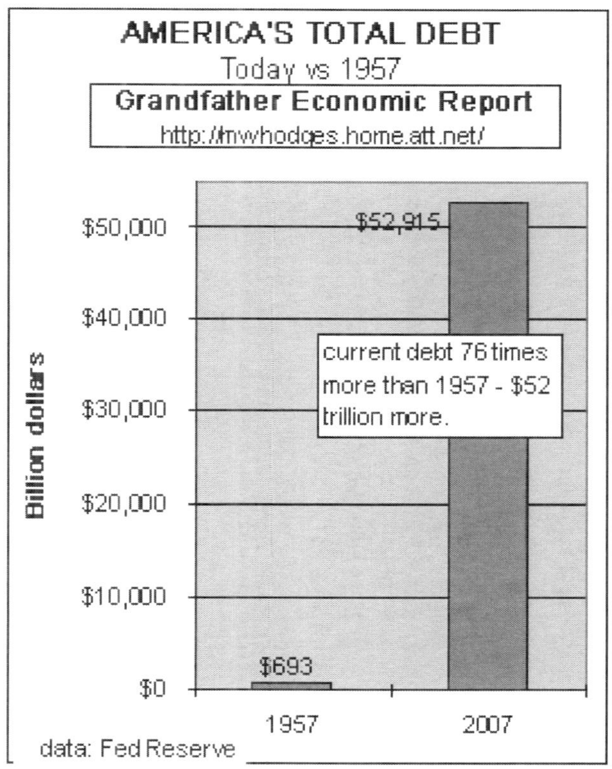

This is A SCARY CHART - showing a 40 year trend of **America's total debt reaching $53 trillion** vs. growth of the economy a measured by net national income adjusted for inflation in today's dollars.

Something is wrong when we suffer under all this debt when we have produced so much wealth!

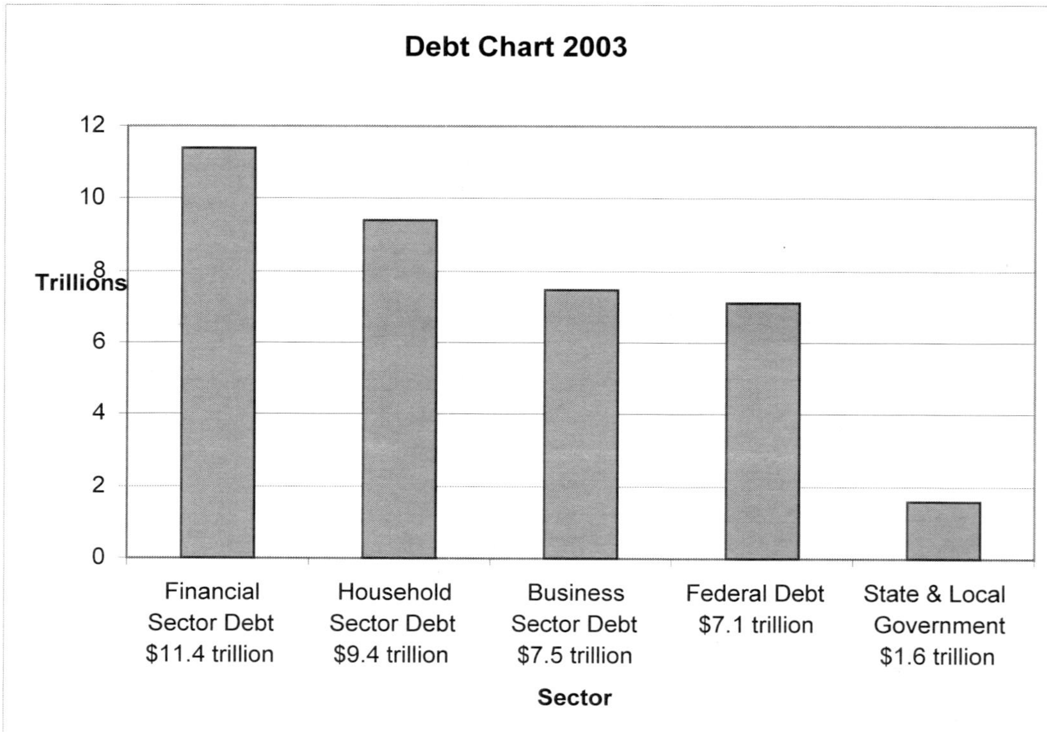

A few years ago I asked the President of the Minnesota Banking Association, Eric Gandrud, if he could name anything that was not produced as an asset. He answered everything is produced as an asset. A fact we agreed on. Then I asked, how in the world did **we collectively end up over 37 trillion dollars in debt, when mostly all we have done is produce material wealth for the last 250 years?** He answered: "It's our screwed up accounting system."

Something is wrong when so many people, who think they have saved enough for their retirement, find that, the seldom talked about costs of interest and taxes, have so eroded the purchasing power of their savings, that it will only buy a fraction of what they thought it would. Because the purchasing power of their savings has been stolen by interest and high taxes, many elderly have been driven from their homes.

Chapter 2
What do we mean by Wealth?

Wealth is all material objects having economic value measurable in price. Wealth is any useful material thing capable of being bought, sold or stocked for future disposition and capable of satisfying human needs and desires in making lives more physically acceptable.

All material wealth stems from our two basic industries, agriculture and mining. If it cannot be grown, it has to be mined either from the ground or from the sea. Everything we have and use (except what we use as **money)** originates from natural resources and consists of known, identifiable chemical substances, including the air we breathe.

By applying our God-given physical and mental energies and abilities to the processes of agriculture and mining, mankind develops nature's natural resources into all of the food, fiber, fuel and materials used to feed, clothe and house all of us. There is simply no debt in this process! We don't borrow our abilities we use them to harvest the natural raw resources and enhance them to make better products.

Most people work all their lives providing labor and services that enhance the basic raw materials that we get from the earth. This enhancement of the raw materials is what gives us a better standard of living. If working people produce all the wealth of a nation, (and they do), **why are we collectively getting deeper into debt?**

In 1998 the household sector debt was up to $6.2 trillion. (Flow of Funds Accounts published by the Federal Reserve Board.) By Jan. 1, 2007 the household sector debt had increased two 12.2 trillion.

Americans are always talking about "making money" in the same glowing terms as producing wealth. But, are money and wealth really the same thing? Most Americans believe that when they work, producing wealth and providing services, they are somehow at the same time creating money. We need to ask is that belief based on fact or fiction?

We all know that the increasing numbers of plants, animals and people comes from natural reproduction. People acquire their energy from consuming good quality food and water. Then working with the elements of the earth they manufacture all kind of things. We call this adding value by using the manufacturing process.

Most people never consider that money as we know it is not something produced by nature nor does it come from any form of natural reproduction. Money is a creation of man. It must be manufactured by someone! Most people do not understand that after money is manufactured it must be moved into circulation and there is only three ways to move money into circulation. Those three ways are: gift it, spend it or lend it.

Why is it that it seems that everyone has to borrow? How can it be that the banking system has trillions of dollars to loan, when at first glance they only provide services and do not manufacture anything. Could it be the banking system never seems to run out of money to loan because it uses an innovative bookkeeping system to create all that we use for money, as a debt owed to itself? **The answer is, yes!** That is the only reason that we owe over 46 trillion (2006). Maybe that is why Eric Gandrud, President of the Minnesota Banking Association, said the problem is "our screwed up accounting system."

By 2007 our total debt grew to **$53 Trillion** and is growing faster than the growth of the total economy. In 2009 the debt seems to be going up by a trillion every time certain people declare the banks need a new bailout or the economy needs a boost. When the banks are the only ones who can create money, why would they need a bailout from the government? Our government does not create money so the only place the government could get the money to give the banks a bailout would be to borrow the money from the banking system. The government would have to borrow it directly from the banking system or tax the money from the people. But the people can't create any money so they would have to borrow it from the banking system before they could pay the taxes.

Modern Money Secrets hiding in plain sight:

All Modern Money is created as interest bearing loans.

What Is Wealth?

Wealth comes from our two most basic

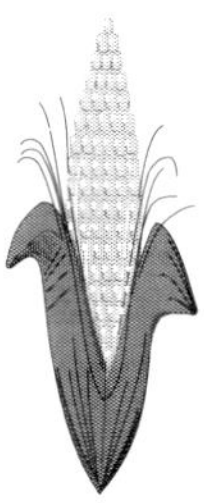

AGRICULTURE | **MINING**

If It Cannot Be Grown—It Has To Be Mined.

Farming, Livestock, Forestry, Fishing

Coal, Oil, Gas, Non-Metals, Metallic, Building Materials

Everything we have and use comes from our natural resources

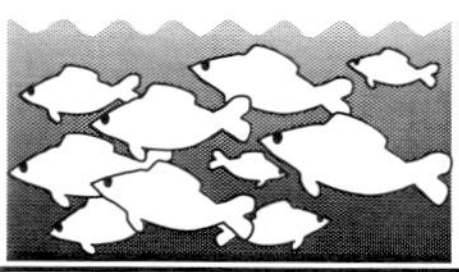

Man, by applying his God-given physical and mental energies to agriculture and mining, develops our natural resources into all other things we use. Labor applied to raw resources produces all the food, fiber, fuel and materials to feed, clothe and house us—<u>all</u> of the materials we use <u>everyday!</u>

We call this WEALTH

Wealth includes ideas and services that enhance the products from agriculture and mining.

Chapter 3
Money

People have been fooled with all the talk about different kinds of money. However, when one scrapes away all the fluff and spin, **money is nothing more or less than a man made tool which should only be used to enhance fair and honest trading of goods and services**. Money, like all tools can be used for good purposes or for evil purposes. Money can be a tool for an honest medium of exchange or for an evil tool for theft by deception **as it is now**.

Fire, when used properly it is a very useful tool. Fire, when used wrongly or let get out of control, can be a very destructive force. Money, like fire, when used improperly, and put into circulation under the wrong principles, can be a very destructive force for the many and a very enriching tool for a few. Unlike fire, the destructive force of money is very hard for most people to recognize.

Most of the things we see in our economy are not really strange nor complicated, neither mysterious nor driven by some unseen hand of complex market forces. The economic events we are seeing have grown from basic economic laws and traditions that have been perverted to form a destructive debt-ridden life for most people.

What is it about the money we use that puts us collectively trillions of dollars in debt while we are constantly and collectively producing wealth? What effect do all these trillions of dollars of debt, and the interest, have on America's spiritual, physical, moral, and financial health?

John Maynard Keynes, whose ideas strongly influenced economic thinking said, ***"There is no subtler, no surer means of overturning the existing basis of society than to debauch (to corrupt) the currency. The process engages all the hidden forces of economic law on the side of destruction, and does it in a manner which only one man in a million is able to diagnose."*** *(to corrupt added)*

The only way money can be debauched is to change it from a representation of wealth into a representation of interest-bearing debt. This is exactly what fractional banking has done to money.

Chapter 4

Types of "Money"

When people talk about money, one may hear them talk about different types of money.

Commodity money is a medium-of-exchange in which the units are fixed amounts, either by law or custom, of an actual commodity that has value other than as a medium-of-exchange. Most people falsely believe commodity money only means gold or silver money. Commodity money is any commodity that had been monetized by the passage of law. The supply of commodity money is tied directly to the production of that commodity by the people.

The <u>most important principle</u> of commodity money is the one least talked about. Commodity money can only be created by man's labor combined with raw resources of the earth.

Under the principles of free coinage, metal commodity money was exchanged into circulation. Metal commodity money is developed when someone takes bullion extracted from the earth to a mint and to be assayed, weighed, and stamped into uniform coins. If taken home and spent it doesn't incur debt to anyone. One of the benefits of the free coinage of commodity money was that it assured that no one receives excess purchasing power or excess profit simply through the issuance of the money.

The problem with gold and silver coined money is not the principle under which it functions it is that there is simply not a large enough supply of it to make a good general medium of exchange.

Fiduciary money is a medium of exchange composed of some intrinsically less valuable substance, usually paper (or cotton/linen), which the issuers promise to redeem in commodity money on demand. The fiduciary money is used for exchanges. The actual physical wealth, usually gold or silver bullion or coin, remained in the vault. Fiduciary money is <u>based on trust</u> and the <u>public's confidence</u> that the issuer can be trusted to honor its promise to pay. Fiduciary money is most commonly issued by private banks and governments.

There would never be a need for fiduciary money if there was truly enough gold and silver to make a good general medium of exchange. There is no need to promise to pay someone if you have the means to pay on the spot. The Gold and Silver Certificates and the early Federal Reserve Bank notes are examples of fiduciary money. Fiduciary money **could be** convenient, honest money if it was always kept on a one-to-one basis with the represented lawful commodity money and exchanged, **not loaned at interest**, into circulation. History has shown that **no** issuer of fiduciary money, in the long run, ever honored its promise to pay.

There was only a few times when it was traded into circulation. Mostly, it has been loaned into circulation at interest. Fiduciary money gains acceptance of the people for the following reasons:

1. The people could not acquire the gold and silver
2. The people consider it more convenient to use
3. The people are always misled into having confidence in the issuers

It's a fact. People consider paper money more convenient to use than gold or silver proving that gold and silver coins is not the best medium of exchange.

The facts prove there has never been enough gold or silver (coined or otherwise) to make a good general medium of exchange. If everyone is not able to have excess to gold and silver money, they must use something else.

The issuers of fiduciary money like it because of the access profit or excess purchasing power they can obtain. Through the issuing of more fiduciary money than there is of the commodity, that they are promising to pay.

The Continental Currency -- Fiduciary money -- is how the Continental Congress financed the American colonies war for independence. It is one of the few examples of Fiduciary money being spent into circulation. Why did the Congress create and spend the bills instead of the coins? The Continental Congress didn't have the coins or the silver or gold to make the coins, therefore they gained immediate excessive purchasing power for funding the war by using the bills.

Banks love Fiduciary money because it gives them the ability to deceive the people and gain excess profit. A bank that has 100 one dollar silver or gold coins will gain 10 dollars profit, per year, by loaning those coins out at 10% simple interest. Using fractional reserve banking and Fiduciary money, banks with 100 one-dollar coins could loan 1000 one dollar denominated bank notes at 10% interest making a tidy profit of 100 dollars. Today bank reserves don't consist of coins. Their reserves only consist of more promises to pay.

When a bank issues an excess of Fiduciary money, the banker increases the money supply. Many people have understood this fact, only a few have seen the excessive profit angle. However, something else happened that almost everyone failed to understand. The quality as well as the quantity of the money changed.

The money had been switched from evidence of wealth, to evidence of interest-bearing indebtedness.

Fiat Money is any thing that is declared money by law. In the United States, at the time of this writing, all money is fiat money. This includes all coins and currency issued by the United States government and Federal Reserve Notes which are not issued by the government. Most writers claim that fiat money is paper money not backed by gold or silver. This doesn't include check-book money which is created on the books of banks and is not declared money by any law.

Money does not occur naturally. It does not reproduce itself by breeding or by sprouting from seeds. Money stems from a manufacturing process. As such, **all** money is fiat in nature and becomes money by law. This includes gold and silver coins because a law set the weight and purity of the coins. Webster's New World Dictionary fourth edition defines fiat as an order issued by legal authority.

All money is a combination of substance and symbol. Commodity money is as more substance than symbol. Paper money is more symbol that substance. What we use for money today, book-entry bank liabilities, are almost all symbol with **very** little substance (maybe a little bit of ink or electricity). It is not fiat money as no law declares the book-entry bank liabilities that we use for our medium-of-exchange (money) to be dollars, money, legal tender, or anything else. It is truly money by common mental deception and enforced as law by our corrupt court system.

Debt money - Money created as a liability. A debt-based monetary system is an economic system where money is created as a liability. Debt money can be created in three different ways. It can be created as a liability to:

- The party issuing the money
- The party receiving the money
- Both the issuing party and the receiving party

This form of money is called debt-based money or debt money because someone must incur a debt in order for the money to exist or before the money can move into circulation.

An example of money that puts both the issuer and the user into debt is the checkbook (demand deposit) money that we use today. As stated by the Federal Reserve below, all checkbook money is created as a numerical promise to pay (a liability) by the banks.

> *"All bank deposits are a form of credit. Basically, they represent amounts* ***owed by banks to depositors.*** *They come into existence by an exchange of bank promises to pay customers for the various assets which banks acquire—currency, promissory notes of business, consumers and other customers, mortgages on real estate, and Government and other securities."* The Third Edition of the Federal Reserve System Purposes and Functions page 6. (emphasis added)

Demand deposit (checkbook) money is created when we go into a bank and borrow by signing a promissory note, promising to pay the borrowed principal plus the interest, back to the bank. The checkbook money goes into circulation when the borrower writes check and spends the money. After the first borrower has spent the checkbook money into circulation it can and will move to non-borrowers checking accounts. Most of them will then not understand that it first had to be borrowed for it to exist.

An example of debt money that puts the issuer, but not the user, into debt was the "Continental" issued by the Continental Congress. These bills stated:

"This bill entitles the Bearer to receive Spanish Milled Dollars or the value there of in gold and silver..." Because the bills were payable on demand, they were a debt upon the Continental Congress. Because the currency was *spent* into circulation they were not a debt to the users.

An example of money that puts the user, but not the issuer, into debt is the coins we use today. The U.S. Treasury takes combinations of copper, zinc, manganese, brass and nickel and stamps these metals into coined money. This procedure doesn't create a debt to the treasury. The treasury sells the coins taking only bank created credit money for payment. Therefore we the users have to be in debt to the banking system before the coins move into circulation. Source Bradford E. Cooper, Associate Director, Manufacturing United States Mint and Alan Keller, Director, Office of Public Correspondence, Department of the Treasury

If the U.S. Treasury would manufacture the coins and spend them into the circulation, there would be no debt to either the issuer or the users.

> *There is no such thing as "debt-free" money under U.S. law."* Thomas Woodward Specialist in Macroeconomics * Economics Division * Congressional Research

Wealth Money – Money that is created and spent or exchanged into circulation and which is not a debt, liability or an obligation to either the issuer or to the user.

Free coinage, as set forth in the 1792 mint act, is a good example of wealth money. Under that law, anyone who had silver or gold or who had dug some gold or silver bullion out of the earth could take it to the United States Mint. The mint would weigh, assay, and coin the bullion into legal tender coins free of charge. If the person took the coins home and spent or exchanged them into circulation, it would be wealth money. If the coins were loaned into circulation the newly minted coins would become debt money. All commodity money started out as wealth money.

Another example of wealth money would be for the government or the banks to create new money and spend it into circulation to pay for building and repairing the nation's basic infrastructure for the people to use, free of taxes or fees.

Most all of the problems Americans and the world suffers from is because as whole, we do not understand the true principles of money and how to use them to provide a money system that will serve all the people fairly and honestly. All that most people understand about money is that they would like to have more of it.

More important than the physical characteristics of money, is how and under what principles money is put into circulation. This, the most important monetary principle, has been missed or purposely ignored by most people who discuss money.

The real issue is not gold or silver -vs- paper, nor commodity money -vs- fiat money. It is about exchanging evidence of wealth or exchanging evidence of debt. It is about I own or I owe, **honesty or fraud**.

The best money system for every country in the world would be for the government of the country to create the money as paper money (or in our modern world, as a computer entry) and spend it into circulation to pay for the basic infrastructure system of that nation in lieu of taxes. A nation can have commerce without money, but a nation can't have commerce without a transportation system.

Modern Money Secrets hiding in plain sight:

Modern Bankers get to buy everything with a promise to pay, a promise they never have to make good.

Chapter 5

A Brief History of Money

From the beginning of mankind, people have strived to make their lives more comfortable. People quickly learned to benefit from the use of tools. People soon learned how to improve the quality of life by utilizing agriculture and mining.

All regions don't contain the same resources. One area may produce agricultural products while another may have an abundance of wood, iron ore or other natural resources.

People have always relied on each others' skills to meet their collective wants and needs. The need for economic interaction enhanced the desire to trade, and commerce grew. Due to differing values of items to be traded and the differing wants and needs of people, direct barter is an inefficient form of commerce.

Value is subjective. It is a mental concept of how much I want to keep something, balanced against what I am willing to give up for something else. When two people agree on that point, value is set. Trade can take place.

All exchanges (commerce) take place in one of two ways: fair and honest trade, where willing and knowledgeable people agree and trade, or theft by force or deception.

A medium-of-exchange (money) is simply anything that people are willing to take in exchange and hold until they find something else that they want. It is preferably something that does not spoil or needs to be fed or cared for. Money has been many things and has changed often over time. For example, a person agreeing to trade a cow for 100 chickens may not want all the chickens at that time. So he might agree to accept 10 chickens and 90 shells for his cow. Later he could trade some of his shells for more chickens or for something else that he decides that he wants.

We have been taught that at one time all these different things have been used as money: fish hooks, salt, cattle, sheep, tobacco, gold, silver, copper, zinc, iron, gems, tobacco, furs, beads, shells, playing cards, cigarettes, IOU's, small pieces of paper with words and pictures on them, and finally just numbers written in an account ledger (check-book money).

The word *pecuniary* (which means related to money) stems from the Latin word *pecunia*, which in turn comes from *pecus*, meaning cattle. *Chattel* (meaning property) stems from the same root word as cattle. The word *fee* is from the old German word, *vieh*, which also means cattle.

In Mediterranean countries where it was easier to raise sheep than cattle, sheep were used as a form of money. Sheep not only provided meat, milk and cheese, also the wool that could be spun and woven into cloth and the skin supplied leather.

At one time, people thought grain would make a good medium of exchange. It could easily be stored and didn't need food to keep it alive. People weighed the grain on a balance scale. This method of weight still survives today. An avoirdupois pound is composed of seven thousand grains.

Until the invention of refrigeration, people needed salt to preserve food. The Romans paid part of their soldiers' wages with salt. The word salary stems from the Latin word, *salarium*. Hence the expression "He's not worth his salt," is quite familiar along with "Salt it away," meaning to save it.

Although many items in the past have been used for money, we have been led to believe that two of the more popular materials used for money were gold and silver. These commodities worked pretty well as money. They were very malleable, easily stamped into coins of varying sizes, very easily stored, almost indestructible and had good eye appeal.

Many of the old western movies referred to people getting gold fever. One day when talking to a fellow, who ran a gold and silver exchange, he told me that he had heard people talk about gold fever. He thought it was just an old wives' tale until the government decriminalized the ownership of gold and he began to handle lots of it. He told me that the feeling that comes over a person when he has a large amount of gold in his hands is almost unbelievable.

S.C. Mooney, in his book MONEY SYMBOL & SUBSTANCE, stated that men valued gold because God valued gold. I don't know if this is true or not, but

I do know that putting this religious connotation on a yellow metal has sure screwed up a lot of people to the point they seem incapable of thinking clearly and rationally about money. If you take a close look, most of the people that push gold as the only true money are the ones who are trying very hard to sell gold for the bank created money that they claim is so bad.

History shows us that kings and rulers liked to use gold because of its eye appeal and to impress others with the wealth and power they possessed. History, however shows that silver, much more than gold was used as a medium of exchange.

Since the founding of the United States of America, bank credits have been used for money than gold and silver combined.

We define wealth as labor and ideas combined with raw elements of the earth. People have to labor to extract the raw resources gold and silver from the ground as wealth. Assaying and stamping the metals into coins of uniform size, weight, and purity, then passing a law declaring those coins lawful money would clearly make the exchange of the metals much more convenient.

When these gold and silver coins are traded or exchanged into circulation, they become a sound, honest and fair medium of exchange.

This principle would have created a debt-free medium-of-exchange of natural wealth just as trading with fish-hooks, salt, cattle, sheep, tobacco, wampum etc. did.

Some of the oldest record records, including the Bible, tell of using silver for money. However, a comprehensive study shows clearly that the supply of gold and silver has been much too small to be a good medium-of-exchange for the total population.

History tells us that the American colonies were founded by Europeans who were using some metal, but mostly paper, as their mediums-of-exchange. The paper used at that time was either a receipt for the metals or a note, a promise to pay, the metal at a later time.

The development of North America by the earliest immigrants from England Spain the Netherlands and France was somewhat like the development of mankind as a whole. The Plymouth colony in modern day Massachusetts, one of the first English settlements in North America, was started by the Pilgrims when the Mayflower landed in 1620. During the very early years, people had little need for money. It was a rough and raw life. It was a struggle just to get food and shelter and other basic needs for survival. In time, through hard work and creativity combined with the natural increase of plants and animals, the people began to produce more than they needed for survival. People began to trade excess goods among themselves for things that they wanted but could not produce for themselves.

British subjects outnumbered all other immigrants to the colonies. Years of struggle by the Englishmen had won for them many guaranties of rights, liberties and immunities, many of which were written into the Magna Carta. This English background had a substantial effect on the thinking of the colonists. However they were a long way from England and had their own problems to deal with and therefore began to rule themselves and enjoy their individual liberties.

As Englishmen they understood the concept of trading with money and most of them held the belief (at least in theory) that gold and silver coins were the only true money. Under the common law of England the minting of coins had long been a royal prerogative.

Royal prerogative: *Those rights and capacities that the king enjoys alone.*

Royal mines: *Royal mines owned by the King at common law as within his prerogative, although on private property. At common law, mines of gold and silver were by the prerogative of the sovereign, the property of the crown, though discovered in the land of private owners. They were termed "Royal mines," and belonged to the sovereign wherever they were found. The prerogative is supposed to have originated as a necessary incident of the King's right of coinage in order to supply him with materials; mines in which there was no gold or silver, however belonged to the proprietor of the soil.* Ballentine's Law Dictionary third Edition

In practice however, the supply of coins in the colonies was so limited that most trades were done with wampum, tobacco and commodities.

Wampum was a bead made from the clam, periwinkle, conch and other shells and was used for money by the America Indians. Wampum was not easy for the Indians to make and the Indian who went to the seashore to find the shells and worked with them until they were of the required size and shape well earned, the value they passed for as money. The settlers soon made their own wampum and because they had better tools to make the wampum and the Indians would still accept them in trade for furs, some families gained a small, if not totally honest, fortune.

The first lawful money of these settlers was in 1634. The court of Massachusetts ordered that musket balls, of full bore, shall pass for a farthing. A farthing was a British bronze coin worth a quarter of a penny. In 1637, wampum was made legal tender when the Massachusetts court ruled that it should pass at six for a penny.

In the 1640's the Massachusetts colony began trading with the Dutch, and the English and the Spanish colonists on the West Indies islands. Many different kinds of silver coins began to enter the Massachusetts colony. In 1642, the Massachusetts court passed an act regulating the value of the different coins in relationship to the British schilling.

The most prominent of these coins were the Spanish American eight reales cob coins called the Spanish dollar by the colonists. These Spanish dollars had crude cobs struck out of a clump of silver without a standard shape. The Spanish minted the cobs as quickly as possible as a way to inventory and ship silver to Spain. The cobs were not designed to be used as circulating money. However, because of the severe shortage of any kind of money, they were used as money in the colonies. The coins were both chipped and debased by counterfeiters.

To address these problems, the general court passed an act authorizing a mint where silver bullion and foreign coins could be melted and used to mint coins of a standard weight and fineness. Individuals could bring anything and everything made of silver to the mint to be coined. If the silver was pure, alloys were added and if the silver was of poor quality alloys were removed. The mint master was allowed to keep 6.5% of the coins he minted. Even with the minting costs, it was advantageous to have the easily chipped Spanish cobs melted then stamped into the new higher quality coins.

The Massachusetts mint was the first, most successful and longest running of all the colonial mints. The mint was opened to provide coinage for the local economy. They made the coins 22.25% lighter than their British counterparts hoping that the coins would not leave the local community. Sadly, they lacked an understanding of how severe the shortage of coined money was. The demand for and the exportation of the coins drained the silver from the area until there was not enough silver to maintain the mint.

Some of the coins made it to England where they caused problems with the king. The king sent his commissioners to Massachusetts requesting a copy of their laws and statutes. After reviewing the laws and statutes, the king's commissioners sent a letter to the Massachusetts General Court informing it that it needed to make 26 changes in their laws. They also informed the court that they had to repeal the minting law as the right to silver coins was a royal prerogative which had not been given to the colonies.

In 1684, England's King Charles II abolished the Massachusetts charter, thereby revoking all of their privileges of self government and placing the colony under royal rule.

Coinage, silver or otherwise, never played a significant role in the colonies monetary system. England was not inclined to send coins to the colonies as coinage was also very short in England. The fact is, there has simply never been a large enough supply of gold or silver to be used for anything except small change.

Under the English common law, the king owned all the gold and silver that came out of all the ground that fell under his jurisdiction. The king was the only one with authority to coin money. The King had the power to tax the people to regain the coins after he spent them. Yet the king ended up having to borrow from people who he believed were richer and had more gold and silver than he did. Under the English common law, these people couldn't have owned any gold or silver mines and didn't have the power to tax. Just how did they get so rich in gold and silver? Hmmm, that seems like a question that could stand some serious thought.

There were many different kinds of coins in circulation in the American colonies including English and French guineas, old Roman Johannes and half-Johannes, Spanish and French pistole, doubloons, English and French crowns, English shillings and the Spanish milled dollars, all of which served as a medium-of-exchange in the colonies. Of all those coins the Spanish milled silver dollar was the most popular. It came across the frontier from Louisiana and was the principal coin of commerce. However, all the coins together were not enough to provide an adequate monetary system for the colonies or the new nation.

This is clearly evidenced by the fact that the colonies of Virginia, Maryland and North Carolina adopted tobacco warehouse receipts as their money. It was declared legal tender and circulated as the principal currency throughout those colonies.

As English colonies, they were bound by the English mercantile system. Under this system, they were forbidden any production or trade outside of sending raw goods to England and receiving finished goods from England. As the desire for tobacco grew in England, the colonists of Virginia, Maryland and

North Carolina were able to obtain most of the finished goods they needed from England.

Tobacco money provided colonial churches and colonial governments with a good source of revenue. When a man wanted to take a bride, he paid the church leader in tobacco money. Colonial governments accepted tobacco money in payments of fines and taxes.

In those colonies, people who were found encouraging Negroes to hold meetings were fined 1000 pounds of tobacco. People who allowed Negro slaves to keep horses were fined 500 pounds of tobacco.

Most of the foreign coinage that came into the colonies also quickly left the colonies in payment to English merchants. For the payment of postage, which had to be paid in silver, the silver went to England.

The shortage of coins and the metals for coining left the colonist with no course of action but to use something else as their circulating medium-of-exchange. All the colonies, beginning with Massachusetts in 1690, turned to paper instruments as their chief medium-of-exchange.

Due to their false belief that silver and gold coins were the only true money, and their complete lack of understanding of the most basic underlying principle of money (money must always represent wealth). They turned down the wrong road. They issued all paper monetary instruments as IOU's with most of those IOU's tied to interest. That caused all these early emissions of paper monetary instruments to be called "Bills of Credit".

Money can only be a payment not a promise to pay. It is simply a tool to make trade easier and it **must** be a **representation of wealth.** True money must be what one uses to make final monetary payment. Therefore true money can never cause anyone to bear the cost of interest to get the money into circulation.

If the colonists would have understood that self-evident fact, they would have printed paper money and spent it into circulation, in lieu of taxes, to build a great transportation system in the colonies. The money would then stay in circulation for the people to use as their medium-of-exchange with out debt or taxes.

Had the founding fathers would have understood the basic principles of money today we would be a great and wealthy nation without any debt and with very little taxation. Instead we are a nation way over its head in debt with a total tax rate of around 60% with the pressures to tax more growing daily.

There is probably no doubt that there would have been a war for the colonists to gain independence from England. There is no doubt the states would have needed to form a union to fight and win that war. There is no doubt that the union of states would have had to print paper money to fund the war, because Britain was, but not as a promise to pay something that they did not have and had no hope of getting.

They would have printed the money as government currency under the authority of a sovereign nation to do so. They would have never allowed private banks to create money based on a promise to pay gold and silver coins that did not exist. If the coins would have existed, there would have been no reason why honest men would not have used them. If the people were so willing to use paper for their medium-of- exchange, as they obviously were and are, why would the paper money need to be a promise to pay some thing else? The paper money we use today proves that paper money doesn't need to be a promise to pay anything else.

If the increase in the money supply to fund the war did happen to cause price inflation (which is very doubtful), all that would have been needed to correct that problem would have been to stop printing any more money until the goods increased.

To be fair to our forefathers, it is a lot easier to sit down and study history in the light of our present day debt and understand what caused it and see what should have been done differently. Than it would have been to set down in 1700 and look 300 years in the future and see the outcome of their decisions.

It appears that in the years between 1600 and the 1890's, most of the people believed, in theory, **but not in practice**, that the only money was silver coin and maybe a little bit of gold. Today, no one can deny that the whole world's medium-of-exchange is a bookkeeping medium of exchange and clearly functions well as a medium-of-exchange, but not as true money. It is not the form of money that is killing the system. It is the debt and the interest and the outrageous manipulations of the debts that are causing all the problems.

The English kings did everything they could to stop the colonists from minting coins and from printing any currency except IOU's that promised to pay coinage. The Kings soon learned that when the colonies issued the IOU's without interest, the colonists were perfectly satisfied to use them. The colonies would take those IOUs in payment of taxes then reissue them, thus keeping them in circulation and using them as money. The bankers, who obviously controlled the kings, did not like that.

In 1751, the king required any issue which was not redeemed within two years, had to pay interest.

The constant efforts by the kings to suppress the colonies money supply led the colonial leaders to violate the king's rules; the colonial leaders issues most of their paper money issues without the king's approval. The shortage of money was probably the biggest reason the colonists claimed exemption from taxation that was imposed by the king. Attempts by the British Parliament to impose taxes and restrict the money supply caused increasing tension on both sides. These monetary conflicts were a major cause of the colonist demanding their independence. Slowly the colonies moved toward separation from Britain. As disputes with Britain worsened, the colonies took steps to join together. These steps led to the Declaration of Independence, the formation of the Continental Congress and finally war.

It takes an enormous amount of funds, to fight a war. The Continental Congress did not have any authority to tax (at that time only the states had the power to tax) to raise the needed funds. The people didn't have the money to pay the amount of taxes that were needed anyway. The nation did not have any gold or silver mines from which to mine and make coins. War, it seems, provides very fertile ground for financial innovation. Men like Alexander Hamilton and Aaron Burr were well aware of the practice of fractional banking and the profits and the power that could be gained by printing paper notes and loaning them at interest.

On May 11, 1775, John Hancock of Massachusetts placed before the Continental Congress a plan to raise funds for the colonies' fight for independence. The plan revolved around the idea of printing and issuing continental currency promising to pay Spanish Milled Silver dollars. On the face of the currency it read, **"This bill entitles the holder to receive Spanish milled dollars or the equivalent in gold or silver bullion."** Why would honest men issue the paper promise to pay gold and silver if they had the gold and silver? The Continental Congress did not have the Spanish Milled dollars or the gold or silver bullion to give to the holder.

I am not so sure that many of our founding fathers were really honest men. However, by issuing and spending the continental currency the Congress gained immediate purchasing power to fund the war effort. Maybe this was not totally honest, but it was effective.

The Robert H. Gore Jr., numismatic endowment records show copies of the actual notes the Continental Congress authorized. Their records show the congress printed $3,000,000 dollars worth of Continental notes (bills of credit) in May of 1775 for the defense of America. By 1780 the Continental Congress had issued around **$140,551,695** in continentals. It is commonly taught and accepted that the Continental Bills began to lose their purchasing power and finally became worthless because the congress (government) issued too many of them. Hence, the old saying "not worth a Continental",

However, James Madison wrote that the Continental Bills lost their purchasing power only when it became obvious to more and more people that the Continental Congress would never be able to obtain enough Spanish Milled Dollars to pay their notes. The English Crown refused to permit continental currency to circulate in areas occupied by the English army. The English loyalists' used every means that they could think of to discredit the continental currency. This included writing letters to the editors demonizing the currency and putting advertisements in papers to sell counterfeit continental currency at a very great discount. It is very hard to know how much that increased the amount of continental currency in circulation.

The following ad re-written here for easier reading appeared in the New York Gazette and Weekly Mercury on Monday, April 14, 1777:

ADVERTISEMENT

Persons, going into the other Colonies, may be supplied with any number of counterfeited Continental Notes for the price of the paper per ream. They are so nearly and exactly executed that there is no risk in spending them, it being almost impossible to discover that they are not genuine. This has been proved by the Bills to a very large amount which have already been successfully circulated. Inquire for Q.E.D. at the coffee house from 11 P.M. to 4 A.M. during the present month.

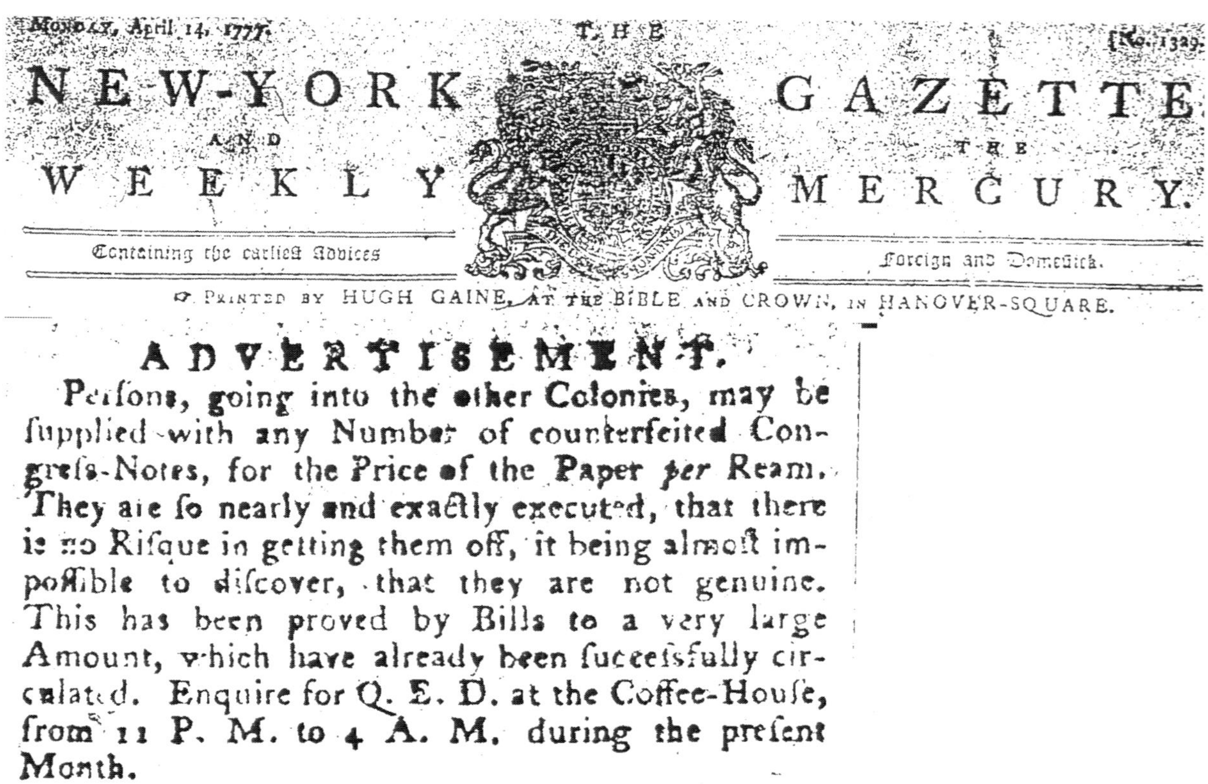

MONDAY, April 14, 1777. THE [No. 1329.

NEW-YORK GAZETTE AND THE WEEKLY MERCURY.

Containing the earliest Advices Foreign and Domestick.

PRINTED BY HUGH GAINE, AT THE BIBLE AND CROWN, IN HANOVER-SQUARE.

ADVERTISEMENT.

Perſons, going into the other Colonies, may be ſupplied with any Number of counterfeited Congreſs-Notes, for the Price of the Paper *per* Ream. They are ſo nearly and exactly executed, that there is no Riſque in getting them off, it being almoſt impoſſible to diſcover, that they are not genuine. This has been proved by Bills to a very large Amount, which have already been ſucceſsfully circulated. Enquire for Q. E. D. at the Coffee-Houſe, from 11 P. M. to 4 A. M. during the preſent Month.

As Bill Maher said the other night on the Larry King show, *"the American people will believe anything if you just tell them the same thing enough times."*

One must be very careful when it comes to the subject of money. The more one reads about moneys history and its effect on people's lives, the more contradictions, half-truths and misinformation one finds. We must also always keep in mind that most books and articles on money are written by apologists for the banking system.

On one hand, writers tell us that the Continentals lost their value because the government issued too many of them. We must understand that the word value used here means purchasing power not weight as it did in the writing of the 1792 coinage act. Seldom, if ever, do they mention that the Continentals lost their purchasing power because the issuer did not have the ability to pay the holder in coin as the notes promised. Nor do they inform us that a large number of the colonist were loyal to the King and opposed and counterfeited millions of dollar worth of the currency as a strategy of war.

On the other hand, writers tell us that at about the same time (1797), the bank of England had issued so many bank notes that they could not pay the holders of the notes in coin as the notes promised. So Parliament passed laws making the notes of the Bank of England a legal tender. Parliament passed additional laws restraining people from redeeming the bank notes meaning the holder of the notes could not ask the issuer to make his notes good. These laws prevented a run on the Bank of England. The notes worked the same in the exchanging of goods and services whether they were redeemable in coin or not, so the people continued to use the notes.

The same thing was done several times between 1789 and present day America. In fact, that is what we are doing now as I proved in my court case with the Federal Reserve Bank of Minneapolis. Before 1963, all Federal Reserve notes stated they would pay dollars to the bearer on demand. In 1963 President Kennedy had the words '*pay dollars to the bearer on demand*' removed and made the note itself the payment. Few people even noticed and everyone went on using them as money. It is like the bank saying we know it is a bad check but it will be ok if you just keep on passing it around. This is fraud on its face.

It is impossible for a promise to pay to become actual payment. The only thing that can happen is to pass the debt onto someone else and watch the compounding interest exponentially grow the debt. This book will prove that is what is happening now in America.

Putting that reality aside, the question is, if it worked so well with bank notes in England **why didn't the same thing work with the government notes, the Continentals of 1776 and the United States notes of 1812 and 1865?**

The answer is very simple! The bankers, through the media and the schools of economic thought, constantly tell the people that government issued debt-free interest-free money can't be trusted; only bank issued interest-bearing money (with the interest going to the bank) is the only sound money. We also have many people who refuse to diligently examine the facts claiming gold is the only sound money.

We are constantly told that a person who holds a public office, who receives no personal gain other than a set wage, cannot control his urge to issue too much money. But a man working **solely for personal gain**, (interest on money issued on someone else's property) in a privately owned banking system, can control his urge to issue too much money. Any thinking person should see the fallacy in this line of reasoning.

Modern Money Secrets hiding in plain sight:

Inflation is NOT a hidden tax.
Interest on modern money is a hidden tax.

Chapter 6
History of the America Dollar

The word dollar was the English name for the German thaler, or Joachimsthaler, which was a large silver coin first minted by Count Schlick in 1519. Our English word "cash" comes from the Persian word *karsha* meaning weight.

From the Oxford English Dictionary we read:

Dollar- Thalar recorded Aberus 1540, with the full term Joachemsthaler of Joachemsthal. A silver coin in Bohemia where they were coined in 1519 from the silver mine opened there in 1516, by a German Count named Stephen Von Schlick. In England before 1600 modified to dollar.

Dollar = 1. The English name for the German Thaler, a large silver coin. Also of the coins of northern countries of Sweden.

2. The English name for the peso or pieces of eight (eight reales) formerly current in Spain and the Spanish American colonies, and largely used in the British North American colonies at the time of their revolt.

3. The standard unit of the gold and silver coinage of the United States of America. In 1782, Thomas Jefferson in <u>Notes on a Money Unit for the United States</u>. Wks. III, 446 stated: the unit of (Spanish) dollar is a known coin and the most familiar of all to the mind of the people. It is already adopted from south to north. In 1785, on July 6, the United States Continental congress resolved that the money unit of the United States of America be one dollar.

In order to determine the initial value of the United States dollar, the newly formed government set up a study to weigh the Spanish coins and found that on the average they weighed 371.25 grains of pure silver. Therefore, 371.25 grains of pure silver was the weight (value) of the dollar set forth in the 1792 Coinage Act.

Setting the value of America Dollar by weight

The Continental Congress turned their attention to the metal monies current in the several states. On April 19, 1776 a committee of seven was appointed by the

Continental Congress to examine and ascertain the value of the species of gold and silver coins, then current in the colonies, and to determine the proportions they ought to bear to the Spanish milled dollars. The committee of the continental congress directed the financier Robert Morris to report to them on a table of rates at which the foreign coins should be received at the treasury. His assistant, Governor Morris, answered with a statement of the denominations of the money current in the several states and of the comparative value of the foreign coin in circulation. Governor Morris explained the necessity of establishing a standard of value and the adoption of a money unit. He proposed for the unit a fraction of pure silver that would be a common measure of the penny of every state. He found this common measure to be 1,440 units or as we would say today 1,440 pennies to a dollar. Congress addressed this issue again in 1784. Jefferson agreed the general views of Morris were sound, and the principle was ingenious, but the numbers were so large it would be too hard to do the math in your head or even with pen and paper. If the price of a loaf of bread would be 1/20th of a dollar or 5 cents, it would be 72 units. A pound of butter at 1/5th of a dollar or 20 cents would be 288 units. A horse or a bull at 80 dollars would be 115,200 units.

Jefferson thought that it would be wiser to adopt the Spanish milled dollar as the unit of account and divide it according to the decimal system. The penny would be one 100th of the dollar and the dime would be one 10th of a dollar.

On September 2, 1776, Thomas Jefferson recommended to the Continental Congress that the United States adopt the silver Spanish Milled Dollar, commonly called "Pieces of Eight" as the monetary unit of value. Jefferson stated: "The Spanish milled dollar is a known coin and the most familiar of all to the mind of the people. It is already adapted from the south to the north." Jefferson further expressed the opinion that in fixing the unit of money, the following circumstances were of principal importance:

> *1. That it be of a convenient size to be applied as a measure to the common money transactions of life.*
> *2. That its parts and multiples be in easy proportion to each other so as to facilitate the money arithmetic.*

3. That the unit and its parts or division be so nearly of the value of some of the known coins so that they may be of easy adoption for the people.

Jefferson concluded the Spanish Milled dollar seemed to fulfill all these conditions. Source: the writing of Jefferson

On July 6, 1785, the Continental Congress resolved that the money unit of the United States of America would be one dollar. On the eighth of August 1786, it was enacted by the Continental Congress that the standard for coinage of gold and of silver should be eleven parts fine and one part alloy, and the money unit or dollar should contain 375-64/100 grains of fine silver.

The dollar was not defined in the Constitution because in the minds of the founding fathers, it was a matter already settled by the Continental Congress.

This fact is proven when we read Article I Section 8 Clause 6 of the United States Constitution. It states that Congress was to provide for the punishment of counterfeiting the securities and current coin (meaning the coin that was in use at the time of the constitutional convention in 1787) of the United States. Congress fulfilled the black letter of their constitutional duty to "coin money" when it passed the Coinage Act of 1792. This act established a mint and regulated the coinage of the United States. However, they did not fulfill the intent of the Constitution which clearly was to establish a good and honest working monetary system for the new nation.

Section 9 of that act states, "Dollar or units each to be the value (value meaning the weight and purity of the metal in the coins not the purchasing power) would be the same as the Spanish Milled Dollar which was a coin current at the time; and to contain three hundred and seventy-one grains and four sixteenth parts of a grain of pure, or four hundred and sixteen grains of standard silver." There was no doubt that in the minds of the founding fathers, the current coin meant the Spanish milled coin. The coin that Jefferson stated was the most familiar to the mind of the people. It was the most familiar coin, but coins were just a small part of the money supply. Just like today.

The Spanish Milled Dollar (1740)

The Silver Dollar (1795-1804)

Many people have become confused over the meaning of the word 'value' as used in the United States Constitution. The dictionary states: *Value is a fair or proper equivalent in money; the worth of a thing in money or goods at a certain*

time. Therefore most people only think of money's value as the purchasing power of money. When the founding fathers wrote in Section 8 clause 5 of the Constitution that the Congress shall have the power, "To coin Money, regulate the Value thereof", they were not talking about regulating the purchasing power of the money. They were talking about regulating the weight and purity of the metals that was coined into money. The value, what something is worth, in reality is only what a willing buyer and a willing seller agree on at any given point in time.

To illustrate: what would you pay for a large glass of water if you were standing by a fresh clean mountain stream? What would you pay for the same glass of water when you had been out in a desert without water for three days and that glass of water would determine whether you lived or died? Look at the stock market. Its value changes minute by minute as buyers and sellers reach agreement.

Debasing coins simply means putting less weight and purity of the valuable material into the coins during the coining process. The most common way to debase coins is to substitute a less valuable metal like copper, nickel, or zinc for the gold or silver when the coins are minted. This is being done in America today. Debasement is the only way that anyone can truly counterfeit coins. Our founding fathers understood debasement and wrote into law a punishment for "'counterfeiting the current coin" as they were instructed to do by Article I Section 8 Column 6 of the Constitution. In Section 19 of the 1792 Coinage Act, they wrote, "If any of the gold or silver coin which shall be struck or coined at the said mint shall be debased or made worse as to the proportion of fine gold or fine silver therein contained every such officer or person who shall commit any or either of the said offenses shall be deemed guilty of a felony and shall suffer death." This constitutionally mandated law, like many other constitutional mandates has not been not adhered to or enforced.

The 1792 Coinage Act goes on to state:

Half Dollars – each to be of half the value of the dollar or unit, and to contain one hundred and eight-five grains and ten sixteenth part of a grain of pure, or two hundred and eight grains of standard silver. Quarter Dollars – each to be one fourth the value of the dollar or unit, and to contain ninety-two grains and thirteen sixteenth parts of a grain of pure, or one hundred and four grains of standard silver. Dismes (Dimes) – each to be of the value of one tenth of a dollar or unit, and to contain thirty-seven grains and two sixteenth parts of a grain of pure, or forty-one grains and three fifth parts of a grain of standard silver. Half Dismes (nickels) – each to be of the value of one twentieth of a dollar, and to contain eighteen grains and nine sixteenth parts of a grain of pure, or twenty grains and four fifth parts of a grain of standard silver. Cents – each to be of the value of one hundredth part of a dollar, and to contain eleven penny-weights of copper. Half Cents - each to be of the value of half a cent, and to contain five penny-weights and half a penny-weight of copper.

Please make a special note that in 1792, the 50¢ coin was just half the weight of the dollar coin. The 25¢ coin was just half the weight of the 50¢ coin. The weight of 10¢ coin was one tenth of the weight of the dollar coin. The 5¢ was one twentieth the weight of the dollar coin.

It is not the intent or the propose of this book to cover all the coins that have been minted in the United States but to just show the overall change in our coinage from 1792 to the present.

In 1982 (the year I started my researched), the Bureau of the Mint, an agency of the Department of the Treasury, spent approximately $201,002,000.00 (operating costs and metal costs) for 16,501,576,624 newly manufactured coins with a face value of $661,514,541.00. In 1983, I wrote a letter to the United States Department of the Treasury and asked them for the metal composition of our coins. Kenneth B. Gubin answered by letter and stated, "As for the metal composition of our coins, please note the following;"

COINS 1982-1983

Total metal fabrication, manufacturing cost & profit for the coins:

Value	Weight	Composition		Cost	Profit (Seigniorage) per coin
$1.00	125.0 grains	109.4 grains copper copper - 87.5%	15.6 grains nickel nickel - 12.5%	0.031	0.969
$0.50	175.0 grains	160.4 grains copper copper - 91.67%	14.6 grains nickel nickel - 8.33 %	0.0404	0.4596
$0.25	87.5 grains	80.2 grains copper copper - 91.67%	7.3 grains nickel nickel - 8.33 %	0.0217	0.2283
$0.10	35.0 grains	82.1 grains copper copper - 91.67%	2.9 grains nickel nickel - 8.33 %	0.0095	0.0905
$0.05	77.16 grains	57.87 grains copper copper - 75%	19.29 grains nickel nickel - 25%	0.0192	0.0308
$0.01	38.58 grains	.96 grains copper copper - 2.5%	37.62 grains zinc zinc - 97.5%	0.0078	0.0022

The mint created $460,512,541.00 dollars as a profit to government while creating small change coinage for the people.

It is clear to see that in 1983, the 50¢ coin was larger and weighed more than the dollar coin. When and where else have you ever seen the half of anything be bigger and weigh more than the whole of the same thing? That is like saying that one half of a gallon of gas would be larger in volume and weight than a whole gallon of gas or that half a bushel of corn would be bigger and weigh more that a whole bushel of coin. During one of my trips to Washington D.C., I was discussing our money system with Congressman Nussel. After showing him the changes in our coinage I asked him if he thought he could get any Iowa farmer to believe that half bushel of corn could weigh more that a whole bushel of corn? He responded that he didn't believe that he could.

Due to upgraded equipment and other cost cutting measures total metal fabrication and manufacturing cost for the coins in 1998 was:

$0.01 coin was $0.0026 generating a profit of $0.0074 profit per coin

$0.05 coin was $0.0066 generating a profit of $0.0434

$0.10 coin was $0.0089 generating a profit of $0.0911

$0.25 coin was $0.0168 generating a profit of $0.2332

$0.50 coin was $0.0379 generating a profit of $0.4621

The people, however, do not receive any, wealth or debt- free money due to the way the government puts the coinage into circulation. After the Mint manufactures the coins they are sold at face value to the twelve Federal Reserve banks. The reserve banks in turn sell them to the local banks at face value. The local banks then sell them to the people at face value. The only way any of the coins are paid for is with demand deposit money (numbers in a checking account). Banks create Checkbook money by simply by writing numbers in their banks ledgers when they make loans.

The coins that we use are made by the government at a profit for the government. The paper currency that we use is printed by another agency of the treasury, the Bureau of the Printing and Engraving. This is done as a, at cost, print job for the 12 private Federal Reserve banks, not as a profit for the government.

In a personal letter to me, Donna Pope speaking for the Director of the Mint stated: "The notes are sold to the Federal Reserve at the cost of manufacture, not at face value. There is no Seigniorage or profit on issuing paper currency from the Bureau of engraving and Printing to the Federal Reserve."

When I first started studying this subject in 1982, the cost of printing a currency note was $0.0206 per note regardless of the face value or denomination, of the currency note. In 1975 the cost was slightly in excess of 1 cent. In 1999 the cost was 4 cent a currency note. When the currency is sold to a commercial bank by a Federal Reserve bank at face value, the profit per currency note for a federal reserve bank would be:

$1.00	bill minus	$0.04	=	profit	$0.96
$2.00	bill minus	$0.04	=	profit	$1.96
$5.00	bill minus	$0.04	=	profit	$4.96
$10.00	bill minus	$0.04	=	profit	$9.96
$20.00	bill minus	$0.04	=	profit	$19.96
$50.00	bill minus	$0.04	=	profit	$49.96
$100.00	bill minus	$0.04	=	profit	$99.96

The Federal Reserve Banks claim that they do not get a profit from buying the bills at the cost of printing. Here is the way Russell L. Munk explained it in a personal letter to me. *"The Federal Reserve notes then become liabilities of the twelve Federal Reserve Banks. Because the notes are Federal Reserve liabilities, the issuing Bank records both a liability and an asset when it receives the notes from the Bureau of Engraving and Printing, and therefore does not show any earnings as a result of the transaction."*

The following is some interesting points on Seigniorage, debt-free, interest free money vs interest-bearing money and other things that I gleaned from a Congressional hearing on redesigning the dollar coin by the subcommittee on domestic and International Monetary Policy, Committee on Banking and Financial Services in the House of Representatives, Representative Michael N. Castle presiding.

Chairman CASTLE. We are here today to attempt to break the impasse over the one dollar coin issue. Some might ask, why bother? The Susan B. Anthony one dollar coin is used in limited transactions around the country, so why shouldn't it continue in that role? The short answer is because the Treasury, the Federal Reserve, and the United States Mint face a looming problem. There's only about a 30-month supply of Susan B. Anthony coins stored at the Mint and the various Federal Reserve banks, and U.S. Mint officials say they need about 30 months to prepare for issuing a redesigned coin.

Everyone would agree that the current coin could be improved. Its color and edge make it too easily confused with a quarter. I have introduced H.R. 2637 to correct design flaws that are often blamed for its poor reception by the public. Giving the coin a golden color and distinctive edge will eliminate confusion between the dollar and the quarter coins. Many people think that the paper one dollar Federal Reserve note, or one dollar bill, must be withdrawn before any dollar coin can be successful, no matter how attractive and well designed. This is only an argument for doing nothing, since several years of debate have shown that neither the public nor the Congress are ready to give up the paper note at this time.

Failure to modernize our money now leaves a mix of currency and coins that is increasingly less convenient. The quarter dollar is our basic coin, and it is called upon to play roles formerly filled by pennies, nickels, and dimes, while still acting as the primary unit for parking meters, toll booths, and vending machines. Accumulated inflation has altered the function of most denominations of money.

We all remember the penny gumball machine from our youth. It now takes a dime, or even a quarter, before it will dispense a gumball. If you try to park for more than an hour at any urban parking meter, you may need an entire roll of quarters to avoid risking a heavy fine.

As hard cash becomes harder to use, it will only encourage the public to shift away from cash toward the increased flexibility of electronic money, stored-value cards, and internet transactions, issues this subcommittee has examined. There's nothing wrong in such a shift, if people want it, rather than having it forced upon them by poor planning. Our Government must also be willing to accept that declining use of coins and currency will jeopardize the $24 billion per year franchise represented by the earnings Treasury now makes from them.

H.R. 2637, the United States One Dollar Coin Act of 1997, simply provides for a redesigned gold colored coin with a distinctive new rim. H.R. 2637 does not give any of the various factions in coin politics everything that they desire. It may be that there is no middle ground between those who insist on the status quo because they profit from supplying the paper and ink for paper money, and the vending and metal interests who would have Congress dictate that the green-back dollar must be taken away before the American people are prepared to truly accept the dollar coin.

Mr. KOLBE. Thank you, Mr. Chairman. Yes, this is a beautiful coin, and is certainly one that I would be very proud to have in my pocket as a dollar, substitute for a piece of dollar paper. As you pointed out, unless Congress acts in the very near future, we will have made the decision, by our inaction, to make more of the Susan B. Anthony one dollar coins. The legislation that you, Mr. Chairman, have introduced would avoid this embarrassment. Additionally, your legislation recognizes one of the great myths about the Anthony dollar: that size was the problem with the coin. Size was not the problem.

H.R. 2637 maintains the Anthony's dimensions, but changes the color to the golden such as you have here in this mockup; calls for a distinctive edge, in this case, it's a smooth edge with it serrated inside. That's exactly what I've been proposing for the last decade. With these changes, the new Liberty dollar would be very much easier to distinguish from a quarter, than a quarter is even from the current nickel.

Mr. Chairman, if I might add one thing, because you mentioned the great reliance of electronic transactions, and this doesn't go to the issue of the coin, specifically, this coin or another coin, it goes to the issue of a modern currency. I just had a little experience over the weekend which I'd like to share with you. I serve on the board of trustees of a university, Embry-Riddle Aeronautical University, which has two campuses, one of them in Florida, in Daytona. I was down there for the board of trustees meeting, and the administration at Embry-Riddle has introduced a new thing which they call "eagle cards." An "eagle card" is an electronic transaction card which all students now can buy and go down to any number of places on campus with cash and get a card that is equal to a certain amount of money. It's like a metro card. You can go down and put $50 on it, $100, or whatever. They have now converted everything on campus to using the eagle card, so that in the dorms—the new dorms we just built—where they have convenience stores, something we didn't have when I was in school—they don't use cash; they use their eagle card. The Laundromat uses the eagle card.

The bookstore uses the eagle card now. You can use cash, but everybody's found that this eagle card works so much better. You don't have to have cash on hand, and each time you use it, it tells you electronically how much you have remaining on your card. I think you can see the advantage.

I know that a few businesses find a coin preferable to a one dollar bill and have lobbied Congress for a new dollar coin. Your bill will allow them to have that in limited quantities tied to actual demand without penalizing the American people. I still think that a dollar coin, no matter what color it is, is too close in size to a quarter, and I don't like the idea of lugging more coins around in my pocket. Judging by the letters I've received over the years, I suspect many of my constituents agree.

It's often said we're the only major industrialized country that still uses a paper dollar. Those who say this are either uninformed or unaware that the U.S. currency is a unique worldwide circulating currency system and that nearly two-thirds of American dollars are held overseas.

I alluded earlier to the fact that this committee held a series of hearings on the future of money. I read the transcripts with interest, particularly in regard to the use of the "smart," or debit cards which seem to be gaining more popular acceptance. As a Member of the House Committee on Transportation, I naturally follow those developments very closely. One thing I've started noticing is that transit systems that have formerly relied on dollar coins are starting to switch to debit cards. This is a recent debit card issued by the Chicago Transit Authority, which I believe has supported the coin in the past. I think we'll find that more and more transit systems will be choosing cards over coins as we move to the 21st century.

Mr. KOLBE. Mr. Chairman, might I just respond to that? He's absolutely correct about the amount of American currency held abroad, but it's not one dollar bills that are held abroad, it's one hundred dollar bills.

Mr. DAVIS. That is what we understand at least.

Mr. DAVIS. Well, if I could just respond. I don't think it matters whether you have a coin or a bill. I think that the future of these cards is inevitable whether it's at turnpikes, tolls, metro systems, or the like, and I think that technology is kind of overtaking us whether it's bills or coins at this point.

Chairman CASTLE. Well, just a closing comment and as a sidelight to all to that, I agree with both of you on that. I think that this whole business of electronic commerce is coming on a lot faster than a lot of experts in this country realize, and it's happened because of the example—and I don't think you were here, Mr. Davis—that Mr. Kolbe used. A lot of these colleges are doing it. You're virtually going to have a whole universe of colleges all doing this, so the higher educated part of our population is going to be used to it by the time they go out into the work world, and that's going to make, in my judgment, a very vast difference over anything that we have seen before. But I'm never going to change either of your minds, I don't think, but I appreciate your testimony.

Mr. LUCAS. Mr. Chairman, I appreciate your calling for this hearing, First of all, change does come to our currency system. I mean, clearly, we are not operating the way the Founding Fathers operated in the beginning. Long ago, we stopped minting half cents and stopped making large one cent pieces, and long ago, after the emergency circumstances of the Civil War, we stopped printing paper dimes and paper quarters and paper half dollars. Things do change.

Mr. METCALF. Thank you, Mr. Chairman. I've long been a strong supporter of the dollar coin. I like the Susan B. Anthony dollar, very frankly. Had they colored that, brass colored or whatever, it would have circulated and been totally acceptable. Color was the problem. I guess there's another reason I like the coins, because we don't pay interest on the coins, but we pay interest, the people and the businesses of America, pay interest directly or indirectly on every Federal Reserve paper dollar in circulation, and that is something that the more coins we use, the less interest we pay; that's one point.

Mr. KOLBE. Well, Mr. Metcalf, I think you want to direct that later here when you have the Mint in front of you,

Mr. METCALF. OK, I think that's all the questions.

Mr. ALLISON. I'll try to lay it out in understandable terms. First, let's assume that a dollar coin costs eight cents—that's a number that's been used in the past—and lasts 30 years. Let's assume that a dollar note costs four cents and lasts a year-and-a-half, I've kind of gone to round numbers on these, but these are ballpark—these are all in the ballpark. To keep a dollar note in circulation, then, for 30 years—that's the amount we use, because that's the assumed life of a coin—to keep a dollar note in circulation for 30 years requires the Government to lay out four cents initially to make the note and then another four cents every year-and-a-half, or 20 more times over that 30-year period; that's a total of 84 cents over the 30-year period. Now, for a dollar coin, it costs eight cents once to make it, and another eight cents at year 30 after it, on average, becomes unfit. At that point; a total of 16 cents. That's quite a difference; that's 68 cents over that 30-year life in favor of the dollar coin. Now, you multiply that—that doesn't seem very much—but you multiply that by, say, a billion coins or so that might convert from notes to coins, and then that gets to be several hundred million dollars.

Suppose the total amount of coins went up. That would provide a means of financing expenditures for the Treasury that didn't exist before; that is, the Treasury can in effect spend. Let's say there were another one billion coins, the Treasury could, in effect, spend—on goods, services, salaries, anything it wants to buy—a billion dollars without having to borrow the money to do it. And, therefore, it would save the interest cost on a billion dollars of debt that is avoided, in the case of a billion more coins. I'm not predicting that there would be a billion more coins, but just to put this in the perspective of some possible number.

Mr. METCALF. Thank you, Mr. Chairman. Very interesting, Mr. Allison. I thank you for that explanation. You said some very interesting things. The dollar coin costs about eight cents, and then it is issued into circulation at face value by the Treasury. That's correct?

Mr. ALLISON. Yes.

Mr. METCALF. And so the Seigniorage, it costs you eight cents, but the Treasury gets, essentially, a full dollar, so it's 92 cents per coin seigniorage; it goes right into the Treasury in effect.

Mr. ALLISON. It's a bookkeeping entry. Seigniorage is a bookkeeping entry, but, yes, the Treasury gets to net 92 cents right away, because it deposits those dollar coins with the Federal Reserve.

Mr. METCALF. Right. It seems to me that we should issue all the coins that are needed out there. Now let's talk about the dollar note. It costs four cents to print, you said.

Mr. ALLISON. Yes. These are rough——

Mr. METCALF. You rounded out, I understand.

Mr. ALLISON. Yes, I said those were ballpark numbers.

Mr. METCALF. But then the Federal Reserve, essentially, issues it into circulation.

Mr. ALLISON. Yes.

Mr. METCALF. And what do they do with that? They get 96 cents for every one dollar bill that goes into circulation, if it costs four cents. What do they do with that 96 cents? What do they buy with it?

Mr. ALLISON. Yes, actually, the Federal Reserve buys a Treasury bill or Government security of some type worth one dollar.

Mr. METCALF. And, thus, we pay interest directly or indirectly on every Federal Reserve note in circulation; over $400 billion.

Mr. ALLISON. Let me make clear that the Federal Reserve buys those notes from the public; that is, those were Government securities that the Treasury had issued in the past; they're already put into circulation. They're a consequence of past budgetary deficits by the Federal Government. So, instead of the Treasury paying interest to the public or some other holder, it's paying to a different holder. This holder, however, the Federal Reserve System, returns all of the interest—unlike all other holders—returns all of the interest to the Treasury.

Mr. METCALF. Not all of the interest.

Mr. ALLISON. At the margin, all of the interest. The Federal Reserve, as you know, keeps an amount necessary to cover our own budget, and that's about the first $2 billion, roughly, of earnings; keeps enough to add a small increment to an account called "surplus," which is retained earnings. That's a few hundred million, and pays a dividend to member banks, another few hundred million, and then 100 percent of the balance over that goes back to the Treasury.

Mr. METCALF. Right. You take out your expenses, and give the rest to the Treasury which is fine. I just wanted to make that clear. It seems like a strange system where we could issue the money directly as we do our coins, and gain the Seigniorage, and, instead, we allow the Fed to issue it, and then we pay interest on it out of the Treasury, and then part of that interest comes back to us. It seems like an arcane system that could have been invented only by somebody who was mentally deranged. I think we're mentally deranged to continue it.

Mr. Allison, sort of change—actually, maybe a little bit of a follow up to Mr. Metcalf's questions—and I've asked you this before, but I haven't, actually, asked you this lately. Has Treasury, in recent months, seriously studied the potential for producing legal tender, electronic forms of money? I mean, I really do think this is starting to take hold a little more than we might have thought a year ago, and I'd be curious as to whether you all contemplate—the Federal Government should contemplate—being a player in this or just stand by and watch it happen? I don't know what—I'm not sure what we should do. I'll be just curious as to your thinking on it.

Mr. ALLISON. The Treasury and the Federal Reserve have, in the past, taken the view that there ought to be less Government intrusion rather than more in this process, especially at the beginning, so that innovation can take place, and that remains the Federal Reserve position, I believe.

Chairman CASTLE. This is going a little beyond my knowledge, perhaps, but aren't we dealing with an impact on Seigniorage eventually. I mean, my understanding is that in many European countries, they've gone to electronic forms of currency to a huge extent, much greater than America, and we could do that here, at which point, you're going to have, sort of, private exchanges and not Federally-issued currency, which would eventually, I would think, impact some of the Seigniorage numbers that we've already talked about here today. I mean, maybe you may need to refine my statement a little bit, but is that not correct, and do we not have to sort of keep an eye on that?

Mr. ALLISON. I would agree with you in this sense. I would agree with you period, and let me elaborate a bit. The Government, neither the Treasury in the case of coins, nor the Federal Reserve in the case of currency, has a monopoly on all of the means of payment in this country. If we think about M2, which is the measure of money that's useful for policy purposes. Total currency, bank notes and coins together comprise only about 10 percent of that, and the rest is bank account money. So, the banks, in effect, are permitted to supply the public with 90 percent of its money as defined by M2.

If the public finds electronic alternatives to either currency or bank account money more efficient, I would say—and provided the other public policy concerns like safety and security and privacy and so forth are taken care of—then I would say that that's an appropriate development. That's a development that is in the public interest.

Mr. METCALF. Interesting point that I just thought of as you people were talking there. Interest is paid on all of the bank of Fed-created money. Is that not correct? Interest is paid directly or indirectly in the system on all of the money—you mentioned that it was about one-fifth. So, we got one-fifth, or we got part of it as coins, and then we're paying interest on the notes, but all the other four-fifths draws interest, directly or indirectly.

Mr. ALLISON. Let me clarify what I mean. One reason the Federal Reserve earns as much as it does, is that it pays no interest to the holders of its liabilities. Its liabilities are mainly currency notes, and the holders of currency notes don't earn any interest on those. By the same token, the holders of some bank account money don't receive interest; strictly checking account deposits, for example. Other holders of bank account money do receive interest. In every case, though, there is a corresponding asset that the financial institution which issues that money holds, which earns a return that, it's hoped, would be greater than the cost of those funds; that is, the earnings on those funds would exceed their cost. So, yes, the Federal Reserve earns interest on assets that fully cover the outstanding currency supply in the case of Federal Reserve notes.

Mr. METCALF. On the outstanding currency supply?

Mr. ALLISON. The outstanding supply of Federal Reserve notes, sure.

Mr. METCALF. Well, thank you, that's very helpful. But the other four-fifths that is essentially bank money, interest is charged directly, is paid by the people in the businesses of America on all of that, indirectly or directly. It's all backed by debt, right? Interest-bearing debt?

Mr. ALLISON. No, it's all backed by assets, loans and investments of commercial banks, and other financial institutions.

Mr. METCALF. But they're assets of the banks.

Mr. ALLISON. So, they're assets of the banks that match the money liabilities, the deposit liabilities of the financial institution.

Mr. METCALF. Sure, but interest is being paid on it by somebody somewhere.

Mr. ALLISON. Well, the banks earn interest on their loans and investments, and they pay interest on many of their deposits so that the holders of that kind of money frequently do earn interest from the bank that issues the money.

Mr. BENFIELD. We must be careful not to delude ourselves, because no matter how beautiful the coin is, we believe it will not circulate in large numbers. There is a technical explanation, and I think it's important to put it on the record. I've created a chart over here, and you can see most people get their cash from an ATM machine or a bank teller, usually in ten- and twenty-dollar bills. These bills are then spent at a grocery store, chain restaurant, convenience and drug stores. During these transactions, coins and bills enter the consumers pockets, and later on the coins and dollar bills find their way to vending machines and transit fare boxes, parking meters, pay phones, and library copy machines.

In a way, the term "circulate" is a very appropriate term. Sometimes we have the idea that money jiggles back and forth in the economy; it doesn't. It goes in very tight circles. The large bills start at the bank; move to the consumer; then, they go to the cash register. From there, the coins are removed by the vending and mass transit industries. There was a notion in the Senate that "Oh, if we give the vending industry and mass transit their coins, they'll be happy, and that's a great compromise." Well, the truth is that transit and vending remove coins from circulation; they don't put them into circulation.

In 1993, I was taking to a young fellow in southern Minnesota who told me that I was wrong about America's coinage. He said that we could still have silver coined into money by the government if we wanted to. He said that his father had done it not very long ago. A few days later, I was telling Greg about that conversation. Greg said *"I have an ounce of silver. I will send it to the mint and see if what the fellow said is true."* on August 9, 1993 Greg sent the following letter and received the answer that follows the letter.

DEPARTMENT of the TREASURY
C/O the UNITED STATES MINT
Washington, D.C. 20220

Dears Sirs,

Enclosed is a one ounce, .999 silver round. Would you please coin this into one U.S. legal Tender Silver dollar for me at no charge? A person told me that you did this recently for his father. Thank you
Sincerely,

Gregory K. Soderberg
2410 4th Dr. SW
Austin, MN. 55912-2866

DEPARTMENT OF THE TREASURY
UNITED STATES MINT
WASHINGTON, D.C. 20220

SEP 15 1993

Mr. Gregory K. Soderberg
2410 4th Drive S.W.
Austin, MN 55912-2866

Dear Mr. Soderberg:

This is in response to your letter of August 9, 1993, regarding coining your one ounce, .999 silver round into a U.S. legal tender silver dollar for you.

The legal authority of the Mint to accept private deposits of silver for coinage was repealed by Congress over a century ago. As a brief historical background, the coinage of gold and silver from private deposits was first authorized by Congress in the Coinage Act of April 1, 1792. By the middle of the last century, however, the coinage of private silver deposits was considerably curtailed by Congress. In the Act of February 21, 1853, Congress expressly provided that the Mint could not accept deposits of silver from the general public for the striking of any coin denomination other than the dollar. Then, in the Coinage Act of February 12, 1873, Congress eliminated the standard silver dollar from our coinage system and, correspondingly, terminated the right of the public to deposit silver with the Mint for coinage into silver dollars. While the Bland-Allison Act of February 28, 1878, restored for the time being the standard silver dollar in our coinage system, the Congress had never reenacted legislation authorizing the Mint to accept private silver deposits for coinage purposes.

I should also point out that the Federal Government no longer has the statutory authority to issue standard silver coins. In the Coinage Act of 1965, as amended by the Act of December 31, 1970, Congress removed all silver from our circulating coinage and substituted a cupro-nickel coinage alloy instead. Accordingly, I am returning your silver round to you.

A I hope this information is helpful.

Sincerely,

Kenneth B. Gubin
Chief Counsel

Enclosure

BM-29
(7/74)

DEPARTMENT OF THE TREASURY
WASHINGTON, D.C. 20220

OFFICE OF
DIRECTOR OF THE MINT

A HISTORY OF THE SILVER DOLLAR

The silver dollar, not as we know it today, but as its progenitor, came prominently to the fore in the days of the American Revolution.

The dollar, or "thaler" (which did not originate with the Spaniards), is short for the "Joachimsthaler" of Joachimsthal, a mining town in the Joachims Valley in Bohemia, where the coins were first struck in the sixteenth century.

On the second day of the Second Continental Congress, May 11, 1775, Mr. John Hancock of Massachusetts placed before that body a plan to raise funds for support of our forces in the fight for freedom, involving the use of Spanish milled silver dollars for payments of notes to be issued by the Congress.

The Journal of the Continental Congress on June 22, 1775, records a "resolve" that a sum not exceeding two millions of Spanish milled dollars be emitted by the Congress in bills of credit for the defense of America.

At the time there were many different kinds of colonial shillings in circulation, all with different values in terms of the English shilling. However, the Spanish silver dollar, which came in by trade across the frontier from Louisiana, which Spain later ceded to France, was the principal coin of commerce. It contained 374 7/8 grains of silver.

A committee of seven was appointed by the Continental Congress on April 19, 1776 to examine and ascertain the value of the species of gold and silver coins then current in the colonies and to determine the proportions "they ought to bear to Spanish milled dollars." This committee filed such a report on September 2, 1776. Included in the report are references to such denominations as English and French guineas, Johannes and half Johannes, Spanish and French pistole, doubloons, English and French crowns, English shillings, and the then popular Spanish milled dollars, all of which served as a medium of exchange in the colonies.

Thomas Jefferson recommended on September 2, 1776, to the Continental Congress, that the United States adopt the silver "Spanish Milled Dollar" called "Pillar Pieces of Eight", as our monetary unit of value, since daily trade was transacted in that coin.

In his notes on the subject, Thomas Jefferson expressed the opinion that in fixing the unit of money the following circumstances were of principal importance:

1. That it be of a convenient size to be applied as a measure to the common money transactions of life.

2. That its parts and multiples be in easy proportion to each other so as to facilitate the Money Arithmetic.

3. That the Unit and its parts or divisions be so nearly of the value of some of the known coins so that they may be of easy adoption for the people.

Mr. Jefferson concluded the Spanish dollar seemed to fulfill all these conditions.

The Superintendent of Finance in the Continental Congress, Robert Morris, wrote in 1777: "The various coins which have circulated in America have undergone different changes in their value, so that there is hardly any which can be considered as a general standard, unless it be Spanish dollars. These pass in Georgia at five shillings, in North Carolina and New York at eight shillings, in Virginia and the four Eastern States at six shillings, and in all the other States except South Carolina at seven shillings and sixpence, and in South Carolina at thirty-two shillings and sixpence."

The dollar was established as the ideal money unit of the United States of America by the Continental Congress, on July 6, 1785. On the eighth of August 1786, it was enacted that the standard for coinage of gold and of silver should be eleven parts fine and one part alloy, and that the money unit or dollar should contain 375-64/100 grains of fine silver.

The Mint Act of April 2, 1792:

1. Authorized coinage of the silver dollar (of the value of Spanish milled dollar) against the deposit of silver and fixed its weight at 371-4/16 grains of pure silver or 416 grains of standard silver;

2. fixed the standard for silver coins as 1485/1664 (.8924) fine;

3. fixed the coinage ratio of gold and silver as 1 to 15;

4. provided for free coinage; and

5. declared silver dollars (and all other coins authorized) lawful tender.

The Act of 1792, in effect, reduced the silver content 1-1/7 percent from the dollar established in 1786.

Coinage of silver dollars commenced in 1794. In his report of October 28, 1794 to the Congress, the first Director of the Mint, David Rittenhouse, reported "A beginning has been made in coining the precious metals * * * * A large parcel of blank dollars is ready for coining, waiting for a more powerful press to be finished, in order to complete them for currency."

From 1794 until 1805, the Mint at Philadelphia produced 1,439,517 silver dollars. During this period, many of these coins were exported to Mexico and the West Indies where they found acceptance in place of Spanish milled dollars. This left the worn and clipped Spanish coins as the chief circulating medium in the United States.

While Secretary of State, Madison wrote Mint Director Robert Patterson on May 1, 1806:

> "In consequence of a representation from the director of the Bank of the United States that considerable purchases have been made of dollars coined at the Mint for the purpose of exporting them, and as it is probable further purchases

> and exportations will be made, the President (Jefferson) directs that all the silver to be coined at the Mint shall be of small denominations, so that the largest piece shall not exceed a half a dollar."

No more silver dollars were minted until 1836, thirty years later, and then only 1000 of them were issued from the Mints, and during this interim period, as indicated, the largest denomination of silver coins issued from the Mint was half dollars.

The Act of January 18, 1837, which consolidated Mint law up to that date, fixed the standard fineness as 0.900 for silver coins and changed the weight of the silver dollar to 412.5 grains. Under this act, 6,590,721 silver dollars were coined, commencing in 1839, and continuing without interruption (except for the year 1858) until 1873.

Coinage of the silver dollar was discontinued by reason of the Act of February 12, 1873, which omitted the silver dollar from the list of coins authorized to be struck by the Mint. When the standard silver dollar was dropped, Congress made provision for a trade dollar.

The trade dollar was exported largely to the Orient, where it competed in circulation with the Mexican peso. This coin was 420 grains in weight, seven and one half grains heavier than the standard weight of the regular silver dollar. Though trade dollars continued to be struck for a period of seven years after the Bland-Allison Act of 1878, these pieces were confined to specimen proof strikings. The total of trade dollars struck amounted to 35,965,924 pieces.

The Act of February 28, 1878 restored coinage of the standard silver dollar (but only on Government account) of the weight of 412.5 grains of standard silver 0.900 fine (371.25 grains of pure silver) as provided by the Act of January 18, 1837, and declared all such dollars (and all those previously coined) to be legal tender except where otherwise expressly stipulated in the contract. The Act also directed the Secretary of the Treasury to purchase each month, at the market price thereof, not less than $2,000,000 nor more than $4,000,000 worth of silver bullion and to coin the bullion so purchased into standard silver dollars. Under this Act, 291,272,018.56 fine ounces of silver were purchased, at a cost of $308,279,260.71, and 378,166,793 standard silver dollars were coined.

Purchases under the Bland Allison Act of 1878 were continued until passage of the Sherman Act of July 14, 1890.

The Sherman Act of 1890 repealed the provisions of the Act of February 28, 1878, which required the monthly purchase and coinage of silver bullion, and directed purchase of silver, to total 4,500,000 ounces of bullion per month at the market price thereof, not exceeding one dollar for 371.25 grains of pure silver, provided for its coinage into standard silver dollars, and authorized the issue of Treasury notes (called Treasury Notes of 1890) in payment for the silver bullion purchased.

Under the Sherman Act, 168,674,682.53 fine ounces of silver were purchased, at a cost of $155,931,002.25 for which Treasury notes were issued. Of the silver purchased, 144,653,722.68 fine ounces, costing $134,192,285.02 were coined into 187,027,345 standard silver dollars. The balance was used for subsidiary silver coinage. (Of the silver dollars coined, 36,087,285 were coined before the repeal of the silver purchase authority by the Act of November 1, 1893; 42,139,872 were coined between November 1, 1893 and June 12, 1898; and 108,800,188 were coined as directed by the Act of June 13, 1898.)

The Acts of March 3, 1891 and March 3, 1887 authorized coinage from trade dollar bullion and trade dollars then in the Treasury. Under these Acts, 5,078,472 standard silver dollars were coined.

The Act of November 1, 1893 repealed the purchasing clause of the Act of July 14, 1890.

The Act of June 13, 1898, directed coinage into standard silver dollars of all the remaining bullion in the Treasury purchased under the Act of July 14, 1890.

The Act of April 23, 1918, (Pittman Act) authorized the conversion of not exceeding 350,000,000 standard silver dollars into bullion and its sale, or use for subsidiary silver coinage, and directed purchase of domestic silver for recoinage of a like number of dollars. Under this Act, 270,232,722 standard silver dollars were converted into bullion (259,121,554 for sale to Great Britain at $1.00 per fine ounce, plus mint charges, and 11,111,168 for subsidiary silver coinage), the equivalent of about 209,000,000 fine ounces of silver. Between 1920 and 1933, under the Act, the same quantity of silver was purchased from the output of American mines, at a fixed price of $1 per ounce, from which 270,232,722 standard silver dollars were recoined.

Under the Thomas Amendment to the Agricultural Adjustment Act, approved May 12, 1933, the President was authorized for a period of five months to accept silver on war-debt account, at a maximum price of fifty cents an ounce, the total amount accepted not to exceed a value of $200 million. Silver certificates were to be issued against the silver so received to the total value at which the silver was accepted. The law further provided that the silver so accepted should be coined into standard silver dollars and subsidiary silver coin sufficient, in the opinion of the Secretary of the Treasury, to meet any demands for redemption of the silver certificates issued.

A further requirement to mint silver dollars was contained in a Presidential Proclamation related to the purchase of newly-mined domestic silver, issued on December 21, 1933, calling upon the Mints to coin this denomination, in payment for the silver received under this Proclamation.

The quantity of silver dollars minted under the Thomas Amendment and the Proclamation of December 21, 1933, was 7,021,528 pieces.

Section 5 of the Silver Purchase Act of 1934 provided that all silver certificates issued thereunder would be redeemed on demand at the Treasury of the United States in standard silver dollars, and gave the Secretary of the Treasury authority to coin dollars for such redemption. Further, the Proclamation of August 9, 1934, nationalizing silver, provided that the silver so received would be added to the monetary stocks of the United States and coined from time to time into standard silver dollars in such amounts as were required to carry out the provisions of the Proclamations. The total quantity of silver dollars minted under these two authorities was 53,029 pieces. The coinage involved took place in 1934 and 1935.

Public Law 88-36, approved June 4, 1963, provided:

"Silver certificates shall be exchangeable on demand at the Treasury of the United States for silver dollars, or at the option of the Secretary of the Treasury, at such places as he may designate, for silver bullion at a monetary value equal to the face amount of the certificates."

On March 25, 1964, the Secretary of the Treasury exercized the option authorized by this act, and it is no longer possible to secure silver dollars from the Treasury. However, holders of silver certificates could continue to avail themselves of their legal right to demand an amount of silver precisely equal to the silver content of a standard silver dollar, that is, .77+ ounce of fine silver. The certificates were redeemed at the U.S. Assay Office in New York in the form of crystals, and at the U. S. Assay Office in San Francisco in the form of pellets or granulations. Redemption was made at the monetary value of $1.292929292 an ounce.

Silver certificates have not been exchangeable for silver bullion since June 24, 1968. They are legal tender, however, and continue to function as a medium of exchange at their face value.

From 1792 until 1873, when silver dollar coinage was discontinued, the manufacture of silver dollars was free for the account of the depositor of silver, and the mint price of silver was $1.2929+ per fine ounce. After restoration of coinage in 1878, coinage of silver dollars was for the account of the United States, and the difference between the cost of the silver and the face value of the dollars coined, termed seigniorage, was covered into the Treasury as a miscellaneous receipt.

President Lyndon B. Johnson signed an historic bill July 23, 1965, providing for the first major change in United States coinage in more than a century. Silver was eliminated altogether from the dime and quarter, and substantially reduced in the half dollar. A world shortage of silver and the necessity of conserving this metal for industrial and military uses was the motivating factor behind passage of the legislation authorizing this departure from the traditional silver alloy.

The Coinage Act of 1965 also contained a provision restricting the minting of silver dollars for a period of five years after passage of the act. Even though no longer produced - the last coinage took place in 1935 - the standard silver dollar continued as an officially authorized coin of the United States.

On December 31, 1970, President Nixon signed into law the Bank Holding Company Act. Appended to the legislation were important amendments to the Coinage Act of 1965.

Section 101(b) removed the silver from the dollar and directed that it be a clad coin composed of cupro-nickel. Continuing production of this denomination for general circulation will be of these metals, i. e., copper and nickel.

Section 101(d) is a special provision authorizing the minting of not more than 150 million clad dollars containing 40 per cent silver and 60 per cent copper, to be sold to collectors. These are produced in both proof and uncirculated condition and may be obtained on a seasonal basis from the U. S. Assay Office in California. The mailing address is: Bureau of the Mint, 55 Mint Street, San Francisco, California 94175.

Section 203 of the Act reads:

> "The dollars initially minted under authority of Section 101 of the Coinage Act of 1965, shall bear the likeness of the late President of the United States Dwight David Eisenhower, and on the other side thereof a design which is emblematic of the symbolic eagle of the Apollo 11 landing on the moon."

---oooOooo---

AUTHORITIES FOR SILVER DOLLAR COINAGE

Authorizing Act	Standard Weight	Standard Fineness
April 2, 1792	416 grains	892.4
January 18, 1837	412-1/2 "	900.0
February 28, 1878	412-1/2 "	900.0
July 14, 1890	412-1/2 "	900.0
March 3, 1891	412-1/2 "	900.0
April 23, 1918	412-1/2 "	900.0
December 31, 1970	379-1/2 "	400.0

SILVER DOLLAR COINAGE

Act Apr. 2, 1792:		
From 1792 to 1805 ----------------------------	$1,439,517	
During 1836 -----------------------------------	1,000	
		$ 1,440,517
Act Jan. 18, 1837: From 1839 to Feb. 12, 1873 ----		6,590,721
Act Feb. 28, 1878 (Bland-Allison Act) ------------		378,166,793
Act July 14, 1890 (Sherman Act), to date of repeal of purchasing clause thereof Oct. 31, 1893 ----	36,087,285	
Act Nov. 1, 1893, to June 12, 1898 ---------------	42,139,872	
Act June 13, 1898, war revenue bill --------------	108,800,188	
		187,027,345
Act Mar. 3, 1887 and 1891, trade-dollar conversion		5,078,472
Act Apr. 23, 1918, Pittman Act replacement (represents equivalent number of dollars converted into bullion - 259,121,554 for export to India and 11,111,168 for domestic subsidiary coin):		
Old design, since Feb. 21, 1921 ------------	86,730,000	
Peace dollar, since Dec. 21, 1921 ----------	183,502,722	
		270,232,722
Act May 12, 1933 (sec. 43), Executive proclamation, Dec. 21, 1933 ----------------------------------		7,021,528
Act June 19, 1934 (sec. 7), Executive proclamation, Aug. 9, 1934 -----------------------------------		53,029
Total ---		855,611,127

As most people know, our money is still expressed in dollars and cents. A few years ago I wrote to the United States Treasury and asked them, what is the current statutory definition of the word dollar? They wrote back and told me that is was 31 USC 5101 which states,

"31 USC 5101. - Decimal system

United States money is expressed in dollars, dimes or tenths, cents or hundredths, and mills or thousandths. A dime is a tenth of a dollar, a cent is a hundredth of a dollar, and a mill is a thousandth of a dollar."

It appears that 31 USC 5101 is a simple rewrite of Section 20 of the 1792 Mint or Coinage Act which states, *"And be it further enacted, that the money of account of the United States shall be expressed in dollars or units, dismes or tenths, cents or hundredths, and mills or thousandths, a disme being the tenth part of a dollar, a cent the hundredth part of a dollar, a mille the thousandth part of a dollar and that all accounts in the public offices and all proceeding in the courts of the United States shall be kept and had in conformity to this regulation."*

That rewrite seems to be the only thing that survived from the 1792 Mint Act. It seemed in the rewriting, our money of account was changed to just numbers expressed by using the decimal system of accounting.

I then went to the United States code, 1994 Edition, which states at 31 USC 5103. *"Legal tender - United States coins and currency (including Federal Reserve notes and circulating notes of Federal Reserve Banks and national banks) are legal tender for all debts, public charges, taxes, and dues. Foreign gold or silver coins are not legal tender for debts."*

31 USC 5111 states, *"(a) The secretary of the Treasury – (1) shall mint and issue coins described in section 5112 of this title in amounts the Secretary decides are necessary to meet the needs of the United States,*

31 USC 5112 states, *"(a) The Secretary of the Treasury may mint and issue only the following coins:*

(1) a dollar coin that is 1.043 inches in diameter and weighs 8.1 grams.

(2) a half dollar coin that is 1.205 inches in diameter and weighs 11.34 grams.

(3) a quarter dollar coin that is 0.955 inch in diameter and weighs 5.67

(b) The dollar, half dollar, and the quarter dollar are clad coins with three layers of metal. The two identical outer layers are an alloy of 75 percent copper and 25 percent with three layers of metal. The inner layer is copper."

31 USC 5112 (7) goes on and states, *"A fifty-dollar gold coin that is 32.7 millimeters in diameter, weighs 33.931 grams, and contains one troy ounce of fine gold. (8) A twenty-five dollar gold coin that is 27.0 millimeters in diameter, weighs 16.966 grams, and contains one-half troy ounce of fine gold. (9) A ten dollar gold coin that is 22.0 millimeters in diameter, weighs 8.483 grams, and contains one-fourth troy ounce of fine gold. (10) A five dollar gold coin that is 16.5 millimeters in diameter, weighs 3.393 grams, and contains one-tenth troy ounce of fine gold."*

31 USC 5112 (e) goes on to state, *"Notwithstanding any other provision of law, the Secretary shall mint and issue, in quantities sufficient to meet public demand, coins that –*

(1) are 40.6 millimeters in diameter and weigh 31.103 grams;

(2) contain .999 fine silver;

(3) have a design –

(A) symbolic of Liberty on the obverse side; and

(B) of an eagle on the reverse side;

(4) have inscriptions of the year of minting or issuance, and the words "Liberty", "In God We Trust", "United States of America", "1 Oz. Fine Silver", "E Pluribus Unum", and "One Dollar"; and

(5) reeded edges. "

31 USC 5112 (h) states, *"The coins issued under this title shall be legal tender as provided in section 5103 of this title.*

This law clearly presents some problems. They define dollars both in terms of clad coins of nickel and copper and coins of silver and gold. The ten dollar gold coin is also not of equal weights and measures. It is 1/4 ounce of gold, when it should be 1/5 of an ounce (or its face value should be 12.50 dollars, since the full ounce coin is stamped as Fifty Dollars).

The gold, silver coins and the nickel copper coins are legal tender by federal law. Go to a bank and lay down a legal tender one dollar Federal Reserve note and the bank will give you a clad coin dollar. Then lay down a $50 Federal Reserve note. The bank will not give you a legal tender $50 gold or silver coin as they should since they are both legal tender for $50.00. Go to a Federal Court and try to pay a filing fee or a fine with the gold or silver coins. The Federal Court may or may not take the coins. If they do, they will only take them at face value because the value of money is set by law not by substance.

The Sacagawea dollar coins and the new dollar coins with pictures of past presidents are golden in color; they are 8.1 grams in weight, 2mm thick and 26.5 mm in diameter. The coins physical makeup is a three-layer clad construction – pure copper sandwiched between a metallurgically bonded outer lay of manganese brass.

I think it is interesting how our coins are made today. The U.S. Mint buys strips of metal already made for each type of coin, called blanking strips. These are used to make all of our dollar, half dollar, quarter, dime, nickel and penny coins. The strips come in a rolled coil about 13 inches wide and 1500 feet long. (Step I) Each coil is fed through a press which punches out round discs called blanks. (Step 2) After the blanks are punched out, they are heated in an annealing furnace to soften, and then run through a washer and dryer. (Step 3) The good blanks are run through an upsetting that raises a rim around the edges of the coins. (Step 4) The blanks go to the coining press where they are stamped with the designs and inscription which make them genuine United States coins. (Step 5) Press operators, using magnifying glasses, spot-check each of newly-struck coins. (Step 6) An automatic counting machine counts the coins and drops them into bags that are sealed and loaded on pallets. New coins are shipped by truck to Federal Reserve Banks and then to commercial banks. <u>Source: The United States Mint website.</u>

The letter below from John Chastain of the Administrative Office of the United States Courts was written in response to questions that arose when Sylvester Ziebarth tendered .999 Fine Silver One Dollar coins issued under 31 USC 5112, (e) to pay a filing fee to the Federal Court in Bismarck North Dakota.

I was with Sylvester on the day that he tendered the coins to the clerk of courts. There was a lot of discussion concerning the Constitution of the United States and the value of the coins and money in general. Sylvester argued that value of the metal in the coins should be taken into account in determining how many coins it would take to pay the filing fee.

The clerk, of the court, argued that the substance of the coin made no difference. The legal tender was the value that was printed on the money whether the money was paper, coin or anything else. I said to the clerk if Sylvester gives you the silver coins in payment of the filing fee, will you be willing to give me the coins in exchange for 120 one- dollar Federal Reserve Notes. The clerk said “yes because to me they are just one dollar coins”. After more discussion, Sylvester gave the clerk 120 of the silver coins to pay the filing fee. However, when I pulled out Federal Reserve notes with the decimal system accounting value of $120 to buy the silver coins back from the clerk as we had agreed, they suddenly became more valuable to him. He would not complete the deal as agreed. This clearly proved that he fit into the mold of too many of the people we have in government, lying means nothing to them.

With this case, it seems like the government has a peculiar precedent. The people working for government will uphold the law and honor the legal tender value of money if it is beneficial. If it is more beneficial to not uphold the law and not honor the legal tender value of money, **they will not**!

ADMINISTRATIVE OFFICE OF THE UNITED STATES COURTS
WASHINGTON, D.C. 20544

L. RALPH MECHAM
DIRECTOR

JAMES E. MACKLIN, JR.
DEPUTY DIRECTOR

WILLIAM R. BURCHILL, JR.
GENERAL COUNSEL

June 25, 1991

RECEIVED
JUL 1 1991
EDWARD J. KL...
U.S. DISTRICT CO...

Mr. Edward J. Klecker
Clerk, United States District Court
Post Office Box 870
Fargo, North Dakota 58107

Dear Ed:

I am writing in response to your letter to Bill Burchill of May 17, 1991, posing several questions about the acceptance of Mr. Sylvester Ziebarth's 120 "silver eagle" dollars in payment of the civil filing fee. I have been unable to determine the fate of the letter I wrote in May on this subject; however, in the event it turns up, I believe it will prove to be consistent with our telephone discussions and with the present missive.

To address Judge Conmy's questions, you may accept 120 "silver eagles" in payment of the $120 filing fee. The coins are legal tender at the face value of one dollar each, despite their bullion value of about six dollars each. 31 U.S.C. § 5103. To treat them as cash, you should receipt them for the face value and deposit them accordingly. Certainly neither the Treasury nor any depositary institution will credit you with more than $120.

In the alternative, as I suggested in my previous conversations and the earlier letter, you may receipt them as tangible personal property other than cash. The court may direct you to sell the coins and apply $120 of the proceeds to Mr. Ziebarth's civil filing fee. The balance of the proceeds may be credited to Fund 129900, Gifts to the U. S. Not Otherwise Classified, or may be held in a registry account pending the outcome of Mr. Ziebarth's case. The court may apply any surplus proceeds to any collateral or registry deposits that Mr. Ziebarth may be required to make in the course of his litigation. Of course, the court may also order the surplus to be refunded to Mr. Ziebarth, since it is essentially a windfall to the Government.

If I can address this matter further, do not hesitate to get in touch. I will be glad to respond promptly.

Sincerely,

John

John L. Chastain
Assistant General Counsel

The Chief Judge of the Court wrote an order on the matter wherein he stated:

"After careful consideration of the matter, the court hereby directs the clerk of this court as follows: The clerk shall accept for payment of the necessary filing fee, plaintiffs 120 silver bullion eagles, and shall forthwith file the action to be designated as civil file number A1-91-071. ………

Said bullion eagles shall be then traded by the clerk for Federal Reserve Notes at an appropriate gold and silver exchange for a price of $5.25 each or $630.00 total. From that amount the clerk shall deduct and remit $120 to pay the necessary filing fee. The remaining balance of $510.00 to be deposited by the clerk into the court's non-appropriated fund account to be used for such purposes as inure to the benefit of the bench and bar in the administration of justice.

The court specifically finds that plaintiffs have caused the filing fee to be paid with silver bullion eagles for whatever reason they may feel such payment accomplishes."

SO ORDERED.

Dated this 1st day of July, 1991.

Patrick A. Conmy, Chief Judge
United States District Court

NOTICE OF ENTRY
Take notice that the original of this copy was entered in the office of the clerk of the United States District Court for the District of North Dakota on the 1 day of July 1991
EDWARD J. KLECKER, CLERK

By: Lena M. Klukart
Deputy

This issue surfaced again in 2003, and the corrupt people working in government showed their true colors again. When there is a monetary gain they pay no attention to the legal tender laws, even if it means destroying the lives of people who are just trying to follow the law as written.

On or around 1996, an outside-the-box thinking, Las Vegas, Nevada, business man, Robert "Bobby" Kahre began using the legal tender 91.67 % pure gold bullion coins that the Gold Bullion Coin Act of 1985 required the U.S. Mint to coin, to pay some of the people he worked with.

According to Joel Hansen, a Las Vegas attorney, Mr. Kahre put a lot of study into the issue before he started to use the gold and silver legal tender coins. After having a personal conversation with Mr. Kahre, I would agree that he had done a lot studying. It seems that Mr. Kahre came to the same conclusion that John L. Chastain did. Writing for the Administrative office of the United States Courts, Mr. Chastain said: The U.S. Treasury nor any depositary institution would not credit anyone with more that the legal tender value of the coins if tendered to them.

Mr. Kahre and people he worked with agreed to pay and receive the gold and silver coins, for certain things, at their legal tender face value. This seemed to be a reasonable conclusion because all other forms of monetary instruments checks, coins, bonds, paper currency, check-book money, etc. are all valued at the numbers written on them not by the value of the material that the numbers are written on.

According to the news (2008) the one cent coin now costs more to mint that it's legal tender face value and no one seems to question that its value could be anything but it face value.

There was no financial gain in doing this for Mr. Kahre and the people he worked with, with the exception that taxes could be calculated on much smaller numbers. The only way that they could obtain the gold and silver coins was to buy them at the market price of gold and silver bullion with bank created debt dollars (bcd) dollars). If they received the gold and bullion legal tender coins in payment of service rendered they could not spend them for everyday living expenses at their legal tender value. They would have to sell the coins back on the bullion market for 'bcd' dollars and then spend the 'bcd' dollars before they could maintain a decent living standard.

Kahre's method of doing business seemed to work well for about 7 years. Then Kahre's actions caught the attention of the IRS. It must have really upset someone when they understood that Mr. Kahre, and others were accounting for transfer of funds at the legal tender value of the gold and silver coins and not the bank created debt money value.

On May 29, 2003 an unknown number of IRS agents, with their guns drawn and ready to fire raided Mr. Kahre's places of business. These, gun in hand, IRS (bank) agents handcuffed over 20 of the people working with Mr. Kahre and held them out in the 106-degree sun while they seized whatever they wanted from Mr. Kahre's business establishments. Mr. Kahre was charged with 109 counts of tax related crimes. Cleary, the characteristic prosecutorial over kill our 'justice' system is so fond of using.

I personally do not think that the Congress intended to create a dual monetary system as some have claimed. It was just another law that Congress passed without reading and without thinking about the unintended consequences. The gold bullion Act states that: *The Secretary shall sell the coins minted under this subsection to the public at a price equal to the market value of the bullion at the time of sale, plus the cost of minting, marketing, and distributing such coins (including labor, materials, dies, use of machinery, and promotional and overhead expenses.)"* I am quite sure that the coins were only intended to be sold into the market as a scheme to sell gold pushed by some big gold dealer(s). The coins were to be paid for by bank created check-book money, the only money that the American courts will let the people use,

We again see the corruption of our court system when the judge would not allow Kahre's attorneys to argue that Kahre was justified in using the coins at their legal tender value ruling that he could only use the coins at their market value in 'bcd' dollars. However the attorneys were able to bring in the legal tender issue through the good faith belief defense of a co-defendant Alex Loglia. In 2005, Alex Loglia, a law school student wrote a 100 page paper on the separation of powers and it's affect on the gold coin issue.

Alex Loglia's studied opinion was that Congress not the judicial branch had the power to coin money and set its value and that Congress had set the coins legal tender value by the passage of law.

The government called three CPA's to the witness stand. In cross examination the defense attorneys ask each one of them "what is the proper way to calculate income for purposes of the Internal Revenue Code if you are paid in a gold coin that has a $50 face value on it? They all answered "I do not know".

Kahre and his co-defendant were very lucky the day the jury was selected. Some of the co-defendants were acquitted and the rest got a hung jury. Under our corrupt court system, a hung jury is called a mistrial. Under the court system our founders gave us a hung jury, was the same as an acquittal.

As American coins have changed over the years, so has the American paper currency. More importantly **the basic principle of what our money represents has changed.** Under sec. 14 of the 1792 coinage act, (free coinage) our coined money represented the production of the people as wealth to the people. Today all our **money represents interest-bearing debt owed to the banking system**.

In the next few pages, we will demonstrate the change. Silver and gold are natural raw elements of the earth, they are not by nature money. Someone has to labor to extract the ore from the earth and have it monetized (declared money by law). It is not the coining that turned silver or gold, or now copper and zinc into lawful money, it is the law that declared the coins money. It is not the metal that has been declared money it is the coins. There are several companies that mint metal into coins today, but those coins are not lawful money.

Under the 1792, Mint Act, when a person mined silver or gold ore out of the earth, they could take it to the mint where it was assayed and weighed and stamped into coins free of charge. Coins, that the law declared was money. When that person took the coins out and spent them, the money would have represented his production free of debt and interest.

In some circles there is a lot of talk about the constitution declaring that we can only use coins as our money. However, history has made it clear that most people have always preferred to carry and trade with the paper rather than coins. If that was not true people would not have started using check around A.D. 1500.

Below is copy of a silver certificate. On its face it states:

> THIS CERTIFIES THAT THERE IS ON DEPOSIT IN THE TREASURY OF THE UNITED STATES OF AMERICA ONE DOLLAR IN SILVER PAYABLE TO THE BEARER ON DEMAND

From my research, it appears that the first silver and gold certificates were first issued in 1853, when Congress endeavored to furnish the people with a more uniform system of silver and gold coinage. An assay office was set up in New York City. The treasurer of that office was authorized to take in foreign coin and gold and silver bullion from importers and others. The assay office would then assay those metals to determine their value based on their weight and the purity of the gold or silver. Then United States silver and gold certificates would be issued in exchange for the foreign coin and the bullion.

This silver and gold was then coined into United States coins of the weight, grade and standard set by law. The people could use these certificates as their medium-of- exchange or they could take them to the treasury and exchange them for United States coins. The principle of debt free money would have been the same. The biggest difference is the matter of trust and honesty. If the treasury is operated by honest men they will not issue any more certificates than there was silver of the fineness set by law. But the same element of honesty and trust comes into play with coins. If the men operating the mint are not honest they could also debase the coinage.

The same is true with the gold certificate shown below: On its face it states

THIS CERTIFIES THAT THERE HAVE BEEN DEPOSITED IN THE TREASURY OF THE UNITED STATES OF AMERICA TEN DOLLAR IN GOLD COIN PAYABLE TO THE BEARER ON DEMAND

However, when a person deposits gold or silver coins or gold and silver certificates into a fractional reserve bank, a totally different principle applies. The bank will hold that deposit as a reserve then increase the money supply by a factor of ten by making interest-bearing loans to individuals, business and government bodies. The factor of ten is not a set number. And is not the factor we are currently using. The banking system has the authority to change it when deemed necessary.

Now the banks loan is a promise to pay nothing. In the past, both state chartered and federal-chartered banks issued paper notes. At this time, only the 12 Federal Reserve banks issue paper notes, which are printed for them by the Federal Governments Bureau of Engraving and Printing for the cost of printing. The rest of the private commercial banks issue credit only, in (decimal system) book-entry form as a liability to themselves. This is their promise to pay nothing.

Below is copy of a 1914 Federal Reserve Bank Note issued by the Federal

Reserve Bank of Minneapolis. On its face it states:

SECURED BY UNITED STATES CERTIFICATES OF INDEBTEDNESS OR UNITED STATES ONE-YEAR GOLD NOTES, DEPOSITED WITH THE TREASURER OF THE UNITED STATES OF AMERICA

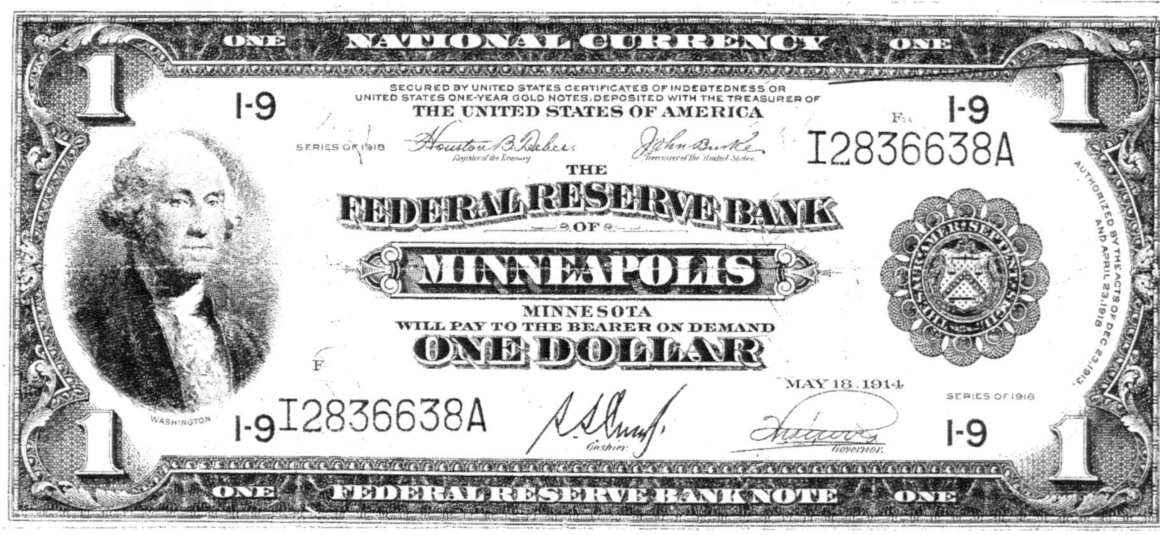

Notice, it states that the Federal Reserve Bank of Minneapolis will pay to the bearer on demand one dollar. It does not claim to be the dollar.

Below is copy of a 1929 Federal Reserve Bank Note issued by the Federal Reserve Bank of New York. On its face it states: The Federal Reserve Bank of New York will pay to the bearer ten dollars.

SECURED BY UNITED STATES BONDS DEPOSITED WITH THE TREASURER OF THE UNITED STATES OF AMERICA OR BY LIKE DEPOSIT OF OTHER SECURITIES

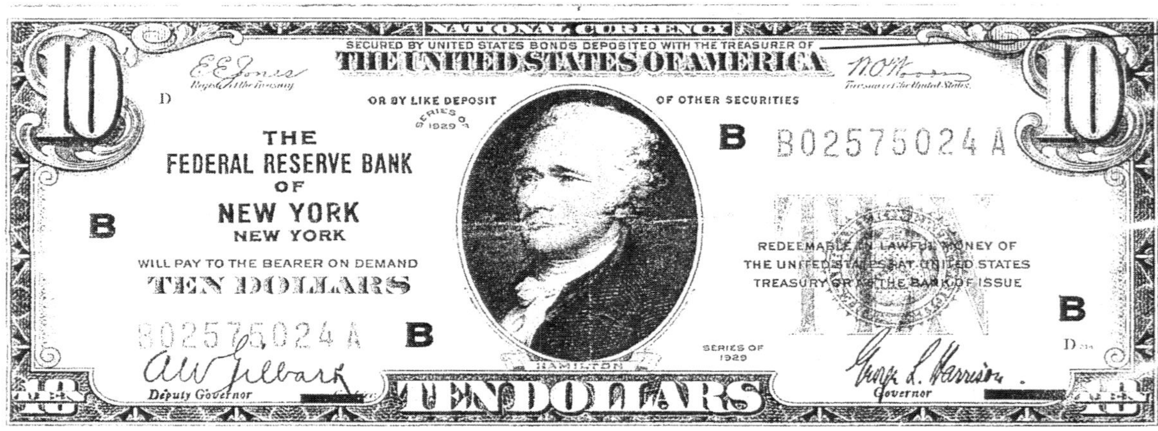

Again, it is very important to note that this bill states that the bank will pay, and it is a promise to pay ten dollars. It does not claim to be ten dollars.

Below is a copy of a 1929 Federal Reserve Note issued by the Federal Reserve Bank of Minneapolis. This bill states on it face it is a Federal Reserve Note and the United States of America will pay. It no longer states that the issuing bank will pay.

REDEEMABLE IN GOLD ON DEMAND AT THE UNITED STATES TREASURY OR IN GOLD OR LAWFUL MONEY AT ANY FEDERAL RESERVE BANK

On April 5, 1933 President Franklin D. Roosevelt issued this Executive order:

Executive Order 6102

BY VIRTUE Of the authority vested in me by Section 5 (b) of the Act of October 6, 1917, as amended by Section 2 of the Act of March 9, 1933, entitled "An Act to provide relief in the existing national emergency in banking, and for other purposes," in which amendatory Act Congress declared that a serious emergency exists, I, Franklin D. Roosevelt, President of the United States of America, do declare that said national emergency still continues to exist and pursuant to said section do hereby prohibit the hoarding of gold coin, gold bullion, and gold certificates within the continental United States by individuals, partnerships, associations and corporations and hereby prescribe the following regulations for carrying out the purposes of this order:

Section 1. For the purposes of this regulation, the term "hoarding" means the withdrawal and withholding of gold coin, gold bullion or gold certificates from the recognized and customary channels of trade. The term "person" means any individual, partnership, association or corporation.

Section 2. **All persons are hereby required to deliver on or before May 1, 1933, to a Federal Reserve Bank or a branch or agency** thereof or to any member bank of the Federal Reserve System **all gold coin, gold bullion and gold certificates now owned by** them or coming into their ownership on or before April 28, 1933, except the following:

(a) Such amount of gold as may be required for legitimate and customary use in industry, profession or art within a reasonable time, including gold prior to refining and stocks of gold in reasonable amounts for the usual trade requirements of owners mining and refining such gold.

(b) Gold coin and gold certificates in an amount not exceeding in the aggregate $100 belonging to any one person; and gold coins having a recognized special value to collectors of rare and unusual coins.

(c) Gold coin and bullion earmarked or held in trust for a recognized foreign Government or foreign central bank or the Bank for International Settlements.

(d) Gold coin and bullion licensed for other proper transactions (not involving hoarding) including gold coin and bullion imported for re-export or held pending action on applications for export licenses.

Section 3. Until otherwise ordered any person becoming the owner of any gold coin, gold bullion, or gold certificates after April 28, 1933, shall, within three days after receipt thereof, deliver the same in the manner prescribed in Section 2; unless such gold coin, gold bullion or gold certificates are held for any of the purposes specified in paragraphs (a), (b), or (c) of Section 2; or unless such gold coin or gold bullion is held for purposes specified in paragraph (d) of Section 2 and the person holding it is, with respect to such gold coin or bullion, a licensee or applicant for license pending action thereon.

Section 4. Upon receipt of gold coin, gold bullion or gold certificates delivered to it in accordance with Sections 2 or 3, the Federal Reserve Bank or member bank will pay therefor an equivalent amount of any other form of coin or currency coined or issued under the laws of the United States.

Section 5. Member banks shall deliver all gold coin, gold bullion and gold certificates owned or received by them (other than as exempted under the provisions of Section 2) to the Federal Reserve Banks of their respective districts and receive credit or payment therefor.

Section 6. The Secretary of the Treasury, out of the sum made available to the President by Section 501 of the Act of March 9, 1933, will in all proper cases pay the reasonable costs of transportation of gold coin, gold bullion or gold certificates delivered to a member bank or Federal Reserve Bank in accordance with Section 2, 3, or 5 hereof, including the cost of insurance, protection, and such other incidental costs as may be necessary, upon production of satisfactory evidence of such costs. Voucher forms for this purpose may be procured from Federal Reserve Banks.

Section 7. In cases where the delivery of gold coin, gold bullion or gold certificates by the owners thereof within the time set forth above will involve extraordinary hardship or difficulty, the Secretary of the Treasury may, in his discretion, extend the time within which such delivery must be made. Applications for such extensions must be made in writing under oath, addressed to the Secretary of the Treasury and filed with a Federal Reserve Bank. Each application must state the date to which the extension is desired, the amount and location of the gold coin, gold bullion and gold certificates in respect of which such application is made and the facts showing extension to be necessary to avoid extraordinary hardship or difficulty.

Section 8. The Secretary of the Treasury is hereby authorized and empowered to issue such further regulations as he may deem necessary to carry out the purposes of this order and to issue licenses thereunder, through such officers or agencies as he may designate, including licenses permitting the Federal Reserve Banks and member banks of the Federal Reserve System, in return for an equivalent amount of other coin, currency or credit, to deliver, earmark or hold in trust gold coin and bullion to or for persons showing the need for the same for any of the purposes specified in paragraphs (a), (c) and (d) of Section 2 of these regulations.

Section 9. **Whoever willfully violates any provision of this Executive Order or of these regulations or of any rule, regulation or license issued thereunder may be fined not more than $10,000, or, if a natural person, may be imprisoned for not more than ten years, or both**; and any officer, director, or agent of any corporation who knowingly participates in any such violation may be punished by a like fine, imprisonment, or both.

This order and these regulations may be modified or revoked at any time. Article IV of the Bill of Rights of The United States Constitution states: The right of the people to be secure in their persons, houses papers and effects, against unreasonable searches and ***seizures*** shall not be violated. Article V goes on to state: nor shall private property be taken for public use without just compensation.

After President Roosevelt issued this executive order the currency was changed. Below is a copy of a 1934 Federal Reserve Note issued by the Federal Reserve Bank of San Francisco. It states:

THIS NOTE IS LEGAL TENDER FOR ALL DEBTS PUBLIC AND PRIVATE AND IS REDEEMABLE IN LAWFUL MONEY AT THE UNITED STATES TREASURY OR AT ANY FEDERAL RESERVE BANK

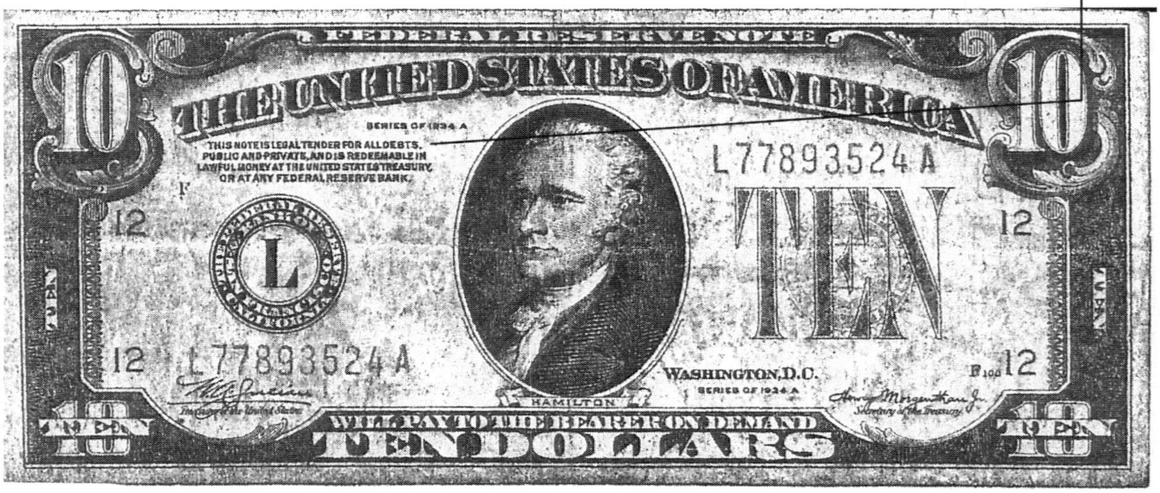

UNDER EXECUTIVE ORDER OF THE PRESIDENT

all persons are required to deliver

ON OR BEFORE MAY 1, 1933

all GOLD COIN, GOLD BULLION, AND GOLD CERTIFICATES now owned by them to a Federal Reserve Bank, branch or agency, or to any member bank of the Federal Reserve System.

Executive Order

CRIMINAL PENALTIES FOR VIOLATION OF EXECUTIVE ORDER
$10,000 fine or 10 years imprisonment, or both, as provided in Section 9 of the order

We find ourselves in a very strange situation. The bill on its face states that it is a note (a financial note is a promise to pay) issued by a private bank. Yet it states on its face that the United States of America will pay ten dollars to the bearer of the note. Three questions come to mind right away.

1. Why is the United States government going to pay the liability of a privately owned bank?
2. What is the definition of the dollar that the United State is going to pay on demand?
3. What is the definition of lawful money?

At the time this Executive Order was signed, the law still declared the term lawful money was gold and silver coin or United States Notes. President Roosevelt had just prohibited the holding, sales, purchases and movements of all gold coins and demanded that all the gold in private hands be turned over to the government so clearly the Federal government was not going to pay in gold coins. There was not enough silver coin in circulation to pay all the notes the private banks had issued. The only other thing left that could have been lawful money were United States Notes. There were not enough of them in circulation either. If there were enough of them to make a good general medium of exchange why didn't the government just use them and not promise to pay the interest bearing note of the banks? It is very clear that the government did not intend to honor that promise.

The next bill is a copy of a 1950 Federal Reserve Note. It looks the same and states the same information as the 1934 note however, the size of the wording regarding legal tender and the promise to redeem the note has be decrease to just three lines instead of four and the print reduced to a small almost unreadable size. Clearly, it was designed so that the people would no longer think about the redemption clause.

Let's examine closely the Federal Reserve Note in use today. Below is a 2004 Federal Reserve Note.

Please notice that now the Federal Reserve seal has changed. It was a seal that stated which Federal Reserve Bank issued the note, now it states: "United States". It has a black seal that states: "United States Federal Reserve System" It still tells what bank issued the note, but now it is in coded letters in the upper left hand corner. It is the J10, The Federal Reserve Bank of Denver. It also has a green seal that states "the Department of the Treasury". It just states: "The United States of America Twenty Dollars". This clearly proves that the Federal government never has any intentions to pay for the gold that was stolen from the people by the Federal government for the benefit of the bankers.

One last thing to consider, If the bills are now the money, not a promise to pay the money, why does the Department of the Treasury print them and sell them to the privately owned banks for the cost of printing? This is currently around 4.2 cents regardless of the face value of the bill. Why borrow book-entry money from the banks and pay interest on it when you can print your own money? I don't know a single person who if he could print up his own money, would sell it to me for just the printing costs, and then borrow it back at face value plus interest before he would spend it. Yet, for some reason the people don't seem to think that it is strange that this is just exactly what the federal government does.

This begs the question, "***If we have a government of the people, for the people, by the people, why are the coins that the government mints not exchanged directly into circulation, in lieu of taxes, for the benefit of the people? Why is the paper currency, we the people through our government print, not spent into circulation in lieu of taxes, for the benefit of the people?***

The answer can only be that Hamiltonian type thinkers don't believe that government should be by the people, for the people. They believe that government is by the rich, for the rich. The Hamiltonian type thinkers are clearly in control, working the money system to benefit themselves at the expense of all the rest of the people.

Modern Money Secrets hiding in plain sight:

Under modern money there is no money until someone borrows from a bank and pays interest on the loan.

Chapter 7

The History of Banking

The concept of banking and debt money originated with the goldsmiths. Goldsmiths were people who worked with gold and silver making jewelry and other things. They had heavily guarded vaults and were willing to store other people's gold and silver coins for a small fee. People would take their gold and silver coins to them for safekeeping. The goldsmith would give the people receipts, certificates of deposit, for the coins deposited in the vault. This was a fair and honest deal between consenting parties. Source: Personal letter from Russell L. Munk

Imagine yourself as a rich person living in the seventeenth century. You have in your possession a large amount of gold and silver coins. You decide to take a trip. You don't want to take all your gold and silver coins with you. After giving it a lot of thought, you decide the best thing to do is to take the coins to the goldsmith and have him store them for you. This way your coins will be safe in a strong vault, and you will have receipts to prove how many coins you have stored. While on your trip you decide to buy something that costs more than the coins you have with you. You work out a deal to sign over to the seller one of the receipts for the coins you have stored with the goldsmith. This is more convenient than going back to the goldsmith's, producing your receipt, obtaining your coins and returning to make your purchase. You tell your friends how well it works to simply trade with the receipts instead of the gold coins.

Appreciating convenience, it soon became common practice to use the receipts as an accepted medium-of-exchange. At this time in history people chose to use paper money over gold and silver coins. Just as they earlier chose to use gold and silver coins over cattle and other forms of exchange. As this practice grew, the goldsmiths found themselves in control of large amounts of other people's gold and silver.

The goldsmiths, like most other men, were open to concepts that might enhance profits. The more wily and dishonest goldsmiths watching what was happening decided they could make more profit by making a few "extra" receipts and loaning them out at interest. Maybe it got started when a friend came by and said, "I decided to buy something but I didn't bring any coins with me. How about giving me a loan?" The goldsmith thought about the gold and silver coins he had stored in his vault that people seldom asked for because they had chosen to use the paper over using the gold and silver. Thoughts of enhanced profits popped into his mind. He replied "Yes, I could loan you some coins but I will have to charge you a small fee for the use of the receipt."

However this fee will be a little different kind of fee. It will not be a one time fee, it will be a renewable percentage fee. In time the fee could be two too three times greater then the principal of the loan. Imagine a real estate agent who said he will find a buyer for your house. He will do it for a small fee that must be renewed and paid each year as long as the buyer owns the house. If the buyer owns the house for 20 years, the seller will owe the agent 2½ times the value of the house. Of course, the borrowers are never taught to think about interest in that way.

Obviously, the amount of gold or silver had not increased, but the promise (obligation/debt) to pay gold or silver did increase. When the goldsmiths created extra receipts and loaned them into circulation, they also created a shortage of gold and silver as the dollar amount of the receipts were soon greater than the dollar amount of the gold and silver. There were more obligations to pay than there was anything to pay with. The people have never really understood that fact. The people have never really cared because they didn't want to use the gold and silver anyway. The paper was so much more convenient.

Russell L. Munk explained it this way:

> *"Modern banking is often explained by analogy with the practices of goldsmiths in early seventeenth century England. These goldsmiths held their customers gold in safekeeping and issued notes to the customers instead, promising to deliver the gold on demand. The goldsmiths discovered that the customers would not all want the gold back at the same time, so it was safe to loan the gold to someone else in the meantime. When the*

goldsmith loaned the gold out, he had created money. Obviously, the amount of gold had not increased, but the note promising to pay gold circulated as money and so did the gold it was based on -- before the goldsmith intervened only the gold circulated as money. It was an easy step to making the loan in the form of a note promising to pay gold, and keeping the gold safely in vaults at all times. Then only the notes circulated as money. Nothing limited the number of notes the goldsmith could issue except the fact that he did have to pay gold if anyone presented them to him. If he issued too many people would not believe that he would be able to pay, and would refuse to accept them. To avoid this problem, prudent goldsmiths -- and, later, prudent bankers -- always kept a certain amount of gold on hand as a reserve.

Modern banks operate in a similar way, with several important differences. One is that they are required by law to keep reserves equal to a percentage of their deposits. The Fed has the power to change this "reserve requirement" ...... In both the goldsmith's practice and in modern banking, new money is created by offering loans to customers. A private commercial bank that has just received extra reserves from the Fed (by borrowing reserves for example) can make roughly six dollars in loans for every one dollar in reserves it obtains from the Fed. How does it get six dollars from one dollar? <u>It simply makes book entries</u> for its bank customers saying you have a deposit of six dollars with us."

When they realized that the people were using their receipts as their medium of exchange the Goldsmith began to loan out some of the coins. They soon realized they did not need to loan the coins, they could just out their promise to pay.

<u>BYRNS STONE ECONOMICS</u> SECOND EDITION, page 289-290 explains it this way:

"The origin of Fractional Reserve Banking

Several centuries ago almost all money was in the form of gold coins ... Goldsmiths were generally willing to store other people's money for a small fee and issued receipts for the gold deposited with them. Buyers found it convenient to transact by exchanging these receipts instead of physically getting the gold, and sellers were happy to take these receipts … as you may have guessed, this was the beginning of checking accounts, the receipts issued by the goldsmiths were 'demand deposits.' Now the plot thickens..... The goldsmiths began lending some of the gold on deposit to borrowers who would pay interest. In fact, it was not even necessary to relinquish physical control of the gold, just like depositors; borrowers generally preferred a receipt to the actual gold."

The people chose to use paper or book-entry money over metal money because it was more convenience. Then they got themselves into real trouble due to their lack of understanding that the paper and book-entry money represents interest-bearing debts, rather than representing wealth as the metal money had. This has made it very difficult to detect and understand the fraudulent, negative, destructive results of the whole debt-money process which is real cause of all bankruptcies. Most people have always believed that paper money represented wealth. They simply don't understand that paper and book-entry money we have now represents debt that they owe to the banking system.

People are slow to catch on to a really good con game. Therefore, in more modern times, it was an easy step from making loans in the form of notes to just making loans as book-entries to the customer's checking account. Now all **NEWLY CREATED MONEY HAD BEEN SWITCHED FROM EVIDENCE OF WEALTH TO AN EVIDENCE OF DEBT. Yet because we can buy anything we want with it, it leaves us with the illusion that money is wealth.**

"Note that although the system of fractional-reserve banking creates money, it does not create wealth. When a bank loans out some of its reserves, it gives borrowers the ability to make transactions and therefore increases the supply of money. The borrowers are also undertaking a debt obligation to the bank, however, so the loan does not make them wealthier. In other words, the creation of money by the banking system increases the economy's liquidity, not its wealth." Source: N. Gregory Mankiw, Ph D., Professor of Economics at Harvard University, Macroeconomics, Fifth Edition, pg 485

It was through this deceptive and fraudulent process that modern banks evolved. Nothing limits the number of loans the bankers can make, all they need are borrowers. Today confidence is enhanced because of the FDIC insurance and the false teaching by college economic professors. The ignorance of most of the people about monetary policy and the principles of money is so high that there is little risk of bank runs. That and the fact today there is no other kind of money to use.

When the goldsmiths started making loans using promises to pay, they changed the money both in *quantity* and *quality*. The change in quantity is very clear and understandable. The money supply increased as soon as the goldsmith made the first loan of someone else's gold coin, because both the gold coin and the receipt for that gold coin were in circulation at the same time, both passing as money. The change in quality is not as easily understood, but it's just as real. When the goldsmith **loaned** the gold coin or an extra receipt into circulation the money supply increased as indebtedness not as an increase of wealth, as occurred when newly mined gold is first coined. At that moment **debt money** was born.

Let's examine closely what really happened when the above took place.

A. The goldsmith/bankers received an unjust gain by misrepresenting the facts. The goldsmiths:

1) did not own the gold they were charging a fee to store it for the owners.
2) began loaning around ten times the monetary value of the other peoples' property as a profit to themselves (fraud and usury).

This is clearly theft by deception.

B. The goldsmith turned into bankers increased the "money" supply as interest-bearing debt owed to them without increasing wealth or goods. This is the most commonly used definition of inflation. The goldsmith/ bankers deceived people into believing that the gold and the receipt for the gold was the same thing. This is **Fraud, the interest on the receipt added theft by deception!**

C. He simply kept the gold and issued multiple receipts, promising to pay gold. Gold he did have. He had to know that he could never honor his promise. **Clearly fraud on its face!**

D. By increasing the receipts, the banker increased his profits through fraud and deception.

E. The banker switched money from wealth, and an evidence of wealth, to an evidence of debt. He debauched (corrupted) the money. The only way that money can be debauched is to create money as an evidence of debt rather than an evidence of wealth. This also created economic servitude.

Very few people understand that there are totally different principles and laws of economics engaged when the money supply is increased through the lending process instead of when money is created as wealth (by labor and ideas combined with raw resources of the earth) and exchanged into circulation. A person can loan a car that has been manufactured to his friend and watch his friend drive it away. It is quite impossible for a person to loan a car that has not been manufactured to someone and watch that person drive the car away.

The only thing that can be done is to deceive a person's mind so badly that when the person walks away he really believes that he is driving a car.

Once the goldsmiths started their practice of loaning multiple receipts many people found it quicker and more convenient to visit the bankers and borrow the money than to labor first and save the money. Of course bankers are more than willing to make loans that net them large windfall profits. The people seldom understand the fraud.

To justify their evil and destructive deeds, bankers rationalize that they are really helping people by expanding the money supply faster and easier than can be done by mining gold and silver ore, refining it and stamping it into coins. This made the life of the banker a lot easier as he didn't have to produce any real wealth to earn a huge income. All he had to do was print promises to pay, loan them out at interest, then sit back and receive the benefits of the other peoples production, created most often by hard labor. He then had time to plan on how the might be able to rule the world though the power of money.

As long as someone was willing to keep mining gold and silver and stamping it into coins (monetized property), and spend it into circulation, it was possible to pay at least part of the interest with the increase of new gold money. This also gave the banker the gold as a free gift. One can give the bankers promise to pay back to the banker to repay the principal of the loan, which will extinguish the debt principal. But when a loaned promise to pay is used to pay the interest, the interest debt is not extinguished. It is only shifted to someone else. Once the debt-free gold and silver coins, were no longer minted, or were demonetized by law it became impossible to pay the interest in money. Today we stamp gold and silver into legal tender coins. They are now truly and fully monetized, because they are legal tender as to the number stamped on the coin, but they are traded at the market value of the metal using the bank created money.

Interest debt can be shifted to other borrowers or roll over and thereby compounding the interest debt to the borrower. Both ways gives a monetary benefit to the banker.

You can give up some non-monetized property through bankruptcy to pay the interest.

The debt and the interest can simply be written off the books through bankruptcy, or otherwise.

If the interest rate was 10% when the banker loaned out ten promises to pay for each coin he had in his vault, his interest rate on the one coin would jump to 100%. No one would see or understand the increase in the lenders profits. This could also spread the risk over more borrowers. To this day few people have really understood what was really happening. The news spread rapidly that if you were a little short of money you could go to the bank and borrow what you needed if you signed a promissory note pledging your property as collateral. Even today very few understand what is really happening.

Smart bankers soon realized that if they demanded that most of the interest on his loans be paid in silver and gold coins, it would not take long until they would own vast amounts, if not all of the silver and gold. Using the rule of 72, we find that if a banker loaned out one coin that belonged to someone else at 10%, it would take him 7.2 years to double his money. In other words, it would take him 7.2 years to own one coin for every one coin that he had in his vault that belonged to someone else. This is not being clever, it is clearly fraudulent.

However, if he loaned out ten, promises to pay for each coin stored in his vault, using the rule of 72, it would only take him 8.6 months to own one coin for every one coin that he had in his vault that belonged to someone else.

If the goldsmith started out by loaning one ounce of gold and doubled his money every year, which he could do by fractionalizing ten to one he could mathematically amass 68,719,476,736 (69 billion ounces of gold in 37 years.) By the way, this would be 17,921,297,158 (18 billion) more ounces of gold than has been mined in the history of the world, according to the world gold council 2006.

If the bankers stared by just loaning one dollar and doubled their money every year for 60 years, this could be done by fractionalizing ten to one, they could mathematically accumulate 576,460,752,303,423,488 (576 quadrillion) dollars. Realistically, this could not be done. However, it shows clearly that though the practice of fractional banking (creating money as a promise to pay) how the bankers have been able to control the world though the power of compound interest. How they have been able

Realistically, this could not be done. It is clear that by practicing fractional banking, one would soon have control of all the money and would be able to loan to kings and governments, fund wars and buy anything and everything that one wanted including congressmen, judges, governors, sheriffs etc.

In Modern Money Mechanics, a workbook on deposits currency and bank reserves published by the Federal Reserve Bank of Chicago it states a least 4 times that banks can increase deposits (create money) by making investments as well as by making loans. Think about that, the bankers can create the money they want for their own investments. At the same time they also create all the money that everyone else uses to pay their loans, their living expenses and the money that people use to make investments as interest-bearing loans to the banks.

It is very easy to see how the goldsmiths turned into bankers and great financiers and gained great wealth and control over the people by criminal thinking and fraudulent activity. It also easy to see why the *"225 richest people in the world own assets worth over $1 trillion, an amount equal to the annual income of the poorest 47 percent of the world's population - 2.5 billion people. Why, the three richest people have assets that exceed the GDP of the 48 least developed countries."* New York, Oxford: Oxford University Press for the United Nations Development Program, 1998

Why, the 225 richest people on the planet now earn the same as the poorest 2.7 billion people, equivalent to 40% of humankind, the report finds. *"The three richest people have assets that exceed the combined GDP [Gross Domestic Product] of the 48 least developed countries."* State of the Future survey by the World Federation of United Nations Associations.

Why, *"the wealthiest 10 percent of households reaped 85 percent of the stock market gains from 1989 until the end of 1997".* Economist Edward Wolff

The very process by which money is now created will in time destroy most Americans' potential for achieving the American dream and force them to live the American nightmare. The math shows clearly why the banking system and the people at the head of it have become the slave masters over all commerce. Today, they either own or hold mortgages on all the property in the world through direct loans or indirectly through loans to governments. It is easy to see how they could control most, if not all the governments of the world, and why the government, especially in America, does not function the way it should.

This also makes it a lot easier to understand how the bankers gained control and ownership of most of the gold and silver through the interest gained from the issuing of excess receipts. It is also easy to see why it is so important for the bankers to keep everyone believing the real money is gold and their checkbook money is wealth owned by the people. That way, few would ever question their right to issue paper and book-entry money that has become the most accepted medium of exchange. Because who else would have enough money to make so many loans?

As time moved on, the men of banking began to really understand and believe in the power of money. Each generation worked to improve and enhance the system for their benefit. The Rothschilds, perhaps the greatest banking family the world has ever known, realized that it was really good business to loan to kings and Governments providing the king or the government had a good taxing system that would ensure them the interest payments.

Meyer Amschel Rothschild said *"Let me issue and control a nation's money and I care not who writes the laws."* He had learned this lesson well from his predecessor William Paterson, who in 1694 created the First Bank of England. In return for giving the King a large loan, Paterson's bank was given a monopoly on the issuance of the nation's currency. This currency was a promise-to-pay gold and silver coins that neither the bank, nor Paterson, owed. If Paterson did have it, he was not about to let it get out of his vault; it was a lot better to loan paper promises.

Over the years, the bankers have learned that the best way to hide this fraud is to tell the people the truth in such a confusing and deceptive way that most people are convinced that the fraud the banking system is pulling over on them is really beneficial to them. Bankers soon realized that the best way to ensure that most economic writing supported their practices was by funding schools of economic thought and the professors who teach in them. Professors who would teach the students, through half truths and deception, that the expansion of the money supply as loans was a very good practice; that creating money as loans was really more beneficial for the borrower than for the lender because it allowed the people and the nation to expand the economy faster than would be possible by restricting the economy to any other money system.

Russell L. Munk put it this way:

"The advantage of creating money by extending loans is that the new money goes to people that the bank believes will be able to pay it back. In general, this means that the money will go to people who are engaged in productive economic activity. Ideally, the new money will serve to channel real resources into productive use and, ideally, the new money will be created by banks when more economic activity is taking place and more money is needed to finance it."

It is often stated, in support of the banking system's fractional reserve method of creating money that it would have been impossible to have the progress of the industrial age using gold for money. Proponents of fractional reserve banking argue that the gold would not have allowed for the expansion of the money supply necessary to fund the industrial age.

Economist and others who support bank-created money like to argue that it's the velocity of money that makes the money supply grow. They fail to acknowledge that if that was true, increasing the velocity of the silver and gold coinage would have also increased the supply of coinage thereby providing the money needed to fund the industrial age. Most of them refuse to acknowledge that real issue is whether the money represents wealth or debt. There is no argument that growth in the money supply was needed to accommodate the growth in population and the growth in the economy that America has experienced. But, who has really gotten the financial benefit of the economic expansion. Was it the lower income people who did all the work that produced the real growth or the moneyed elite? For the answer, we need only to look at the total national debt and acknowledge the well-known fact that the moneyed elite is getting exponentially richer than everyone else.

It is very important to the banking system to have people believe that banking and high finance is too complicated to be understood by the average person and that the whole subject is best trusted in the hands of the financial 'experts'. It is also very important to the banking system that no rational debate about how the money system really works ever gets any national news coverage. If it did, every open-minded person listening would see how big a fraudulent ponzi scheme the banking system really is.

It is very easy to control the minds of people by controlling what is taught in the schools they attend and by what they hear in news reports.

College banking and economic courses teach that the goldsmiths simply increased the money supply. They leave out the fact the so-called, 'increased' money supply was in the form of interest accruing debts to the people and a 100% fraudulent gain to the bankers. College economic professors never talk about the effect of interest in a debt money system. They never teach that the debt money needs perpetual expansion and constant inflation to keep it working. College economic professors never even let it be hinted that the country, and the people living in it, would be served much better if the government issued the money (debt-free and interest-free) and spent into circulation in lieu of taxes to build the basic public transportation infrastructure that the nation needs.

"The controversy over the burden of the debt has not yet produced precise answers about the impact of interest cost." Source: Two Faces of Debt, Federal Reserve Bank of Chicago. Yet, we continue to use an interest-bearing system without knowing its effects.

When most people talk about how the money system works, they make a big deal about the reserves that the banks must have. I understand that today it is roughly 12 dollars in loans for every dollar in reserves. However, the reserves are not gold and silver coins or anything else, they are just another promise to pay. An economist that I talked with recently explained that today reserves have practically no monetary effect with the exception maybe of a mental and emotional effect on the people when banking is explained to them. We are now witnessing this in the sub-prime loan business. When the bankers and their funded lending agencies over loan, or make non-practical loans, the Central bank working through the government just steps in and adds liquidity as more loans.

I have talked to people with economic training who truly believe that money can only be what a bank creates. In their minds, they believe nothing can work for money except a bankers promise to pay. That actual payment would not work as money. They believe that nothing can be accomplished until the banks create money. In 2009, here may be a little truth in that statement. For history as a whole that has not been true.

That nothing can be accomplished until one has money can be quickly proven false if one just does a little studying about the first gold discovered in the United States. The first gold was found just lying in a creek bed in what is now North Carolina.

Little Meadow Creek at Reed Gold Mine, site of first discovery of gold in the U.S.

John Reed lived on a farm with a creek. One Sunday in 1799, his son Conrad found a 17-pound yellow rock while playing in the creek. The family thought it was pretty and used it for a doorstop. In 1802, a jeweler stopped by the house, noticed the rock and identified it as gold.

The following year John Reed formed a partnership with three neighbors and started a mining operation. At that time unlike today, there was very little food to eat unless you raised it yourself. You could not go to the story and buy all your food. So although the gold was there and could be mined by hand, the partners did not do any mining until their crops were planted and harvested, because raising their food was so much more important to survival than having gold.

To get really rich, the bankers needed to deceitfully teach the people that it was a very good idea for the people to use paper money or bookkeeping money (this part is true). The bankers also needed to teach that this form of money can only work if the banking system created it as interested-bearing loans. The people must never understand that it would much better for them if the government created debt-free and interest-free in lieu of taxes to build the transportation system. The bankers need to teach that people working in government simply can not be trusted to create paper money or bookkeeping money without debt and interest. Although they would not gain directly or personally by the creation of the money they would surely create too much of it and cause wild inflation. Only men working as bankers, who get a personal gain for each loan made, can be trusted to create just the right amount. What deception that is!

Above all else, monetary education had to be done in a way that disguised, evaded, and definitely did not reveal the truth. Throughout history, the key to success of monetary fraud has been in keeping the masses confused, uninformed and totally ignorant of the real facts! Keeping the pockets of key government people very full of the bank created money also helps a lot.

No doubt! If the American people ever **really** understand the facts about what has been done (the amount of wealth that has been stolen from them, this includes at least two thirds of their time at work) through the manipulation of money--a lot of heads would roll.

It would be impossible to have the vast diversity of labor we have in the economy without a money system to enhance exchange. Simple barter is too ineffective.

The supply of gold or silver is simply not large enough to be used as a general medium-of-exchange. There is only one way to give people an honest money system with which they can conduct honest commerce, with no false inflation or constant loss of purchasing power. That is a money system that is based on the wealth produced by the people for the benefit of all the people in lieu of taxes and <u>exchanged</u> not loaned into circulation. Then outlaw the charging of interest, if **anyone** is allowed to loan money at interest, you will soon have a dishonest, tyrannical oppressive and confiscatory monetary system where the lenders will oppress everyone.

What makes for an honest monetary system is not the form of the money. It is how the money is put into circulation and whether or not a debt is incurred and interest is charged.

If a nation's money system consisted of only gold and silver coin and every commercial transaction was settled with that coin it would be a debt money system, if the miners or the coining processer simply loaned the coins into circulation with interest.

Debt money systems are based on principles of theft by deception. As soon as the interest comes due, the debt has grown but the money supply has not. This makes it impossible for all the borrowers to pay their debt with money. The borrowers are forced to give up their production (property) to the lender without receiving any production from the lender. **This is the end of barter and fair trade and the beginning of confiscation.** With enough time the lender owns everyone's production by deception.

When a few are loaning any form of money at interest to other to use as there medium-of- exchange it will only take a few decades before the lenders will control the nation. One only has to do the math for proof.

A monopoly on the issuance of the nation's money as interest-bearing debt is the best and most effective way to steal from everyone and get control of everything. It makes no difference whether the money is gold coin, silver coin, paper representing gold or silver, or just paper bills or the banks accounting system called book-entry money. Loaning money at interest into circulation is a sure way for the lender to get a share in every transaction that takes place in the country. The lender will in time gain ownership of all property through purchase from the profits or foreclosure on delinquent loans. This is what has happening now in America.

We have been told that the elite believe that only those in the highest stratum of society know what is best for everyone. They believe that the common person is not capable of making good decisions and therefore not capable of self-government. However, I have come to believe that the elite really believe that people are very capable of self- government. Therefore the elite must be very careful that the people are not *allowed* self-government. Because if the people did have self-government they would not let the rich and powerful steal from them.

Alexander Hamilton, one of the founding fathers, believed in government by

the wealthy elite and pushed hard and successfully for central banking. Thomas Jefferson was a staunch believer in the capacity of the common people to make good decisions for themselves and capable of self-government. Jefferson in his later years was against central banking.

The difference in these two concepts is whether governments are formed for the purpose of bestowing benefits on the rich or formed to protect the God-given rights of individuals to get the benefit of their own production. It is clear to me what kind of government we have today.

This difference in thinking caused the two men to be at odds on almost everything. The clash between those two concepts still rages today. That is what the so called 'new world order' and the 'liberal left' and the establishment right is all about. They are simply Hamiltonian thinkers.

Up to now, Hamiltonian type thinkers have clearly won the day. Our government is and has been run by and for the benefit and desires of the super rich.

This is mostly because Jeffersonian thinkers have never understood how to use the benefits of paper or electronic money for the common man. The common man has never understood fractional reserve banking or the power of interest. They don't see how the super rich have used those powers and the authority of the courts and governmental laws to provide and protect those benefits for themselves.

Thomas Jefferson stated: *"If the American People ever allow the banks to*

control the issuance of their currency, first by inflation and then by deflation, the banks and corporations that will grow up around them will deprive the people of all property until their children will wake up homeless on the continent their fathers occupied." Source: Olive Cushing Dwinell, The Story of Our Money (Boston: Forum Publishing Company, 1946), page 202. The Truth in Money Book by Theodore R. Thoren. Today we see the fulfillment of Jefferson's words. Americans no longer really own anything. Corporate lawyers run most businesses while the banking system finances it all and has the equity right to everything by a mortgage through either private or public debt.

As an example of how it works, let's look at the Merritt family of northern Minnesota. Lewis Merritt arrived in Minnesota in 1856 with his family that included seven sons. He was a lumberjack with an interest in mining. Before his death, he convinced his sons that there was iron ore on the Mesabi Mountain. One day twenty years later as they were hauling lumber off the mountain, a wagon wheel went through the top soil and sunk into funny looking powdery reddish subsoil. After getting the wagon out, they took a sample of the subsoil and had it assayed. It assayed to be 64% iron. Hard rock miners didn't see how they could mine the soft sand-like iron ore. The Merritt brothers decided the way to do it was to get a large steam shovel and just scoop up the ore.

However, they faced several problems. They needed a road capable of get the large shovel in and the heavy ore to Duluth. They needed a dock to get the ore onto ships. For this the Merritt brothers needed money lots of it. In 1893 they issued $1, 600,000 worth of bonds. John D.

Rockefeller, one of the **big** banking men, bought one-fourth of the bonds.

Then what do you know - a money panic. Money suddenly seemed to get scarce. The Merritt Brothers and much of the rest of the nation were in financial trouble. But for some 'strange' reason, it did not seem to affect the **big** banking men. Rockefeller stepped in agreeing to supply the needed money if a new company was started. Rockefeller would put up the money the Merritt family's contribution to the new company would be the ore, the railroad and the dock. Within a year the Merritt family was out and Rockefeller had it all. Source: Building Minnesota by Theodore C. Blegen

Another example is how David Rockefeller, Chase Manhattan Bank and a couple of insurance companies took control of Trans World Airlines from Howard Hughes. Mr. Hughes needed money to buy some jet planes to keep up with other airlines. Like the Merritt brothers, he turned to a Rockefeller for funding. As with the Merritt brothers David Rockefeller, through the Chase Manhattan Bank and Insurance Companies was more than willing to provide the funding. On the condition that if some unforeseen undesirable situation happened to occur Mr. Hughes would have 90 days to correct the problem or he would lose his voting rights. Just as with the Merritt brothers, the undesirable situation occurred and Mr. Hughes was not allowed to vote his shares. Therefore he was removed from his Airlines management. The lenders soon had it all. Source: David by William Hoffman

Every money panic every money crisis, every recession and every depression occur because of the manipulation of the money supply or manipulation of interest rates or the manipulation of the stock market. First, loan the money. Get them in debt. Next, pull back the money supply or change the rules a little then take the property. It seems to work every time. The people never seem to catch onto the game. It is all so easy when you get to create money for your own investments and create money to make loans to others for their investments. Then you get to pull back the money supply any time you want too.

Chapter 8

The history of banking in the United States

The whole monetary history of the United States is about a nation with lots of raw resources and productive people. Unfortunately, the United States doesn't have a sustainable money system and most people don't have a clue on how to create one!

The first bank, in what became the United States, was the Massachusetts Land Bank in 1721. The landowners created a bank where they could mortgage their land and receive a letter of credit that they could use as their medium-of-exchange. The new Land Bank emitted 50,000 pounds of old tenor (paper credit). This may have given them a short-term fix but for obvious reasons it clearly could not work for the long haul and it didn't last long. A mortgage on land is a debt against the land. If you don't remove the mortgage you will never truly own your own land. However, if you remove the mortgage, you destroy the money supply. If interest is charged on the mortgage, the debt owed will grow greater than the supply of money. There will never be enough money to remove the mortgage. These facts are so basically simple. Yet to this day, the people have never understood them.

According to the U.S. Department of the Treasury, the first private bank notes were issued in New London, Connecticut, and were backed by the assets of the New London bank. Those assets would have been the mortgages and the promissory notes of the borrowers given to the bank to obtain the loan of bank notes.

The bank notes were a promise to pay gold and silver coins which the bank didn't have. The people who borrowed the banks promise to pay had to pay interest. It was the same old goldsmith's game, different time different place.

In 1799, Aaron Burr founded the Bank of the Manhattan Company. JPMorgan Chase traces its beginning to the Bank of Manhattan Company.

Now this seems a little strange. One source shows that the Continental Congress spent $37 million and the states spent $114 million, for a total of $151 million, on the war of independence. The best source I could find, shows that the Continental Congress issued $140,551,695 of currency. We have been told, this was so much that it became worthless. Yet it was not enough to finance the war. Our founding father felt they had to start a bank so they could create more money.

Source: of picture The Story of Banks fed bank NY

In 1781 The Bank of North America was formed as an incorporated financial institution and given a federal charter by the Continental Congress to help the war for independence.

In 1784, the first banking company in New York State was organized with a capital of $500,000. Hamilton personally drew up the articles of co-partnership. But the people had been so badly cheated in depredated paper currency, that the Legislature was afraid to charter banks. John C. Hamilton, says 'A memorial,' to incorporate the bank of which the constitution had been written by Hamilton, was presented to the Legislature early in 1784, but so prevalent was the jealousy of moneyed influence that the bank was compelled to conduct its affairs during six years without corporate immunities. So anxious was Hamilton to start his bank, that he opened it even before he had obtained lawful authority and without waiting for those legislative favors by which directors were individually exempted from being sued. From 1784 to 1788 he, personally, was a director. Up to the very day of his death he controlled that institution. It held a monopoly of banking powers, in New York, and, like the Bank of North America it was of the greatest service in facilitating great land speculations, and exercising pressure upon merchants in elections.

It was not until March 21, 1791, that Hamilton was able to secure a charter from the New York Legislature. How, did he get it? Was it given as a partisan present by his Federalist associates? Or was some stronger more metallic inducement necessary to influence the legislators to defy public opposition, as was revealed by Aaron Burr in 1799 when he obtained the charter for the Manhattan bank. Source: The Supreme Court under John Jay

I also learned that when Hamilton was the Secretary of the Treasury he dealt extensively with Dutch bankers. The same Dutch bankers to whom Robert Morris sold three million acres of New York land. Source: A History of the Bank of New York,

The ink was hardly dry on the Constitution and Bill of Rights when Hamilton led the charge to establish the first central bank in America. Hamilton's plan was for Congress to authorize the incorporation of a bank. Federal debt certificates would then be used as 'reserves' against which the bank could lend its own private bank notes into circulation. A multi-million dollar debt would become a multi-million dollar money supply (Monetizing the debt). The plan was passed into law as the Funding Act and the Bank Act.

The following is a little history of how Hamilton carried out his plan.

According to the United States Constitution Sesquicentennial Commission Representative, Sol Bloom, Director General, the meeting of the First Continental Congress was on September 5, 1774, in Carpenters' Hall in Philadelphia Pennsylvania. The Second Continental Congress met at Philadelphia on May 10, 1775, and endured until superseded in 1789 by the government organized under the new Constitution.

The Declaration of Independence was unanimously adopted in General Congress assembled in Philadelphia July 4, 1776, and states: *"We hold these truths to be self-evident, that all men are created equal, that they are endowed by their Creator with certain inalienable rights that among these are life, liberty and the pursuit of happiness."*

On January 21, 1786, the legislature of Virginia, ignoring entirely the requirements of the Articles of Confederation, suggested a general convention of Commissioners from the states to view the trade of the Union. The

Commissioners considered if a uniform system in their commercial relations would be necessary to their common interests.

The convention thus projected, met at Annapolis Maryland in September of 1786. Representatives of New York, New Jersey, Pennsylvania, Delaware and Virginia attended the convention Because of the limited attendance, nothing was done except to make a report drafted by Alexander Hamilton. On February 21, 1787 with eleven states being represented, the Congress took this report into consideration and resolved that a convention appeared to be the most probable means of establishing a firm national government in these states. The legislatures of all the states except Rhode Island appointed deputies to this Convention.

On May 29, 1787, Randolph from Virginia opened the main business by introducing the Virginia Plan drafted by James Madison and worked on by the rest of the Virginia delegation. The deputies who feared a too strong central government introduced the "Paterson Plan" on June 15. On July 16, 1787, came the adoption of the Great Compromise urged by the Connecticut deputies. Eleven of the states ratified the Constitution by 1788. Washington was inaugurated as President April 30, 1789.

The Constitution of the United States reads: "We the people of the United States in order to form a more Perfect Union, establish Justice, insure Domestic Tranquility, provide for the common Defense, promote the General Welfare, and secure the blessing of Liberty to ourselves and our posterity, do ordain and established this Constitution."

The first Congress convened in New York. Without delay, the members engaged in the work of creating the State, War, and Treasury Departments. For the head of the Treasury Department, Hamilton was wisely chosen. All though only thirty-two years old, public opinion had marked him for the place and the hour. He possessed pre-eminent genius for organization and for creation. Robert Morris had long before discovered these qualities in him. The old board of the Treasury had not done anything toward ascertaining the nature and amount of the public debt. A revenue system was to be created and the public indebtedness was to be ascertained, and provision made for its payment. The machinery of the Treasury Department needed to be organized for collecting and disbursing the public revenues. The old Board had bequeathed to the Treasury Department a vast chaotic mass of accounts that had accumulated under the confederation. *Gibb's administrations of Washington and Adams, vol.i.p28. sited in Financial History of the United States Financial History of the United States*

"How he fulfilled the duties of his position, the whole country perceived with delight, and the world saw with admiration. He smote the rock of the national resources, and abundant streams gushed forth. He touched the dead corpse of the public credit, and it sprung upon its feet. The fabled birth of Minerva from the brain of Jove was hardly more sudden or more perfect than the financial system of the United States as it burst forth from the conception of Alexander Hamilton." Webster's Speeches, vol. i. p. 199 cited in Financial History of the United States

Two hundred and seventeen years later in 2008, it is quite easy to see that Hamilton's perfect financial system has not turned out to be so perfect for the American people. Unless one thinks a nation of financial slaves is a perfect system.

The Constitution in Article I Sec. 8 states:

The Congress shall have Power To lay and collect Taxes, Duties, Imposts and Excises, to pay the Debts and provide for the common Defense and general Welfare of the United States; - - - - To borrow Money on the credit of the United States; - - - - To coin Money, regulate the Value thereof, - - - - To establish Post Offices and post Roads;

The ink that formed these words was hardly dry when Alexander Hamilton and his backers, men who clearly understood the benefits and the profits that could come to them through banking practices, moved to place 'his perfect financial system' into the newly formed nation.

Hamilton's plan had four parts:

Part (1) Establish a Federal Tax System.

Part (2) Guarantee holders of Revolutionary War debt they would be paid interest on that debt until the debt was paid. They were not going to be paid in Spanish milled dollars or an equivalent weight of gold and silver but with a bank note payable in gold or silver that the bank didn't have. Hmmm, that sounds like the continental notes.

Part (3) The Federal Government would assume the war debts of the states.

Part (4) **Pass the Bank Act. This created a mostly privately owned bank and authorized the use of debt certificates to purchase bank stock. The certificates would serve as assets against which the bank could make loans, at interest, of money that the bank did not have: right from the playbook of William Paterson.**

Hamilton stated: *(quotes have been reworded a little to flow better in today's English)* "*It is a well-known fact that countries in which the national debt is properly funded,* ***(properly funded means that the government has the taxing power to ensure the interest payments)*** *answers most of the purposes of money. Transfers of public debt are equivalent to payments in specie, or in other words passes as money* (monetizing public debt). *The same thing would, in all probability, happen here under like circumstances." "The benefits of this are various and obvious. Trade is extended by it because there is a larger debt-based interest-bearing money supply to carry it. Agriculture and manufacturing are also promoted by it for like reasons."*

From 1791 to 1796, prices rose 72% in response to the flood of new interest-accruing money loaned by the bank. A big loan makes most people feel rich until the debt comes due. It seems that borrowed money is easier to spend than hard earned money.

Part (1) of his plan was implemented. In July 1789, Congress passed a tax law mostly written by Hamilton.

Part (2) was needed to get his fourth part passed. James Callender, a reporter for the Philadelphia Gazette charged:

"The funding law was passed through Congress by the influence of a majority who purchased certificates from the army at under value and who voted for the law with the single view of enriching themselves. It is firmly believed and

loudly asserted by at least one half of the citizens of America, that the funding system was devised, not for the sake of paying real creditors but of wronging them. Hamilton planned, Congress voted. The president approved". Taylor, 1950, pp.61-4.

Part (3) of Hamilton's plan was needed to ensure that the wealthy supported the federal government over the state governments because that would be the source of their interest payments.

It seems the First Secretary of the Treasury, The First Congress, and First President supported a money supply based on debt because the majority of them had purchased depreciated debt certificates before the Funding and Banking acts were passed into law. This provided them with the ability to secure windfall profits for themselves. Source: Financial History of the United States 1789 – 1860.

The first congressman from Georgia, James Jackson, seemed to have been one of the few people that understood where Hamilton's plan would take the young nation. On February 9, 1790, he stated:

"The funding of the debt will occasion enormous taxes for the payment of the interest. These taxes will bear heavily both on agriculture and commerce. It will be charging the active and industrious citizen, who pays his share of the taxes, to pay the indolent and idle creditor who receives them. It is doubtful with me whether a permanent funded debt is beneficial or not to any country.

Some of the first writers in the world, who are most admired on account of the clearness of their perceptions, have thought otherwise and declared that wherever such funding systems have been adopted in a Government, they tend more to injure posterity. This principle is demonstrated by experience. The first system of the kind that we have any account of originated in the State of Florence in the year 1634. That Government then owed about £60,000 sterling, and being unable to pay it, formed the principal into a funded debt, transferable with interest at five per cent. What is the situation of Florence in consequence of this event? Her ancient importance is annihilated. Look at Genoa and Venice; they adopted a similar policy, and are the only two of the Italian Republics, who can pretend to an independent existence, but their splendor is obscured. They have never since the period at which said funding system was introduced, been able to raise themselves to the formidable state they were before. Spain seems to have learned the practice from the Italian Republics, and she, by the anticipation of her immense revenue, has sunk her status beneath that level which her natural situation might have maintained. France is considerably enfeebled, and languishes under a heavy load of debt. England is a melancholy instance of the ruin attending such engagements.

The same effect must be produced here that has taken place in other nations. It must either bring on a national bankruptcy, or annihilate our existence as an independent empire. Hence I contend that such a funding system in this country will be highly dangerous to the welfare of the Republic. It may, for a moment, raise our credit, and increase our circulation by multiplying a new form of currency, but it must hereafter settle upon our posterity a burden which they can neither bear nor relieve themselves from. It will establish a precedent in America that may, and in all probability will, be pursued by the Sovereign authority, until it brings upon us that ruin which it has never failed to bring, or is inevitably bringing, upon all the nations of the earth who have had the temerity to make the experiment. Let us take warning by the errors of Europe and guard against the introduction of a system followed by calamities so universal. Though our present debt be but a few millions, in the course of a single century it may be multiplied to an extent we dare not think of ." *Source: Annals of Congress, Vol. I, February 1790 sited in the Financial History of the United States*

Hamilton's plan did establish a precedent that has been pursued and refined by the sovereign authority to a point where the Federal Reserve banking system (the third central bank of the United States) and the corporations that have grown up around it have become an unelected, all powerful, fourth branch of government that controls all the other branches, as well as the news stations, the press and all most everything else. Today, in 2008, it is easy to see we have the best government corrupt money can buy, and we only get to hear about the presidential candidates that the big money boys and the big TV news and the big press want us to hear about.

The Bank of the United States opened in December 1791. The First Bank of the United States had a capital stock of $10 million, of which $2 million was subscribed by the Federal government. The remainder was subscribed by the private individuals. Five of the twenty-five directors were appointed by the United States government, the other twenty were chosen by the private investors. It was a nation-wide bank with branches in other major cities. It performed basic banking functions accepting deposits and making loans by issuing bank notes. Source: Historical beginnings ... Federal Reserve Bank of Boston written by Roger T. Johnson The subscriptions of the of private investors were payable, one-fourth in gold and silver and three-fourths in government bonds. The subscription of the government was to be paid by borrowing (issuing more bonds). From the beginning, the bank of the United States was very accommodating to the government. The bank immediately loaned $2,000,000 to the government. By 1795, the bank had loaned $6,200,000 to the government. Source: Financial History of the United States from 1789 to 1860 by Albert S. Bolles **Because of the fraudulent monetary system Hamilton introduced, from the day of its inception to the present each generation has been forced deeper into debt than the generation before it.** Until now the total debt is over $53 trillion and is growing at a rate of more then $4 trillion a year.

Just as James Jackson envisioned, the same effect has happened here that has always taken place in other nations. By 2016, the debt will be so great that the interest on the debt at just 6% will be over a billion dollars greater that the total consumer income! As a nation, we are facing a very dismal financial future.

The 1791, Congress passed a law creating a central bank. Money was created by turning government debt into a circulating medium-of-exchange. Taxes were levied on the general population so the interest could be paid to the very rich who controlled that bank.

In 1792, the same Congress passed a law that stated a dollar was a measure, a weight of pure silver. Therefore, under the 1792 act a debt in dollars was to be measured by how much silver it took to satisfy the debt. If that act would have been enforced, a debt of a thousand dollars of loaned bank credit would have to been paid with a thousand coins weighing 371.25 grains of silver. It would have been impossible for such a process to work.

The creation of a central bank and the passage of the 1792 Coinage Act produced a terrible conflict in law. This conflict of law forced the courts to be corrupt from day one. For the money and banking system to function, the courts could never uphold the bank's promise to redeem the circulating medium in silver or gold. At the same time, the corrupt courts chose to uphold the peoples promise to pay a debt owed to the banking system.

The government and the courts chose to simply disregard the 1792 Coinage Act to keep the economy functioning, instead of addressing the conflict.

If many people had gone to the bank to get coined gold or silver to use for their money instead of the bank notes, they would have soon discovered that the bank didn't have enough silver or gold to satisfy its obligations. Remember the bank was funded with only $2,000,000 in gold and silver. When Thomas Jefferson became President, he would not renew the Charter of the First United States bank when it expired in 1811.

In 1810, it was estimated that the money in circulation in the United States was around fifty million dollars. It was also estimated that there were not even 10 million dollars of gold and silver money in the entire country.

When the charter of the first United States Bank expired, its $24 million in notes were withdrawn. This means that the loans that were made to move the money into circulation would have to be called or shifted to state banks that could create the money. If too many of the loans were called it would cause a recession or a depression.

In 1811, just before the charter of the United States bank expired there were eighty-eight state banks possessing a capital of $42,610,000. During 1811, and the two succeeding years one hundred and twenty state banks were chartered and went into operation. In 1813, the currency of the United States was about seventy million dollars, of which sixty-two million were in bank notes. In 1815, after the suspension of specie the amount of bank notes totaled over one hundred and ten million. Source the financial History of the United States

This clearly proves there was not enough gold and silver money to pay the loans. The rationale for creating the national bank in the first place was for the new government to be able to borrow enough new money to pay off the war debts of the Continental Congress and the states. These debts would have never existed had there been enough gold and silver money, or if the Continental Congress would have created new money as a payment not as a bill of credit (a promise to pay) payable in silver or gold, they did not have, and could not obtain.

Soon after the first bank of the United State charter expired, the war of 1812 started. To fund the war, the Secretary of the Treasury issued United States Notes in 1812, 1813 and 1814 totaling $36,680,000. These notes were not payable on demand. They were receivable in payment of taxes due to the Federal Government. When the government needed supplies it would pay for them with a note. Then, it would receive the note back in payment of taxes. This would give the note value and acceptance to pass from person to person as money. Source the financial History of the United States

This would have increased the ‘money’ supply, until all of the Treasury Notes were removed from circulation, through the payment of taxes and fees.

Money issued on the above basis and on the basis of loans from a bank never provides the people with a stable sustainable money system because when the people pay their taxes, they destroy their money supply. With bank loaned money, when the people make payments of loan principal they destroy that part of their money supply. The difference is banks charge interest and charging interest always increases the debt load, but it does not increase the money supply. Money put into circulation as interest-bearing obligations always forces greater indebtedness on the people.

On Oct. 1, 1816, the government debt was right at one hundred and nine million dollars (not a cent of it was gold or silver coin). Source: Financial History of the United States

A sustainable money system is one where the money stays in circulation without debt and grows as the production of the population grows.

In 1816, the big moneyed men were able, under President James Madison, to get a second United States Bank chartered. The Second Bank of the United States was very much like the first, except that is was much larger. Its capital was $35 million. Like the first bank, the federal government owned one-fifth of the stock. Private investors owned the rest. The President appointed one-fifth of the directors. The private investors chose other directors. Three-quarters of its privately held shares were to be purchased with government securities. It was also chartered for 20 years. Source: (Historical Beginnings ... The Federal Reserve by Roger T. Johnson for the Federal Reserve Bank of Boston) and (The Region published by the Federal Reserve Bank of Minneapolis)

The Second Bank opened on January 7th 1817, in the same building that had housed the first United States Bank. The bank's charter provided that United States funds held in state banks be deposited in the new bank. The bank was to keep the deposits and make loans to the government. On April 30, 1816, the Congress resolved that all taxes due the government be in 'legal currency'. Of course, this included treasury notes and notes of the second Bank of the United States. So much for the 1792 Coinage Act. At that time none of the paper money was redeemable in gold or silver coin and was moved in circulation at varying rates of discounts. Very little, if any, silver and gold coins circulated.

In 1817 and 1818, the government transferred around eleven million dollars from state banks to the United States Bank. One of the hoped for benefits of having a United States Bank was to get a more uniform paper currency. Source: Financial History of the United States. The only way to achieve this would be to transfer funds from state banks to the national bank. Then the national bank would have to make some kind of, behind closed doors, exchange of liabilities with the state bank, then destroy the state bank notes and reissue United States Bank Notes.

During the years 1815 and 1816, the circulation of notes increased to $110,000,000. Then, in 1819, on the pretense that the Second United States bank was going to resume redemption of bank notes in species the circulation of bank notes was reduced to $65,000,000, a reduction of fifty-nine percent.

In a study of money's history, we seldom read about the above mentioned facts or about how the amounts of bank notes increase and then how the number of bank notes decreased. At first glance the numbers don't sound so bad until one really understands that all bank notes go into circulation, only, when banks make interest-bearing loans. When the bank notes are decreased bank loans are called (immediate payment in full, principal and interest demanded). This always results in foreclosures and sheriff's sales. Because the money to pay the interest was never put into circulation. Therefore all the people cannot make full payment of their loan on demand. This causes many hard-working and industrious people to lose everything that they have labored years for, their land, their homes and their merchandise, in the hope of obtaining a better life for themselves and their children. That is what happened in 1819 and 1820 and that happens every time the amount of bank created money is decreased. Just like what we are seeing in 2008.

McDuffie, a house member from South Carolina, stated:

> "T*he Bank of the United States actually furnished a circulating medium more uniform than specie. Funds could be transported from one part of the Union to another, through the aid afforded by the bank, at an expense not exceeding one-half, and frequently less than one-quarter, of the cost of carrying silver.*
>
> *For all the purposes of revenue, it furnished a national monetary circulation of perfect uniformity, attaining that ideal perfection which even a currency of gold and silver, in a country so extensive, cannot possess. All the funds of the government are transported form one point to another free*

of expense: thus furnishing, both to the government and to the people, a currency of absolutely uniform in value in all places, for all the purposes of pay the public contribution, and disbursing the public revenue.

Upon the whole then, concluded a committee of investigation in 1830, it may be confidently asserted that no country in the world has a circulating medium of greater uniformity than the United States, and that no country of any like the geographical extent has a currency at all comparable to that of the United States, on the score of uniformity". *Source: McDuffie's Report, April13, 1830, 21 Congress, first session. Clark and Hall, p. 734.* Financial History of the United States 1789 – 1860.

It is beyond question that what McDuffie and the investigation committee stated was and is true when it comes to the uniformity of a properly-printed circulating medium- of-exchange (money).

Money does not need to be a weight of gold or silver. Paper money and checkbook money has proven to be a very workable medium-of-exchange. It is historically proven that the people as a whole clearly prefer paper to metal money. However, up to this time in the history of America, paper money has been put into circulation as an obligation and most of the time as an interest-bearing debt owed to a bank. Please keep in mind, as long as money is put into circulation as an interest–bearing debt, each generation must get deeper into debt than the generation before it. Eventually, the interest load becomes so great that it becomes impossible for most of the people to survive financially. Then the financially system will fail, not because it is a paper money system, but because it is a debt money system.

In 1830, the total amount of bank loans was $200,451,214. In 1838, the total amount of bank loans was $525,115,702. The total amount of gold and silver coin in the country at that time was less than $6,000,000, and most of that was not in circulation. Source: Financial History of the United States 1789 – 1860

Andrew Jackson, who became President in 1829 when the bank's charter still had seven years to run, made it clear that he was opposed to the bank. On the 8th day of December, 1829, in his first annual message to Congress,

President Jackson stated the he didn't favor a renewal of the bank's charter. Senator Benton, from Missouri presented a resolution in the United States senate requesting that the charter of the bank not be renewed. The resolution failed by a vote of twenty-three to twenty. The narrow defeat of the resolution alarmed Nicholas Biddle, President of the Bank.

To gain support for the bank, Biddle shrewdly expanded the bank's loans, reaching the amount of seventy-one million dollars, to leading merchants and manufacturers so a powerful force would be put on Jackson to renew the bank's charter to insure that their bank loan would not be recalled. Source: The Coming Battle by M.W Walbert. Jackson's opponent in the 1832 presidential election, Senator Henry Clay, was able to push a bill through Congress to re-charter the bank. Source: Historical Beginnings ... The Federal Reserve by Roger T. Johnson. When the bill got to his desk President Andrew Jackson vetoed the bill. The Charter of the 2nd United States Bank was not renewed in 1836 and it passed from the scene.

PRESIDENT ANDREW JACKSON'S VETO MESSAGE

The bill "to modify and continue" the act entitled "an act to incorporate the subscribers to the Bank of the United States" was presented to me on the 4th July instant. Having considered it with that solemn regard to the principles of the Constitution which the day was calculated to inspire, and come to the conclusion that it ought not to become a law, I herewith return it to the Senate, in which it originated, with my objections.

A BANK of the United States is in many respects convenient for the Government and useful to the people. Entertaining this opinion, and deeply impressed with the belief that some of the powers and privileges possessed by the existing Bank are unauthorized by the Constitution. Subversive of the right of the States, and dangerous to the liberties of the people, I felt it my duty, at an early period of my administration, to call the attention of Congress to the practicability of organizing an institution combining all its advantages, and obviation these objections. I sincerely regret that, in the act before me, I can perceive none of those modifications of the Bank charter which are necessary, in my opinion, to make it compatible with justice, with sound policy, or with the Constitution of our country.

The present corporate body, denominated the president, directors and company of the Bank of the United States, will have existed at the time this act is intended to take effect twenty years. It enjoys an exclusive privilege of banking under the authority of the General Government, a monopoly of its favors and support, and, as a necessary consequence, almost a monopoly of the foreign and domestic exchange. The powers, privileges, and favors bestowed upon it in the original charter, by increasing the value of the stock far above its par value, operated as a gratuity of many million to the stockholders.

An apology may be found for the failure to guard against this result in the consideration that the effect of the original act of incorporation could not be certainly foreseen at the time of its passage. The act before me proposed another gratuity to the holders of the same stock, and in many cases to the same men, of a least seven million more. The donation finds no apology in any uncertainty as to the effect of the act. On all hands it is conceded that its passage will increase at least 20 or 30 per cent more the market price of the stock, subject to the payment of the annuity of $200,000 per year secured by the act, thus adding on a moment one-fourth if its par value. It is not our own citizens only who are to receive the bounty of our government more than eight millions of the stock of this bank are held by foreigners. By this act the American Republic proposes virtually to make them a present of some millions of dollars. For these gratuities to foreigners and to some of our own opulent citizens the act secures no equivalent whatever. They are the certain gains of the present stockholders under the operation of this act, after making full allowance for the payment of the bonus.

Every monopoly and all exclusive privileges are granted at the expense of the public, which ought to receive a fair equivalent. The many millions which this act proposes to bestow on the stockholders of the existing Bank must come directly or indirectly out of the earnings of the American people. It is due to them, therefore, if their Government sell monopolies and exclusive privileges, that they should at least exact for them as much as they are worth in open market. The value of the monopoly in this case may be correctly ascertained. The twenty-eight million of stock would probably be at an advance of 50 per cent, and command in market at least $42,000,000 subject to the payment of the present bonus. The present value of the monopoly, therefore, is $17,000,000 and this the act proposes to sell for $3,000,000 payable in 15 annual installments of $200,000 each.

It is not conceivable how the present stockholders can have any claim to the special favor of the Government. The present corporation has enjoyed its monopoly during the period stipulated in the original contract. If we must have such a corporation, why should not the Government sell out the whole stock, and thus secure to the people the full market value of the privileges granted? Why should not Congress create and sell twenty-eight millions of stock, incorporating the purchasers with all the powers and privileges secured in this act, and putting the premium upon the sales into the Treasury.

But this act does not permit competition in the purchase of this monopoly. It seems to be predicated on the erroneous idea that the present stockholders have a prescriptive right not only to the favor but to the bounty of Government. It appears that more than a fourth part of the stoic is held by foreigners and the residue is held by a few hundred of our own citizens, chiefly of the richest class. For their benefit does this act exclude the whole American people from competition in the purchase of this monopoly and dispose of it for many millions less that it is worth. This seems the less excusable because some of our citizens not now stockholders petitioned that the door of competition might be opened, and offered to take a charter on terms much more favorable to the Government and country.

But this proposition, although made by men whose aggregate wealth is believed to be equal to all the private stock in the existing bank, has been set aside, and the bounty of our government is proposed to be again bestowed on the few who have been fortunate enough to secure the stock and at this moment wield the power of the existing institution. I can not perceive the justice or policy of this course. If our Government must sell monopolies, it would seem to be its duty to take nothing less than their full value, and if gratuities must be made once in fifteen or twenty years let them not be bestowed on the subjects of a foreign government nor upon a designated and favored class of men in our own country. It is but justice and good policy, as far as the nature of the case will admit, to confine our favors to our own fellow-citizens, and let each in his turn enjoy an opportunity to profit by our bounty. In the bearings of the act before me upon these points I find ample reasons why it should not become a law.

It has been urged as an argument in favor of re-chartering the present Bank, that the calling in its loans will produce great embarrassment and distress. The time allowed to close its concerns is ample; and if it has been well managed, its pressure will be light, and heavy only in case its management has been bad. If, therefore, it shall produce distress, the fault will be its own: and it would furnish a reason against renewing a power which has been so obviously abused. But will there ever be a time when this reason will be less powerful? To acknowledge its force is to admit that the Bank ought to be perpetual: and, as a consequence, the present stockholders, and those inheriting their rights as successors, be established a privileged order, clothed both with great political power and enjoying immense pecuniary advantages from their connection with the Government.

The modifications of the existing charter, proposed by this act, are not such, in my views, as make it consistent with the rights of the States or the liberties of the people. The qualification of the right of the bank to hold real estate, the limitation of its power to establish branches, and the power reserved to Congress to forbid the circulation of small notes are restrictions comparatively of little value or importance. All the objectionable principles of the existing corporation, and most of its odious features, are retained without alleviation.

The fourth section provides "that the notes or bills of the said corporation, although the same be, on the faces thereof, respectively made payable at one place only, shall nevertheless be received by the said corporation at the bank or at any of the offices of discount and deposit thereof if tendered in liquidation or payment of any balance or balances due to said corporation or to such office of discount and deposit from any other incorporated bank." This provision secures to the State banks a legal privilege in the Bank of the United States and have notes issued by the St. Louis branch, it can pay the debt with those notes, but if a merchant, mechanic, or other private citizen be in like circumstances he can not by law pay his debt with those notes, but must sell them at a discount or send them to St. Louis to be cashed. This boon conceded to the State banks, though not injust in itself, is most odious because it does not measure out equal justice to the high and the low, the rich and the poor. To the extent of its practical effect it is a bond of union among the banking establishments of the nation, erecting them into an interest separate from that of the people, and its necessary tendency is to unite the Bank of the United States and the State Banks in any measure which may be thought conducive to their common interest.

The ninth section of the act recognizes principles of worse tendency than any provision of the present charter. It enacts that "the cashier of the bank shall annually report to the Secretary of the Treasury the names of all stockholders who are not resident citizens of the United States, and on the application of the treasurer of any state shall make out and transmit to such treasurer a list of stockholders residing in or citizens of such State, with the amount of stock owned by each. "Although this provision, taken in connection with a decision of the Supreme Court, surrenders, by its silence, the right of the States to tax the banking institution created by this corporation under the name of branches throughout the Union, if is evidently intended to be construed as a concession of their right to tax that portion of the stock which may be held by their own citizens and residents. In this light, if the act becomes law, it will be understood by the States, who will probably proceed to levy a tax equal to that paid upon the stock of banks incorporated by themselves. In some States that tax is now 1 percent, either on the capital or on the shares, and that may be assumed as the amount which all citizen or resident stockholders would be taxed under the operation of this act. As it is only the stock held in the States and not that employed with them which would be subject to taxation as the names of foreign stockholders are not be reported to the treasurers of the States, it is obvious that the stock held by them will be exempt from this burden. Their annual profits will therefore be 1 percent more than the citizen stockholders, and as the annual dividends of the bank may be safely estimated at 7 percent, the stock will be 10 or 15 percent more to foreigners than to citizens of the United States. To appreciate the effects which this state of things will produce, we must take a brief review of the operations and present condition of the Bank of the United States.

By documents submitted to Congress at the present session it appears that on the 1st of January, 1832, of the $28,000,000 of private stock in the corporation, $8,405,500 were held by foreigners, mostly of Great Britain. The amount of stock held in the nine Western and South-western States in $140,200, and in the four Southern States is $5,623,100, and in the Middle and Eastern States is about $13,522,000. The profits of the bank in 1831, as shown in a statement to Congress, were about $3,455,598; of this there accrued in the nine Western States about $1,640,048; in the four Southern States about $352,507, and in the Middle and Eastern States about $1,463,041. As little stock is held in the West, it is obvious that the debt of the people in that section to the bank is principally a debt to the Eastern and foreign stockholders; that the interest they pay upon it is carried into the Eastern States and into Europe, and that is a burden upon their industry and a drain of their currency, which no country can bear without inconvenience and occasional distress. To meet this burden and equalize the exchange operations of the bank, the amount of specie drawn from those States through its branches with the last two years, as shown by its official reports, was about $6,000,000. More than half a million of this amount does not stop in the Eastern States, but passes on to Europe to pay the dividends of the foreign stockholders. In the principle of taxation recognized by this act the Western States find no adequate compensation for this perpetual burden on their industry and drain of their currency. The branch bank at Mobile made last year $95,140, yet under the provisions of this act the State of Alabama can raise no revenue from these profitable operations, because not a share of the stock is held by any of her citizens. Mississippi and Missouri are in the same condition in relation to the branches at Natchez and St. Louis, and such, in a greater or less degree, is the condition of every Western State. The tendency of the plan of taxation which this act proposes will be to place the whole United States in the same relation to foreign countries which the Western States now bear to the Eastern. When by a tax on resident stockholders the stock of this bank is made worth 10 or 15 percent more to foreigners than to residents, most of it will inevitably leave the country.

Thus will this provision in its practical effect deprive the Eastern as well as the Southern and Western States of the means of raising a revenue from the extension of business and great profits of this institution. It will make the American people debtors to aliens in nearly the whole amount due to this bank, and send across the Atlantic from two to five millions of specie every year to pay the bank dividends.

In another of its bearing this provision is fraught with danger. Of the twenty-five directors of this bank five are chosen by the government and twenty by citizen stockholders. From all voice in these elections the foreign stockholders are excluded by the charter. In proportion, therefore, as the stock is transferred to foreign holders the extent of suffrage in the choice of directors is curtailed. Already almost a third of the stock in foreign hands and not represented in elections. It is constantly passing out of the country, and this act will accelerate its departure. The entire control of the institution would necessarily fall into the hands of a few citizen stockholders, and the ease with which the object would be accomplished would be a temptation to designing men to secure that control in their own hands by monopolizing the remaining stock. There is danger that a president and directors would them be able to elect themselves from year to year, and without responsibility or control manage the whole concerns of the bank during the existence of its charter. It is easy to conceive that great evils to our country and its institutions might flow form such a concentration of power in the hands of a few men irresponsible to the people.

Is there no danger to our liberty and independence in a Bank that in its nature has so little to bind it to our country? The president of the bank has told us that most of the State banks exist by its forbearance. Should its influence become concentered, as it may under the operation of such an act as this, in the hands of a self-elected directory, whose interests are identified with those of the foreign stockholders, will there not be cause to tremble for the purity of our elections in peace, and for the independence of our country in war. Their power would be great whenever they might choose to exert it; but if this monopoly were regularly renewed every fifteen or twenty years, on terms proposed by themselves, they might seldom in peace put forth their strength to influence elections or control the affairs of the nation. But if any private citizen or public functionary should interpose to curtail its powers, or prevent a renewal of its privileges, it cannot be doubted that he would be made to feel its influence.

Should the stock of the Bank principally pass into the hands of the subjects of a foreign country, and we should unfortunately become involved in a war with that country, what would be our condition? Of the course which would be pursued by a bank almost wholly owned by the subjects of a foreign power, and managed by those whose interests, if not affections, would run in the same direction, there can be no doubt. All its operations within would be in aid of the hostile fleets and armies without. Controlling our currency, receiving our public moneys, and holding thousands of our citizens in dependence, it would be more formidable and dangerous that the naval and military power of the enemy.

If we must have a bank with private stockholders, every consideration of sound policy and every impulse of American feeling admonishes that it should be purely American. Its stockholders should be composed exclusively of our own citizens, who at least ought to be friendly to our Government and willing to support it in times of difficulty and danger. So abundant is domestic capital that competition in subscribing for the stock of local banks has recently led almost to riots. To a bank exclusively of American stockholders, possessing the powers and privileges granted by this act, subscriptions for $200,000,000 could be readily obtained. Instead of sending abroad the stock of the bank in which the Government must deposit its funds and on which it must rely to sustain its credit in times of emergency, it would rather seem to be expedient to prohibit its sale to aliens under penalty of absolute forfeiture.

It is maintained by the advocates of the Bank, that its constitutionality, in all its features ought to be considered as settled by precedent and by the decision of the Supreme Court. To this conclusion I cannot assent. Mere precedent is a dangerous source of authority, and should not be regarded as deciding questions of constitutional power, except where the acquiescence of the people and the States can be considered as well settled. So far from this being the case on this subject, an argument against the Bank might be based on precedent. One Congress, in 1791, decided in favor or a bank; another, in 1811, decided against it. One Congress, in 1815, decided against a bank; another, in 1816, decided in its favor. Prior to the present Congress, therefore, the precedents drawn from that source were equal. If we resort to the States, the expressions of legislative, judicial, and executive opinions against the Bank have been probably to those in its favor as 4 to 1. There is nothing in precedent, therefore, which, if its authority were admitted, ought to weigh in favor of the act before me.

If the opinion of the Supreme Court covered the whole ground of this act, it ought not to control the coordinate authorities of this Government. The Congress, the Executive, and the Court, must each for itself be guided by its own opinion of the Constitution. Each public officer, who takes an oath to support the Constitution, swears that he will support it as he understands it, and not as it is understood by others. It is much the duty of the House of Representatives, of the Senate, and of the President to decide upon the constitutionality of any bill or resolution which may be presented to them for passage or approval as it is of the supreme judges when it may be brought before them for judicial decision. The opinion of the judges has no more authority over Congress than the opinion of Congress has over the judges and on that point the President is independent of both.

The authority of the Supreme Court must not, therefore, be permitted to control the Congress or the Executive when acting in their legislative capacities, but to have only such influence as the force of their reasoning may deserve.

But in the case relied upon the Supreme Court have not decided that all the features of this corporation are compatible with the Constitution. It is true that the court have said that the law incorporating the bank is a constitutional exercise of power by Congress; but taking into view the whole opinion of the court and the reasoning by which they have come to that conclusion, I understand them to have decided that inasmuch as a bank is an appropriate means for carrying into effect the enumerated powers of the General Government, therefore the law incorporating it is in accordance with that provision of the Constitution which declares that Congress shall have power "to make all laws which shall be necessary and proper for carrying those powers into execution." Having satisfied themselves that the word "necessary" in the Constitution means "needful," "requisite," "essential," "conducive to," and that " a bank" is a convenient' useful, and essential instrument in the prosecution of the Government's fiscal operations," they conclude that to use one must be within the discretion of Congress" and that the "act to incorporate the Bank of the United States is a law made in pursuance of the Constitution;" "but," say they, "where the law is not prohibited and is really calculated to effect any of the objects intrusted to the Government, to undertake here to inquire into the degree of its necessity would be to pass the line which circumscribes the judicial department and to tread on legislative ground."

The principle here affirmed is that the "degree of its necessity" involving all the details of a banking institution, is a question exclusively for legislative consideration. A bank is constitutional, but it is the province of the Legislature to determine whether this or that particular power, privilege, or exemption is "necessary and proper" to enable the bank to discharge duties to the Government, and from their decision there is no appeal to the courts of justice. Under the decision of the Supreme Court, therefore, it is the exclusive province of Congress and the President to decide whether the particular features of this act are necessary and proper in order to enable the bank to perform conveniently and efficiently the public duties assigned to it as a fiscal agent, and therefore constitutional, or unnecessary and improper, and therefore unconstitutional.

Without commenting on the general principle affirmed by the Supreme Court, let us examine the details of this act in accordance with the rule of legislative act in which they have laid down. It will be found that many of the powers and privileges conferred on it can not be supposed necessary for the purpose for which it is proposed to be created, and are not, therefore, means necessary to attain the end in view, and consequently not justified by the Constitution.

The original act of incorporation, section 21, enacts "that no other bank shall be established by any future law of the United States during the continuance of the corporation hereby created, for which the faith of the United States is hereby created, for which the faith of the United States is hereby pledged: Provided, Congress may renew existing charters for banks within the District of Columbia not increasing the capital thereof, and may also establish any other bank or banks in said District with capital not exceeding in the whole $6,000,000 if they shall deem it expedient." This provision is continued in force by the act before me fifteen years from the 3d of March, 1836.

If Congress possessed the power to establish one bank, they had power to establish more than one if in their opinion two or more banks had been "necessary" to facilitate the execution of the powers delegated to them in the Constitution. If they possessed the power to establish a second bank, it was a power derived from the Constitution to be exercised from time to time, and at any time when the interests of the country or the emergencies of the Government might make it expedient. It was possessed by one Congress as well as another, and by all Congresses alike, and alike at every session. But the Congress of 1816 have taken it away from their successors for twenty years, and the Congress of 1832 proposes to abolish it for fifteen years more. It can not be necessary" or "proper" for Congress to barter away or divest themselves of any of the power vested in them by the Constitution to be exercised for the public good. It is not "necessary" to the efficiency of the bank, nor is it "proper" in relation to themselves and their successors. This restriction on themselves and grant of a monopoly to the bank is therefore unconstitutional.

In another point of view this provision is a palpable attempt to amend the Constitution by an act of legislation. The Constitution declares that "the Congress shall have power to exercise exclusive legislation in all cases whatsoever" over the District of Columbia. Its constitutional power, therefore, to establish banks in the District of Columbia and increase their capital at will is unlimited and uncontrollable by any other power that which gave authority to the Constitution. Yet this act declares that Congress shall not increase the capital of existing banks, nor create other banks with capital exceeding in the whole $6,000,000. The Constitution declares that Congress shall have power to exercise exclusive legislation over this District "in all cases whatsoever" and this act declares they shall not. Which is the supreme law of the land? This provision can not be "necessary" or "proper" or constitutional unless the absurdity be admitted that whenever it be "necessary and proper" in the opinion of Congress they have a right to barter away one portion of the powers vested in them by the Constitution as a means of executing the rest.

On two subjects only does the Constitution recognize in congress the power to grant exclusive privileges or monopolies. It declares that "Congress shall have power to promote the progress of science and useful arts by securing for limited times to authors and inventors the exclusive right to their respective writings and discoveries." Out of this express delegation of power have grown our laws of patents and copyrights. As the Constitution expressly delegates to Congress the power to grant exclusive privileges on these cases as the means of executing the substantive power "to promote the progress of science an useful arts," it is consistent with the fair rules of construction to conclude that such a power was not intended to be granted as a means of accomplishing any other end. On every other subject which comes within the scope of Congressional power there is an ever-living discretion in the use of proper means, which can not be restricted or abolished without an amendment of the Constitution. Every act of Congress, therefore, which attempts by grants of monopolies or sale of exclusive privileges for a limited time, or a time without limit, to restrict or extinguish its own discretion in the choice of means to execute its delegated powers is equivalent to a legislative amendment of the constitution, and palpably unconstitutional.

This act authorizes and encourages transfers of its stock to foreigners and grants them an exemption from all State and national taxation. So far from being "necessary and proper" that the bank should possess this power to make it a safe and efficient agent of the Government in its fiscal operations, it is calculated to convert the Bank of the United States into a foreign bank, to impoverish our people in time of peace, to disseminate a foreign influence through every section of the Republic, and in war to endanger our independence.

The several States reserved the power at the formation of the Constitution to regulate and control titles and transfer of real property, and most, if not all, of them have laws disqualifying aliens from acquiring or holding lands within their limits. But this act, in disregard of undoubted right of the States to prescribe such disqualifications, gives to aliens stockholders in this bank an interest and title, as members of the corporation, to all the real property it may acquire within any of the States of this Union. This privilege granted to aliens is not "necessary" to enable the bank to perform its public duties, nor in any sense "proper," because it is vitally subversive of the rights of the States.

The Government of the United States have no constitutional power to purchase lands within the States except "for the erection of forts, magazines, arsenals, dockyards, and other needful buildings," and even for these objects only "by the consent of the legislature of the State in which the same shall be." By making themselves stockholders in the bank and granting to the corporation the power to purchase lands for other purposes they assume a power not granted in the Constitution and grant it to others what they do not themselves possess. It is not necessary to the receiving, safe-keeping, or transmission of the funds of the Government that the bank should possess this power, and it is not proper that Congress should thus enlarge the powers delegated to them in the Constitution.

The old Bank of the United States possessed a capital of only $11,000,000, which was found fully sufficient to enable it with dispatch and safety to perform all the functions required of it by the Government. The capital of the present bank is $35,000,000 – at least twenty-four more than experience has proved to be necessary to enable a bank to perform its public functions. The public debt which existed during the period of the old bank and on the establishment of the new has been nearly paid off, and our revue will soon be reduced. This increase of capital is therefore not for public but for private purposes.

The Government is the only "proper" judge where its agents should reside and keep their offices, because it best knows where their presence will be "necessary." It can not, therefore, be "necessary" or "proper" to authorize the bank to locate branches where it pleases to perform the public service, without consulting the Government, and contrary to its will. The principle laid down by the Supreme Court concedes that Congress can not establish a bank for purposes of private speculation and gain, but only as a means of executing the delegated powers of the General Government. By the same principle a branch bank can not constitutionally be established for other than public purposes. The power which this act gives to establish two branches in any State, without the injunction or request of the Government and for other than public purposes, is not "necessary" for the due execution of the powers delegated to Congress.

The bonus which is exacted from the bank is a confession upon the face of the act that the powers granted by it are greater than are "necessary" to its character of a fiscal agent. The Government does not tax its officers and agents for the privilege of serving it. The bonus of a million and a half required by the original charter and that of three millions proposed by this act are not exacted for the privilege of giving "the necessary facilities for transferring the public funds from place to place within the United States or the Territories thereof, and for distributing the same in payment of the public creditors without charging commission or claiming allowance on account of the difference of exchange," as required by the act of incorporation, but for something more beneficial to the stockholders. The original act declares that it (the bonus) is granted "in consideration of the exclusive privileges and benefits conferred by this act upon the said bank," and the act before me declares it to be "in consideration of the exclusive privileges and benefits" conferred for their own use and emolument, and not for the advantage of the Government, that a bonus is exacted. These surplus powers for which the bank is required to pay can not surely be "necessary" to make it the fiscal agent of the Treasury. If they were, the exaction of a bonus for them would not be "proper".

It is maintained by some that the bank is a means of executing the constitutional power "to coin money and regulate the value thereof." Congress have established a mint to coin money and passed laws to regulate the value thereof. The money so coined, with its value so regulated, and such foreign coins as Congress may adopt are the only currency known to the Constitution. But if they have other power to regulate the currency, it was conferred to be exercised by themselves, and not to be transferred to a corporation. If the bank be established for that purpose, with a charter unalterable without it is neither necessary nor proper to transfer its legislative power for a term of years, during which the Constitution itself is a dead letter. It is neither necessary nor proper to transfer its legislative power to such a bank, and therefore unconstitutional.

By its silence, considered in connection with the decision of the Supreme Court in the case of McCulloch against the State of Maryland, this act takes from the States the power to tax a portion of the banking business carried on within their limits, in subversion of one of the strongest barriers which secured them against Federal encroachments. Banking, like farming, manufacturing, or any other occupation or profession, is a business, the right to follow which is not originally derived from the laws. Every citizen and every company of citizens in all of our States possessed the right until the State legislatures deemed it good policy to prohibit private banking by law. If the prohibitory State laws were now repealed, every citizen would again possess the right. The State banks are qualified restoration of the right which has been taken away by the laws against banking, guarded by such provisions and limitations as in the opinion of the State legislatures the public interest requires. These corporations, unless there be an exemption in their charter, are, like private bankers and banking companies, subject to State taxation. The manner in which these taxes shall be laid depends wholly on legislative discretion. It may be upon the bank, upon the stock, upon the profits, or in any other mode which the sovereign power shall will.

Upon the formation of the Constitution the States guarded their taxing power with peculiar jealousy. They surrendered it only as it regards imports and exports. In relation to every other object within their jurisdiction, whether persons, property, business, or professions, it was secured in as ample a manner as it was before possessed. All persons, though United States officers, are liable to a poll tax by the States within which they reside. The lands of the United States are liable to the usual land tax, except in the new States, from whom agreements that they will not tax unsold lands are exacted when they are admitted into the Union. Horses, wagons, and beasts or vehicles, tools, or property belonging to private citizens, though employed in the service of the United States, are subject to State taxation. Every private business, whether carried on by an officer of the General Government or not, whether it be mixed with public concerns or not, even if it be carried on by the Government of the United States itself, separately or in partnership, falls within the scope of the taxing power of the State. Nothing comes more fully within it than banks and the business of banking, by whomsoever instituted and carried on. Over this whole subject-matter it is just as absolute, unlimited, and uncontrollable as it the Constitution have never been adopted, because in the formation of that instrument it was reserved without qualification.

The principle is conceded that the States can not rightfully tax the operations of the General Government. They can not tax the money of the Government deposited in the State banks, nor the agency of those banks in remitting it; but will any man maintain that their mere selection to perform this public service for the General Government would exempt the States banks and their ordinary business from State taxation? Had the United States, instead of establishing a bank at Philadelphia, employed a private banker to keep and transmit their funds, would it have deprived Pennsylvania of the right to tax his bank and his usual bank operations? It will not be pretended. Upon what principle, then are the banking establishments of the Bank of the United States and their usual banking operations to be exempted form taxation? It is not their public agency or the deposits of the Government which the States claim a right to tax, but their banks and their banking powers, instituted and exercised within State jurisdiction for their private emolument – those powers and privileges for which they pay a bonus, and which the States tax in their own banks. The exercise of these powers within a State, no matter by whom or under what authority, whether by private citizens in their original right, by corporate bodies created by the States, by foreigners or the agents of foreign governments located within their limits, forms a legitimate object of State taxation. From this and like sources, from the persons, property, and business that are found residing , located, or carried on under their jurisdiction, must the States, since the surrender of their right to raise a revenue from imports and exports, draw all the money necessary for the support of their governments and the maintenance of their independence. There is no more appropriate subject of taxation than banks, banking, and bank stocks, and none to which the States ought more pertinacious to cling.

It cannot be necessary to the character of the Bank as a fiscal agent of the Government that its private business should be exempted from that taxation to which all the State banks shall be thus attacked and annihilated as a means of executing the powers delegated to the general government. It may be safely assumed that none of the sages who had an agency in forming or adopting our Constitution, ever imagined that any portion of the taxing power of the States, not prohibited to them nor delegated to Congress, was to be swept away and annihilated as a means of executing certain powers delegated to Congress.

If our power over means is so absolute that the Supreme Court will not call in question the constitutionality of an act of Congress the subject of which, is not prohibited, and is really calculated to effect any of the objects entrusted to the Government, although, as in the case before me, it takes away powers expressly granted to Congress and rights scrupulously reserved to the States, it becomes us to proceed in our legislation with the utmost caution. Though not directly, our own powers and the rights of the States may be indirectly legislated away in the use of means to execute substantive powers. We may not enact that Congress shall not have the power of exclusive legislation over the District of Columbia, but we may pledge the faith of the United States that as a means of executing other powers it shall not be exercised for twenty years or forever. We may not pass an act prohibiting the States to tax the banking business carried on within their limits, but we may, as a means of executing our powers over other subjects, place that business in the hands of our agents and then declare it exempt from State taxation in their hands. Thus may our own powers and the rights of the States, which we can not directly curtail or invade, be frittered away and extinguished in the use of means employed by us to execute other powers. That a bank of the United States, competent to all the duties which may be required by the Government, might be so organized as not to infringe on our own delegated powers or the reserved rights of the States I do not entertain a doubt. Had the Executive been called upon to furnish the project of such an institution, the duty would have been cheerfully performed. In the absence of such a call it was obviously proper that he should confine himself to pointing out those prominent features in the act presented which in his opinion make it incompatible with the Constitution and sound policy. A general discussion will now take place, eliciting new light and settling important principles; and a new Congress, elected in the midst of such discussion, and furnishing an equal representation of the people according to the last census, will bear to the Capital the verdict of public opinion, and, I doubt not, bring this important question to a satisfactory result.

Under such circumstances the bank comes forward and asks a renewal of its charter for a term of fifteen years upon conditions which not only operate as a gratuity to the stockholders of many millions of dollars, but will sanction any abuses and legalize any encroachments.

Suspicions are entertained, and charges are made, of gross abuse and violation of its charter. An investigation unwillingly conceded, and so restricted in time as necessarily to make it incomplete and unsatisfactory, disclosed enough to excite suspicion and alarm. In the practices of the principal bank partially unveiled, in the absence of important witnesses, and in numerous charges confidently made, and as yet wholly uninvestigated, there was enough to induce a majority of the committee of investigation -- a committee which was selected from the most able and honorable members of the House of Representatives -- to recommend a suspension of further action upon the bill and a prosecution of the inquiry. As the charter had yet four years to run, and as a renewal now was not necessary to the successful prosecution of its business, it was to have been expected that the bank itself, conscious of its purity, and proud of its character, would have withdrawn its application for the present, and demanded the severest scrutiny into all its transactions. In their declining to do so, there seems to be an additional reason why the functionaries of the Government should proceed with less haste and more caution in the renewal of their monopoly.

The bank is professedly established as an agent of the executive branch of the Government, and its constitutionality is maintained on that ground. Neither upon the propriety of present action nor upon the provisions of this act was the Executive consulted. It has had no opportunity to say that it neither needs nor wants an agent clothed with such powers and favored by such exemptions. There is nothing in its legitimate functions which makes it necessary or proper. What ever interest or influence, whether public or private, has given birth to this act, it can not be found either in the wishes or necessities of the executive department, by which present action is deemed premature, and the powers conferred upon its agent not only unnecessary, but dangerous to the Government and country.

It is to be regretted that the rich and powerful too often bend the acts of government to their selfish purposes. Distinctions in society will always exist under every just government. Equality of talents, of education, or of wealth can not be produced by human institutions. In the full enjoyment of the gifts of Heaven and the fruits of superior industry, economy, and virtue, every man is equally entitled to protection by law; but when the laws undertake to add to these natural and just advantages artificial distinctions, to grant titles, gratuities, and exclusive privileges, to make the rich richer and the potent more powerful, the humble members of society – the farmers, mechanics, and laborers – who have neither the time nor the means of securing like favors to themselves, have a fight to complain of the injustice of their Government. There are no necessary evils in government. Its evils exist only in its abuses. If it would confine itself to equal protection, and, as Heaven does its rains, shows its favors alike on the high and the low, the rich and the poor, it would be an unqualified blessing. In the act before me there seems to be a wide and unnecessary departure from these just principles.

Nor is our Government to be maintained or our Union preserved by invasions of the rights and powers of the several States. In thus attempting to make our General Government strong we make it weak. Its true strength consists in leaving individuals and States as much as possible to themselves – in making itself felt, not in its power, but in its beneficence; not in its control, but in its protection; not in binding the States more closely to the center, but leaving each to move unobstructed in its proper orbit.

Experience should teach us wisdom. Most of the difficulties our Government now encounters and most of the dangers which impend over our Union have sprung from an abandonment of the legitimate objects of Government by our national legislation, and the adoption of such principles as are embodied in this act. Many of our rich men have not been content with equal protection and equal benefits, but have besought us to make them richer by act of Congress. By attempting to gratify their desires we have in the results of our legislation arrayed section against section, interest against interest, and man against man, in a fearful commotion which threatens to shake the foundations of our Union. It is time to pause in our career to review our principles, and if possible revive that devoted patriotism and spirit of compromise which distinguished the ages of the Revolution and the fathers of our Union. If we can not at once, in justice to interests vested under improvident legislation, make our Government what it ought to be, we can at least take a stand against all new grants of monopolies and exclusive privileges, against any prostitution of our Government to the advancement of the few at the expense of the many, and in favor or compromise and gradual reform, in our code of laws and system of political economy.

I have now done my duty to my country. If sustained by my fellow citizens, I shall be grateful and happy; if not, I shall find in the motives which impel me ample grounds for contentment and peace. In the difficulties which surround us and the dangers which threaten our institutions there is cause for neither dismay nor alarm. For relief and deliverance let us firmly rely on that kind Providence which, I am sure, watches with peculiar care over the destinies of our republic, and on the intelligence and wisdom of our countrymen. Through His abundant goodness, and their patriotic devotion, our liberty and Union will be preserved.

The rottenness of the Second Bank of the United States was exposed when the stockholders instituted a complete investigation into its management from 1830 to 1836. This investigation uncovered an astonishing degree of corruption and rascality that sustained the charges made by President Jackson. It was discovered that Biddle had spent hundreds of thousands of dollars bribing members of Congress, subsidizing the press to influence elections. After the investigation some of the stockholders filed a lawsuit against Biddle for spending $1,018,000 for which vouchers could not be found. Source: The Coming Battle

In 1836, the Second Bank of the United States passed into history. Banking and money creation passed to state-chartered private banks where with a minimum of regulation, a proliferation of one thousand six hundred banks issued over seven thousand varieties of paper currency with over thirty thousand varieties of colors and designs. Source: U.S. Treasury

All this paper currency was issued as interest-bearing notes promising to pay gold or silver. In 1828, the seventeen banks chartered in Mississippi circulated notes with a face value of $6,000,000 from a base of gold and silver of only $303,000, which is a little over 19 %. The norm for all the banks at that time was around 10% to 25%. My guess is that there were a lot more 10% banks than there where 25% banks. In 1833, the amount of banks notes in circulation was around ten million dollars in 1837 it had risen to almost one hundred and fifty million dollars. Source Jacksonian America E. Pessen through www.maths.ted.ie.html

It is always the same old story. When the banks can't pay the gold and silver their notes promise, they just suspend payment in specie. The people continue using the notes as their medium-of-exchange because in reality they have no other option. However when the borrowers, mostly farmers and laborers can't pay their debt to the bankers, the bankers working through their lawyers, foreclose. Then they send the out the police to seize by force, if necessary, everything they can get their hands on.

The financial history in America, after the adoption of the Constitution repeated itself. First, a national bank is chartered to issue the money as loans. Then the president doesn't renew the charter to the national bank. Thousands of state-chartered banks pop up to issue the money as loans. This leads to a lot of confusion and a lack of uniformity. We have another war, in 1812, and the government decides to issue treasury notes to fund the war. When the government decides to issue it own money, the moneyed elite get very active and pressure the congress to start a national bank. The congress bows to the will of the moneyed elite, because they are the ones who pad the politician's pockets, and the people get a national bank that issues money for the benefit of the banks and not for the benefit of the people. The president doesn't renew the national bank's charter and we return to state banks and the same debt money, all we lose is uniformity and centralized power.

However, all this time the moneyed elite are gaining power for obvious reasons. The bankers continue to get interest on their promise to pay. The banks don't have to honor their promises to pay; but their borrowers do. Some of the big banks have been in continuous business since the days of Hamilton and Burr.

Abraham Lincoln took office in March of 1861. The Civil War started in April of 1861. The government again was very short of money to fund the war.

By an act of July 17th 1861, Congress authorized the Secretary of the Treasury to issue demand notes. The notes were made a full legal tender for all financial transactions. Source: The coming battle. Feb 6, 1862, Congress provided for the issue of non-interest bearing notes to the amount of $150,000,000 with full legal tender power for the payment of all financial transactions. Source: The coming battle. These notes were traded into circulation. They maintained their value and were a favorite of the people with the exception of the banking crowd. The notes were nick-named greenbacks because the backs of the notes were green in color. The people didn't have to go into debt to the bankers to have that money to use. A multitude of bankers traveled to Washington D.C. requesting the Committee on Ways and Means of the House and the Finance Committee of the Senate to meet with them at the office of the Treasury. The meeting was held February 11, 1862.

Following the meeting the legal tender clause was changed to read:

"That the amount of the two kinds of notes together shall at no time exceed the sum of $150,000,000, and such notes herein authorized shall be receivable in payment of taxes, internal duties, excises, debts and demand of every kind due to the United States, except duties on imports and of all claims and demands against the united States of every kind except for interest upon bond and notes which shall be paid in coin, and shall also be lawful money and a legal tender in the payment of all debts, public and private, within the United states, except duties on imports and interest as aforesaid". Source: The Coming Battle

The United States notes issued in 1861 were first issued as full legal tender money. They were not redeemable in gold or silver. Then, as we have just seen in 1862, they were changed so that they were no longer a full legal tender. They were legal tender for every thing except interest on the debt and duties on imports. Then under the Gold Resumption Act of 1879, the United States Notes became redeemable in gold. Source: The Coming Battle and A personal letter from Russell L. Munk

I feel that I must make it clear here that these demand notes were not issued a monetized wealth, but were issued on the credit of the United States. They had to be taxed out of circulation to cancel out the debt on the books of the government.

It is pretty easy to see why the bankers wanted the interest paid in coin. When the government pays the interest to the bankers in coins, they can put the coins in the vault and then loan out, at interest, about ten times the face value of the coins in their bank notes.

Mr. Stevens a federal legislator from Pennsylvania asked: "How is this gold to be raised? The duties and public lands are to be paid for in United States notes, and they or bonds are to be put up at auction, to get coin from the very brokers who would furnish the coins to pay themselves by getting twenty percent discount on the notes thus bought." Source: The Coming Battle

As a result of this act as amended, the merchant who paid duties on merchandise imported from abroad was compelled to pay the taxes levied thereon, in coin. To obtain that kind of money he must proceed to the bullion broker, and pay him a large premium for the coins to make payment of the customs levied on his merchandise. The interest on government bonds was paid in gold, which was sold by him to the importer, at a high premium. Source: the Coming Battle

Once again the moneyed elite pressured congress to charter national banks. **The bankers seem to really get energetic when the government starts to issue its own currency.** On February 25, 1863, Congress passed a National Banking Act that mandated the circulating bank notes, issued by the bank, be backed by holdings of United States government securities. It seems strange that Lincoln who has been given credit for issuing United States Notes is also given credit for being a promoter of a national bank system. Six days later on March 3, 1863, Congress authorized the Secretary of the Treasury to issue $900,000,000 in bonds, at six percent interest.

These bonds could be purchased by lawful money, meaning United States notes treasure notes. Source: The Coming Battle. It didn't say it in the book *The Coming Battle* but of course at that time in history lawful money would have also included gold and silver coin which was controlled by the national bankers and the bullion dealers. It is pretty clear why bankers didn't want congress issuing too many greenbacks.

Let me explain why I am so sure the banks controlled or soon would control most of the gold and silver. If the money supply were one hundred percent gold and silver, and the bankers lent out just ten percent of it, at ten percent interest compounded annually, it would only take twenty-five years for the bankers to own all the gold. Under Fraction banking banks were supposed to have gold and silver to back or to support all the paper money they loaned. They would need to control most of the gold or silver to control the money supply so they could cause booms and busts through the making and calling in loans.

To farther illustrate, the total production of gold from the mines of the United States, from 1848 to 1861 inclusive, reached the grand total of $700,000,000. In 1867, $13,500,000 of silver was produced from the mines of the west. The production of gold for that year was $51,725,000. At this period, the national debt had reached the enormous sum of $2,700,000,000, the interest of which was payable in coin. The whole annual product of the gold mines in the United States would scarcely suffice to pay one-half of the annual interest charge upon the national debt held by the national banking money power. The control of the gold and silver supply of the country was in the firm grasp of the national banking system.Source: The Coming Battle

By 1863, the old banking families had been loaning bank notes for around 200 years at a rate of at least six times the amount of gold and silver they owned or stored. All this time, most of the people were using bank notes as their medium-of-exchange because they didn't understand they were debt money and because they preferred the paper over carrying the metal. **As long as a nation allows lending at interest, the money lenders will run and rule that nation.**

Congressman Kellogg from Illinois underscored the greed of these men when he stated: *"I am pained to sit in my place in the House and hear members talk about 'the sacredness of capital,' that the interests of money must not be touched. Yes, sir, they will vote six hundred thousand of the flower of the American youth for the army to be sacrificed without a blush, but the great interests of capital, of currency, must not be touched."* Source: The Coming Battle

Andrew Jackson in his farewell address warned the people against the moneyed elite and that special privileges must not ever be granted to any class of citizens. Justice and fairness must be the basis of public and private conduct.

Jackson went on to point out that if the money power ever again gained total control of the money system that they would dictate the choice of your highest officers and would compel the nation to make peace or war, as best suits their own wishes. We have clearly seen this in the last few years and in the 2008 elections.

After the Federal Congress and President Lincoln opened wide the door and restored the power over the nations money system to the national bankers, by the passage of the National Banking Act. The bankers began moves to remove other forms of money from the nation. The banker knew that free coinage was a handicap to the banks. They saw the rich deposits of silver in the western states as a danger to their power and total control over the nation's money. They had already stopped the free coinage of silver with an act of February 21, 1853 with the exception of the silver dollar. Then in 1873, congress terminated the right of the public to deposit silver with the mint for coinage of the silver dollar. It took them until December of 1970 to completely take all the silver out of the coinage. There was a huge political fight over demonetizing silver and move to what was called the gold standard. To understand it better, I recommend that you read The Coming Battle written by M.W. Walbert in1899 and republished by Walter Publishing & Research in 1997. To give you a little taste of the political fight I include the following cartoon.

TAKE YOUR CHOICE OF THE TWO BILLS!

The national banks moved to destroy the states banks by having the federal Congress, on March 3, 1865, impose a ten percent tax on State-chartered bank notes. That tax did take the state bank notes out of existence. However, the state-charted banks were able to stay in business by switching to creating money by adding numbers to checking accounts instead of printing bank notes. By 1866, seventy-five percent of all bank deposits were held by nationally chartered banks.

The National Bank Notes were not predominantly backed by gold. They were backed by bonds upon which the government paid interest.

On May 30, 1908, Congress passed the Aldrich-Vreeland Act which permitted the national chartered banks to issue currency on State, County, City, Town bonds and commercial paper, as well as Federal Government Bonds. Black's Law Dictionary defines Commercial paper as: Bills of exchange, promissory notes, bank checks, and other negotiable instruments for the payment of money. This includes short-term notes issued by corporate borrowers.

Once money becomes your god there seems to be no end to greed. The motto of a greedy man is always *'just a little more.'*

Once the moneyed elite gains control of a nation's money system, the same things happen over and over again. First the money flows out as loans, and the country booms. The nation then has a money panic or crisis, the money becomes very scarce and the nation has a recession or depression. *In a recession, you lose every thing you have worked for. In a depression, I lose everything that I have worked for.*

Let's use the history of Minnesota as an example of what greed and manipulation had done to this nation. The fur trade was the first raw resource that was utilized in the state. John Jacob Astor was a German immigrant who came to America when he was twenty. He quickly gained control of the fur trade from the vast lands where the Indians lived to the European market where the furs were used. His company soon had almost a monopoly of the fur trade. His company not only dealt in furs but it acquired and sold land. It produced agricultural produce of all kinds including, but not limited to, maple sugar, cranberries and fisheries. He engaged in the mining of lead and copper. In time, furs ran out. Source: Building Minnesota by Theodore C. Blegen

It seems this left Astor **very** rich. But the people who did the work that made him so rich did not fair **nearly** so well. It is strange that nobody ever wondered where he got all the contacts and the money to accomplish all this starting at the tender age of twenty.

Then came the railroads, it took thousands of people working very hard to build. Yet the working people received little, and a few at the top became very wealthy.

After that came the logging industry and the raping of the timbered lands required thousands of people to move through the country cutting down trees by the millions. In time the prime trees, just like the prime furs came to an end. Again a few became very rich, but most of the working people ended up just making a living.

Then came the wheat, the flour and the iron ore industries. The story of the Merritt family tells how they all ended. A few ended up with most of the benefits while the majority who did the work ended up just making a living while the overall debt continued to grow.

Just stop and think about all the money needed to buy and sell all those furs, lumber, wheat, flour, and coal that were newly produced in Minnesota.

You must fully understand that the banking system created every dollar of it as interest-bearing loans. This has left the people of Minnesota collectively owing around $29,000,000,000 as of 2007, after producing all that new wealth that came by combining the labor and ideas of the people with the natural raw resources of the earth.

The moneyed elite used all their booms (by making lots of loan) and busts created by increasing the interest rates and/or refusing to make as new loans and foreclosing on loans. Like they did to the farmers in the 1980's and like they are doing with housing in 2008, to that you can add the federal bailouts that are used to transfer the wealth from the producer to the moneyed elite.

They also used their money crises as tools to gain more power and as a reason to establish the third central bank of the United States, in 1913, called the Federal Reserve System. Only this time they did not make the mistake of chartering it for just twenty years.

In a few years we should be able to see and understand what new powers or what changes the banking elite want to obtain through the financial crises of 2008.

Chapter 9
THE GOLD STANDARD

Many people have been led to believe that the gold standard was some kind of a check on the banker's creation of money. My research of monetary history has revealed that gold was never a standard of value nor was it a check upon the creation of money by the banking system. The gold standard was never anything but an act of deception by the banking system.

The 1792 Mint Act created by law but not by practice, a money system consisting of a specified weight of both silver and gold coins for the United States. The gold standard came into existence in the United States in 1900 when the Gold Standard Act made it the duty of the Secretary of the Treasury to maintain all forms of money issued by the United States at parity with gold (31 U.S.C. 314,31 Stat. 45). This was done by exchanging gold for each type of money and vice versa at a fixed ratio. This Act officially replaced bimetallism with the gold standard.

The banking system has always pushed their notes as just another form of money to help enhance trade. The bankers claimed their notes were backed by silver or gold only to hide the fact that their notes were put into circulation as interest-bearing debt owed to the banking system for the sole purpose of robbing the people. People have been led to believe that the gold standard means gold is the ultimate and the only honest money and gold was what was really loaned because the banks held enough gold to redeem all of the bank notes that they issued. Gold backed notes held back inflation because the banks could not issue more notes than they had gold. The bank notes were just a more convenient form of money for the people to use as their medium-of-exchange. The facts are the very concept of fractional reserve banking is that banks loan out at <u>least</u> five times more, in face value note money, than they have in gold or any other reserve. The banks notes were and are simply a deceptive way for the banks to get something for nothing.

"In 1933, while this country was on a gold coin standard, our money supply was $20 billion, while our total gold stock was only $4 billion." Paul M. Horvitz Director of Research Federal Deposit Insurance Corporation. Very little of that gold was in general circulation as money. In 1933, my dad was thirty-seven years old and a very active trader. During his life time he could only remember seeing one gold coin in general circulation. In the early 1980s Larry Becraft, a lawyer, called and told me that he had found proof that in the 1930's that the banks in Iowa had loaned $30 dollars for every dollar they had in reserve.

To loan out more than you have, you must somehow deceive the borrower. That is what the banking system has always done. First by loaning gold they didn't own and then by loaning multiple receipts for gold they may or may not have owned.

Today the people running the banking system have deceived the people into believing the bank's promise to pay is money, although it is easily proven that the banks didn't loan anything. Our corrupt court system will always uphold the banker's fraud.

Under the banking system's gold standard, for gold to be monetized it had to be sold to the United States Treasury. The Treasury paid for it with a check drawn on a reserve bank (checkbook money). The seller of the gold would deposit this check at his bank, (a member bank of the Federal Reserve Banking system), which in turn would deposit it with a Federal Reserve Bank. It was added to the reserve balance of the bank and charged to the account of the United States Treasury. The Treasury would then replenish its account at a Federal Reserve Bank by issuing an equivalent amount of gold certificates to the Federal Reserve Bank. When this was done, the gold stock of the Treasury, the gold certificate holdings of a Federal Reserve Bank, the reserve balance of a member bank and the bank deposit of the seller of the gold had each increased by the amount of the check. Source: The Federal Reserve System Purposes and Functions Third Edition pages 100 and 101. This was true whether the gold was produced in the United States or imported from abroad.

Let's think about that for a few minutes. With one check drawn on a reserve bank the United States Treasury got more gold. A Federal Reserve Bank received a gold certificate from the Treasury promising to give the gold to the Federal Reserve Bank when and if the bank demanded it. So, the true owner of the gold was the bank, not the Treasury. A private commercial bank (which was a member of the Federal Reserve System) received new reserves in its reserve account at one of the 12 Federal Reserve Banks and the seller of the gold got a new checking account balance at his bank. Now let's look at what each of the four: the Treasury, a Federal Reserve Bank, a commercial bank and the seller of the gold could do with the benefits it received from that one check.

The Treasury could not do anything with the gold but hold it for the Federal Reserve Bank. The Federal Reserve Bank could use the gold certificate as collateral to have the Bureau of Printing and Engraving print Federal Reserve Notes at the cost of printing, not the face value of the notes. The Federal Reserve Bank could sell their notes to a private commercial bank at face value. The commercial bank could use the notes as reserves to make at least 9 times the face value of the Federal Reserve Notes in loans of checkbook money to the American people. The seller of the gold could spend his checkbook money to buy anything he wanted.

These loans from the commercial banks would put the American people deeper in interest-bearing debt with no way to create the money needed to rid themselves of the debt. This will force the American people to live in economic servitude forever unless the people wake up and demand freedom. The proof that we live in economic servitude is the fact that we now suffer under and pay interest on $53 trillion of debt when all we the people have done is produce wealth with our knowhow, our labor and the resources of the earth.

As we have just seen under the gold standard, gold was monetized as everlasting interest-bearing debts the people owed to the banking system, not as a monetary asset of the people, based on and representing the people's production. **Real, true, honest money can only be an asset to all the people based on their production of real wealth.**

Under the bimetallism free coinage standard set up under the 1792 Coinage Act gold and silver were monetized as wealth to the people based on the production of gold and silver bullion. A bimetallic standard is one in which the monetary unit is defined in terms of both gold and silver. Sec. 11 of the 1792 Coinage Act stated *"the proportional value of gold to silver in all coins which shall be current as money within the United States shall be as fifteen to one, according to quantity in weight, of pure gold or pure silver; that is to say, every fifteen pounds weight of pure silver shall be of equal value in all payments, with one pound weight of pure gold".* However, that standard was never used as the money supply in America. Before the 1792 Coinage Act was enacted, the first Congress had already set up a fractional reserve central banking system. The young nation, in 1792, did not have any mines that produced gold or silver (the first gold was found in 1799). There was an insufficient supply of gold and silver in the country and most all of it was owned by very wealthy Europeans.

Fractional reserve banking has always ruled the monetary system in America from 1791 to today.

"All bank deposits are a form of credit. Basically, they represent amounts owed by banks to depositors. They come into existence by an exchange of bank promises to pay customers for the various assets which banks acquire--- currency, promissory notes of business, consumer, and other customers, mortgages on real estate, and government and other securities." Federal Reserve System Purposes and Functions Third Edition page 6.

Clearly the gold standard was not what most people think it was. Most of the money in circulation from about 1790 to today has been bank notes or demand deposits (interest-bearing money issued by private banks under state or federal government charters).

State Bank Notes, National Bank Notes and Federal Reserve Bank Notes were all issued under the fractional reserve banking practice of creating new money by issuing a promise to pay. The banking system calls it money expansion. But the fact is, it is only an expansion of unpayable interest-bearing debt owed to the banking system.

Under the gold standard the reserve was gold and government bonds. The government claimed that it would redeem all the currency in gold. Therefore, the currency was said to be backed by gold. However, there was always a lot more government debt (bonds) backing (used as collateral for) the notes than there was gold. Imagine you have ten dollars in your checking account and you write checks for one hundred dollars then claim all your checks can be paid with the ten dollars.

The trick to making this work is to convince the holders of the banker's promises to pay, to keep passing the notes around as payment. But never take them to the bank and demand payment from the issuer. Under the fractional reserve banking practices, the banks are never able to pay more than twenty-five percent of their promises to pay.

The banking system has somehow convinced most of the people to believe that **their promises to pay** are the only real money and anyone that thinks that it could be done any other way is truly deceived.

Beginning in 1900, the Gold Standard Act made it the duty of the Secretary of the Treasury to maintain all forms of money issued by the United States at parity with gold (31 U.S.C. 314). History and personal experience have proven that part of the Act was never enforced. It is impossible to have banks issue currency as interest bearing loans, using the principles of fractional reserve banking and at the same time maintain the value of the currency at parity to the reserves, be it gold government bonds or something else. I repeat. The very concept of fractional banking is to expand the currency in volume and value, as interest bearing loans, beyond the reserves base. Interest on money always makes the debt grow. It never makes the money supply grow. Interest is a cost of doing business and it always causes the cost of production to increase.

The United States officially abandoned the domestic gold standard in 1933-1934, pursuant to the authority provided in the Emergency Banking Relief Act of March 9, 1933. If the gold standard was as great as some people would have us believe, why did it only last thirty three years?

When the banks began to shrink the money supply to create the great Depression of the 1930's, many people tried to go to the bank and withdraw gold as the currency stated on its face could be done. The banks, of course, did not have enough gold. To protect the banks and the bankers, President Roosevelt pursuant to the authority provided in the Emergency Banking Relief Act (sounds like what is happening in 2008) of March 9, 1933 did the following:

- Outlawed the ownership of gold held by private persons
- Seized the gold from the people under the threat of 10 years in jail and/ or up to $50,000.00 in fines
- Stopped the domestic redemption of the currency in gold
- Stopped the stamping of gold into coinage (thereby demonetizing gold) and officially abandoned the domestic gold standard
- Forced the people to accept 'notes', evidence of debt as their medium-of-exchange

Congress by Section 43 (b) (2) of the Act of May 12, 1933 (48 Stat. 52), gave the President the authority to change the gold content of the dollar. After President Roosevelt had forced the American people to turn their gold over to the banking system by proclamation No. 2072, dated January 31, 1934 (48 Stat.) he exercised his powers under the 1933 statute, as amended by Section 12 of the Gold Reserve Act of 1934 (48 Stat. 342), to change the gold content of the dollar from 25.8 grains of gold 9/10ths fine that corresponded to a price of $20.67 per ounce, to 15 5/21 grains, of gold 9/10ths fine, that corresponded to $35 dollars per ounce. This means when the American people where forced to turn in an ounce of gold they got $20.67 worth of Federal Reserve Bank credit. As soon as the banking system gained control the same ounce of gold became worth 35 dollars of bank credit on the international market. Source: A personal letter from Russell L. Munk, Assistant General Counsel, Department of the Treasury

Under the Bretton Woods agreement, the United States government was still obligated to surrender one ounce of gold for every thirty-five dollars worth of Federal Reserve notes presented by a foreign central bank. The United States government was obligated to pay one ounce of gold for every thirty-five dollars of credit created by the Federal Reserve Banking system. However, anyone outside of the domestic United States could buy or sell gold with bank created money for any price agreed on by the buyer and the seller.

As Marriner Eccles, Chairman of the Federal Reserve Board in the 1930's stated: *"There is no limit to the amount of money that can be created by the banking system."* As long people are willing to borrow it at interest, most bankers can think of few reasons why they should not create more of it. However, there is a limit to the amount of gold that is produced. A split between the official price of gold and what speculators could be hyped into paying for it had to come sooner or later.

With the expansionary money policies of Arthur Burns, Federal Reserve dollars flew overseas to buy goods. Strong demand to change Federal Reserve dollars into European currencies forced the European central banks to hold the Federal Reserve Notes and issue more of their own currencies. The same thing is happening now in China.

In January of 1971, foreign central banks held $20,000,000,000 worth of Federal Reserve Bank created credit. Fear that the United States government could not pay its obligations (debt) in gold caused many more people to exchange the American currency for the currency of their own country. By May of 1971, the holding of Federal Reserve Notes held by other countries central banks had climbed to a face value of 32,000,000,000 dollars. Those central banks held a legal claim to 914,285,714 ounces of gold. The United States only had about 285,714 ounces of gold.

I remember when Charles De Gaulle of France began to make waves about redeeming his Federal Reserve Notes, but at the time, I didn't understand what was going on. On Sunday evening August 15, 1971, Nixon did what has always been done when demands are put on the banks to honor their promises to pay gold or silver. He announced that the United States would no longer permit a foreign government or their central bank to redeem Federal Reserve Bank credits in gold. The United Stated defaulted on its obligations!

In February of 1973, the United States government changed the legal value of gold to $42.22 worth of Federal Reserve Bank credit, which is its legal value today. It was just a symbolic change because neither the United States government nor the Federal Reserve Banks will honor its obligations or the redemption set forth in 12 U.S.C. Sec. 411 states:

Issuance to reserve banks; nature of obligation; redemption

Federal reserve notes, to be issued at the discretion of the Board of Governors of the Federal Reserve System for the purpose of making advances to Federal reserve banks through the Federal reserve agents as hereinafter set forth and for no other purpose, are authorized. The said notes shall be obligations of the United States and shall be receivable by all national and member banks and Federal Reserve Banks and for all taxes, customs, and other public dues. They shall be redeemed in lawful money on demand at the Treasury Department of the United States, in the city of Washington, District of Columbia, or at any Federal Reserve Bank.

It's hard to believe that our grandparents and great-grandparents couldn't see the theft that was going on when Roosevelt confiscated and revalued the peoples gold and were willing to accept it. Such wholesale theft should have sparked a revolution.

It was forty years before the people could again own gold. When they could, gold was no longer money. It had been demonetized and was once again just a commodity. Money is not a thing of nature; money is a man-made concept. Gold is always just a commodity until it is declared money by man's law. We must understand that the value of anything is only what is agreed on by two or more people at a given point in time and really does not have any bearing on any other trade at any other time. What would be the value of a glass of water to a person standing beside a cool clear mountain stream? What is the value of a glass of water to a person that has been out in a hot desert for a couple of days?

Gold is nothing more or less than a raw natural resource. Because it doesn't rot, spoil or corrode and is very easily divided into small parts (not unlike many other metals) it could work as a medium-of-exchange and enhance barter. That does not necessarily make it a good general medium of exchange.

If gold was mined out of the ground, assayed and stamped into coined money then traded into circulation (as called for under the 1792 Coinage Act), it would have been an honest debt-free money, but not necessarily a very good general medium of exchange. The supply of gold is too limited to be a good general medium-of-exchange for the total production people accomplish with their ideas, labor and nature's raw resources.

Keep in mind that we are discussing the *volume of gold not the value of gold.* To illustrate - if the total population is ten men and the total supply of cows is only eight cows; it would be impossible for each man to have one cow. It doesn't make any difference what value is placed on the cows. The same is true of gold. If there are 10 men and the total supply of gold is only 8 ounces it would be impossible for each man to have one ounce of gold.

Don't be fooled by the nonsense spewed forth by people like Murray N. Rothbard, The Ludwig von Mises Institute, Edwin Vieira Jr. G. Edward Griffin and the many other gold bugs who have accepted the banker's lies.

> "*We must remember that the limited supply of gold as a monetary base is an advantage, not a disadvantage. If it were not scarce, it would not have utility as money. The smaller the supply, the more valuable it is. As pointed out in* "The Creature from Jekyll Island", *any amount of gold or silver will work just as well as any other amount. The only difference is how valuable each unit of measure will be.*" G. Edward Griffin

Let's think about Griffin's statement for a few minutes. If the supply of gold was so small that only one-half of the population could have a piece of gold, and the gold was so valuable that only the very wealthy could have any, what good would gold be as a general medium-of-exchange for the total population?

Gold scarcity is why it doesn't have utility as a good general medium of exchange. If there was a sufficient supply of debt-free, interest-free gold to use as the general medium of exchange, why would the people be so willing to pay the banking system interest just to have a medium-of-exchange?

Let's look at this report:

FREEMARKET
GOLD & MONEY
REPORT

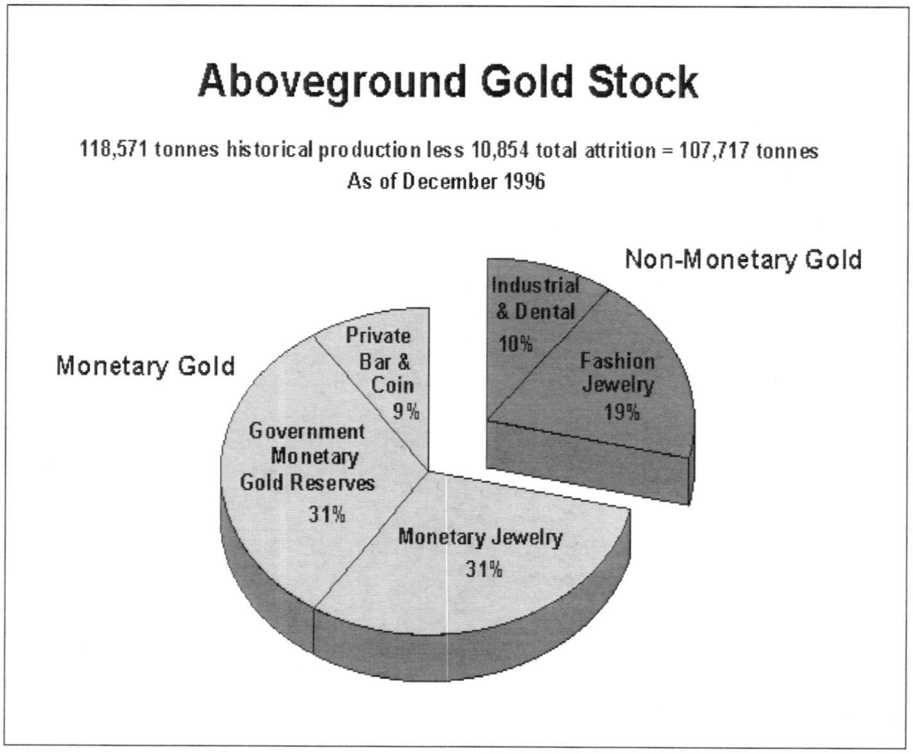

Notice from this report, we learn that total gold supply after attrition in 1996 was 1,823,812,539,840 grains of gold. From another website gold-eagle.com, I learned that in the last few years gold production has been about 2500 tons a year, or 4,232,880,000 grains. Therefore the world aboveground stock of gold in 2006 should be about 1,866,141,339,840 grains. If we divide that by the August 2006 world population of 6,540,106,621 people, we come up with 285 grains of gold per person. If we divide that into one dollar coins **the size of the American dime** (35 grains), we would have a money supply of **eight dollars** per person or a total world money supply of $52,320,876,968 (52 billion). If the total world savings equaled two dollars a person, that would leave just six dollars per person as circulating money. To see what would happen if silver was added. I went to the Silver Institute web-site. There I learned that in 2006 the total supply of silver was 911.9 million ounces (moz). Industrial Applications needs 409.3 moz. Photography needs 164.8 moz. Jewelry and silverware require 249.6 moz.. That would leave 88.2 moz. to coin into money. If we would divide that into one dollar coins, **the size of the American dime** (35 grains) that would increase the money supply by twenty cents per person.

There is not enough of gold and silver to use as the world's money. Gold could be easily manipulated into an interest bearing debt medium-of-exchange. If those who mined the gold and silver out of the ground had it assayed and coined it into money, then loaned the coins at interest into circulation. The gold and silver coins would then be interest-bearing debt money. All the miners would need to do is have the politicians pass a law that only licensed miners could mine gold and silver. If no one else could mine gold and silver and have it assayed and stamped it into coined money, there would be no way to obtain the gold and silver money needed to pay the interest on the money that was borrowed.

Issuing paper or book entry money, loaning it into circulation at interest is much easier for dishonest people than mining gold having it assayed and coined then loaning out the coins at interest. Plus the benefits are a lot greater if you loan and get interest on something that you don't have. The trick was to simply fool the people into believing that money loaned into circulation works the same as money that is spent or traded into circulation. **The moneyed elite have been very successful at fooling the people.**

It makes very little difference what is used as money. It makes a huge difference what principles are used when putting money into circulation. **<u>It's clear that people value money because they can buy anything they want with money and not because of what the money is made of.</u>**

If the money is loaned into circulation with interest charged and the interest has to be paid back in the same thing that was loaned, the thing that is borrowed must have natural reproductive powers. If not, it becomes impossible for the borrower to create more of what was borrowed to repay the loan plus the interest. One last fact about gold and interest: if most of the people were using gold as their medium-of-exchange and the people who had 10% of the gold loaned the gold out at 10%, then re-loaned their profit it would only take 25 years for these people to own all the gold.

We often hear gold bugs righteously proclaim that we should let the market determine what we should use for money. If those people ever took the time to review history, they would realize that people decided a long time ago that they would rather use paper as their medium-of-exchange than gold and/or silver. Had they not done so, the bankers would have never have gained their strangle hold in the first place. Most people have never understood that the paper money and metal money have not operated on the same principles. Metal was produced and traded into circulation as a wealth asset. Paper for the most part, has been loaned into circulation as interest-bearing debts. If those principles were reversed, metal money would be the problem money and paper would be the good money. With only one small difference, the numbers might not be as big, but the debt would be just as hard to pay.

What really matters is whether the money represents wealth or debts and whether the money is spent into circulation or loaned in at interest. There are all kinds of wealth other than metals. It also makes a difference whether that production produces peace or war. You can bomb a nation and its people into submission and destruction but you can't bomb a nation and its people into peace and prosperity.

Modern Money Secrets hinding in plain sight:

Currently, there is no way to create money to get out of debt, because all money is created as debt principal. Therefore there is no way to create the money needed to pay the interest on loaned principal.

Chapter 10

Dale & Soderberg
vs
The Minneapolis Federal Reserve Bank

Federal Reserve Notes are by law a liability of a Federal Reserve Bank and an obligation of the government *(a promise to pay dollars on demand)*. In fact, those words were written on the face of the Federal Reserve Notes before 1962, and the law has never been changed.

However, if you take a Federal Reserve Note to either a Federal Reserve Bank or to the United States Government and ask them to pay the note in dollars, they will tell you that Federal Reserve Notes are legal tender and therefore they are the payment of the dollars that they promise to pay. In other words they say that the notes are now the evidence of the debt the banks and the government owe you. At the same time, the notes are the payment of the debt the Federal Reserve Bank and the U. S. Government owes you. Talk about double talk.

I sent the following letter to the Department of the Treasury:

September 24, 1997

Department of the Treasury
l5th St. & Pennsylvania Ave
Washington DC 20220

Dear Sirs,

I am enclosing a 1950 promissory note, serial no. 133332304 A, signed by Elizabeth Rudel Smith Treasurer of the United States and C. Douglas Dillion, Secretary of the Treasury. This note states on its face: THE UNITED STATES OF AMERICA WILL PAY TO THE BEARER ON DEMAND TWENTY DOLLARS.

Please send to me twenty of what the United States Code defined as dollars when the promissory note was signed and dated in 1950. Please enclose a copy of the United States Code that defined the dollar in 1950.

What is the difference between the Treasurer of the United States and the

Secretary of the Treasury? What is the difference in the duties between the Treasurer of the United States and the Secretary of the Treasury? How are the Treasurer of the United States and the Secretary of the Treasury paid and who pays them?

Thanking you in advance for your prompt payment of this promissory note, this direct obligation of the United States.

Sincerely,

Byron C. Dale
7007 Lynmar Lane
Edina MN 55435

cc: Senator Tom Daschle, SD and Senator Rod Grams MN

I received the following letter:

DEPARTMENT OF THE TREASURY
WASHINGTON

TREASURER
OF THE
UNITED STATES

Mr. Byron C. Dale
7007 Lynmar Lane
Edina, Minnesota 55435

Dear Mr. Dale

Thank you for your letter of September 24, 1997, in which you enclosed a $20, Series 1950c Federal Reserve Note. You would like payment for the $20 note in what the United States Code defined as dollars when the note was signed and dated in 1950. You also ask about the duties and responsibilities of the Secretary of the Treasury and the Treasurer of the United States.

As a major policy advisor to the President, the Secretary of the Treasury has primary responsibility for formulating and recommending tax policy, participate in formulating broad fiscal policies that have general significance for the economy, managing the public debt, and formulating policies for and generally oversee all operations of the Department.

The Treasurer reviews currency and redemptions, signs currency and participates in the promotion of the selling and holding of United States Savings Bonds. The Treasurer oversees the operations of the U.S. Mint and the Bureau of Engraving and Printing.

Both the Secretary of the Treasury and the Treasurer of the United States are federal employees and are paid from the general funds of the Treasury.

With regard to your request for redemption of the 1950 $20 Federal Reserve note, the United States code (12 U.S.C. 411) provides that the note is to be redeemed in lawful money. This statutory provision is also reflected on the face of the note. Federal Reserve Notes, whether current or issued in 1950, are lawful money. The note you submitted is not unfit for circulation; therefore, we are returning it to you under separate cover at the address of this letter. If it was indeed your intent to redeem this note for a more recent Federal Reserve Note, you may resubmit the note or redeem it through a Federal Reserve Bank.

I Trust that this information is helpful to you

Sincerely,

Mary Ellen Withrow

Mary Ellen Withrow

Mary Ellen Withrow's answer brings up a few interesting questions, Webster's New World Dictionary defines redeem - as "to pay off (a mortgage or note), to fulfill (a promise or pledge)". How can trading an old promise to pay for a new promise to pay be called paying off the debt? How can a promise to pay be the lawful payment for the promise?

An <u>obligation to pay cannot become the payment</u> in and of itself. Oh! How easy it is to deceive those that have eyes but will not see, those that have ears but will not hear and those whose minds have not been trained to distinguish good from evil, the truth from fallacy, honesty and fact from fraud - the very minds that are produced by today's educational system.

On May 10,1999, I sent this letter to the Federal Reserve Bank of Minneapolis.

Federal Reserve Bank of Minneapolis
90 Hennepin Ave.
PO Box 291
Minneapolis MN 55480-0291

Dear Sirs:
Enclosed is a promissory note, serial no. I3332304 A, signed by Elizabeth Rudel Smith Treasurer and C. Douglas, Dillion Secretary of the Treasury of the United States of America. This promissory note states on it face: THE UNITED STATES OF AMERICA WILL PAY TO THE BEARER ON DEMAND TWENTY DOLLARS.

It is my understanding from the wording on the promissory note that it was issued from the Federal Reserve Bank, Minneapolis, Minnesota, and is payable at said Federal Reserve Bank.

As I am the bearer of this promissory note, please send to me twenty of what the United States code defined as dollars when this promissory note was signed. To insure there is no misunderstanding between you the debtor and me the creditor, please enclose a copy of the United States Code that defined the monetary word dollar when this promissory note was signed.

Thanking you in advance for your prompt payment of this promissory note which is due on demand.

Sincerely,

Byron Dale

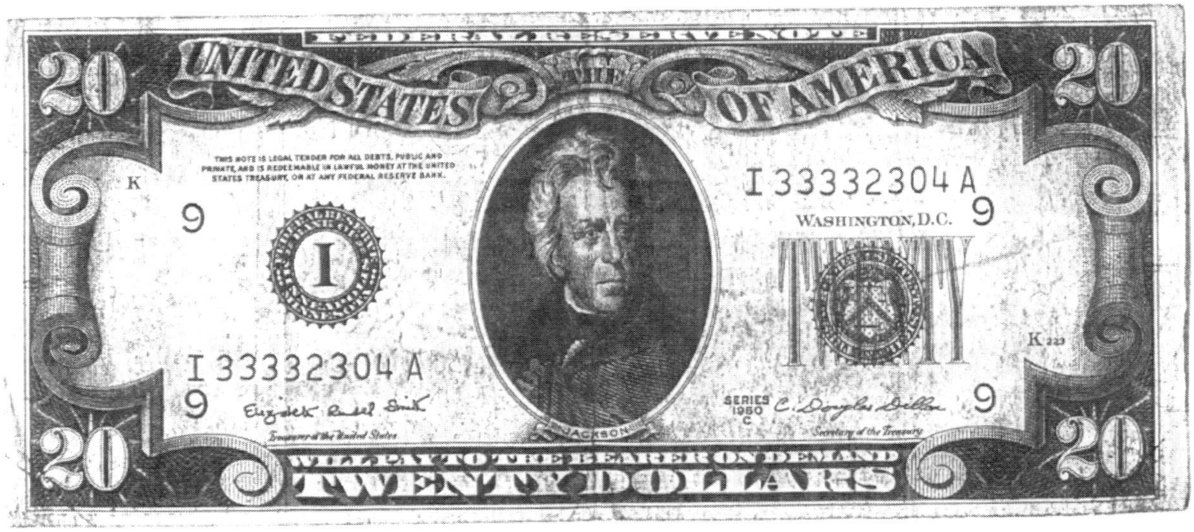

Upon the receipt of my letter, the Minneapolis Federal Reserve Bank called me and said that they did not understand my letter. I told them that it was simply a demand for payment of the note they had issued, just as the note said it would do on its face. The man that had made the call said that I had better talk with an attorney for the bank. He said that he would transfer the call for me. Soon a woman was on the phone. She had not seen the letter so I explained it to her. Suddenly she screamed and slammed down the phone. They sent the note back to me without any letter.

After thinking over what had transpired, Greg and I sent another letter, on June 7, 1999, saying basically the same thing. This time we enclosed an older Federal Reserve note that on its face stated: WILL PAY TO THE BEARER FIVE HUNDRED DOLLARS.

The Federal Reserve Bank of Minneapolis responded by sending us the following letter:

Gentlemen:

Enclosed you will find the Five Hundred Dollar Bill/Federal Reserve Note that you forwarded to the Federal Reserve Bank of Minneapolis for payment. This Five Hundred Dollar Bill is being returned with the following clarification.

As provided in the "Mint Act" of 1792, this country's earliest monetary statute, the "money of account" of the United States is expressed in dollars or units of dollars. The dollar therefore, is the standard of unit of value in our monetary system. Although the dollar as the standard unit of value has been defined through the years in terms of a gold or silver content (31 USC 314). There is no requirement that the monetary system of the United States consist of gold or silver coin or currency backed by gold or silver. As a practical matter, since the United States abandoned the domestic gold standard in 1933-

1934 and demonetized silver in the 1960's, the value of a dollar today should be viewed in terms of the goods or services that it will purchase. Therefore, this note can purchase up to $500.00 worth of goods or services. The enclosed Federal Reserve note that we are returning to you is also considered lawful money. Although not defined by statute, the term "lawful money" is generally regarded as meaning any medium of exchange that circulates freely from hand to hand as money under sanction of law. The decisions of the courts indicate that "lawful money" includes the classes of money which are declared by the United States to be a legal tender. In this regard, 31 USC 392 provides that coins and currencies of the United States, including Federal Reserve notes, regardless of when coined or issued, are legal tender for all debts. Accordingly, this Federal Reserve note is legal tender, and therefore, is "lawful money".

This information should be responsive to your request.

The letter was not signed.

On January 19, 2000, we filed an action in the fourth Judicial District Conciliation Court, State of Minnesota, County of Hennepin. The complaint read:

Plaintiffs are holders in due course of promissory notes payable on demand issued by the defendant. Pursuant to the contract, plaintiff presented the promissory notes to the defendant and demanded payment. Defendant did not and has not denied that payment is due. Defendant has simply refused to render payment to plaintiffs.

After I had filled out the forms needed to file the action, the clerk that was helping me said: "You can't file this, the Federal Reserve Bank of Minneapolis is a government agency and you can't sue them." I replied "I don't think that the bank is a government agency. I am sure that it is a private bank and that I can sue them. However I don't want to have a disagreement with you, so how about I just pay the filing fee and you file it. I will give you my phone number and if the court sends it back saying that it can't be filed, you just give me a call and I will come get my money back and that will be the end of that. She said OK she would do that.

A few days later we received notice that a hearing would be held at the courthouse at 350 5th St Minneapolis MN on 3/9/2000 at 8:00 AM.

June 7, 1999

Gregory K. Soderberg
2410 4th Dr SW
Austin, MN 55912

Byron C. Dale
7007 Lynmar Lane
Edina, MN 55435

Federal Reserve Bank of Minneapolis
90 Hennepin Avenue
PO Box 291
Minneapolis, MN 55480-0291

Dear Sirs,

Enclosed a promissory note, serial # I00002541 A.

This promissory note states on its face: THE UNITED STATES OF AMERICA WILL PAY TO THE BEARER ON DEMAND FIVE HUNDRED DOLLARS.

I understand from the wording on this promissory note that it was issued by the Federal Reserve Bank of Minneapolis, Minnesota and is payable at the same Federal Reserve Bank.

Since we are the bearers of this promissory note, please send to us at 2410 4th DR SW, Austin MN. 55912, five hundred of what the United States Code defined as dollars when this promissory note was signed. So that there is no misunderstanding between you the debtor and we the creditors, please enclose a copy of the United States Code that defined the monetary word "dollar" when this promissory note was signed.

Your prompt payment of this promissory note which is due on demand is appreciated.

Thank you,

Gregory K. Soderberg

Byron C. Dale

Greg and I arrived at the court house a little before 8:00. Court convened at 8:30. There were about ten cases on the docket for the day. The clerk read the docket to see who was present. Our case was about half-way down on the docket. However, our case was not called until almost the end of the docket.

When our case was called, Greg and I stood behind the podium on the right side of the courtroom facing the judge. Kristina Stierholz, the attorney for the Federal Reserve Bank, stood behind the podium on the left side of the courtroom.

The judge opened the case by reading our complaint. When he finished, he had a puzzled look on his face. Then, he said to Greg and me "What is this all about?" I responded saying, *"This is a simple case. We hold promissory notes issued by the defendant that are due and payable on demand. We sent letters to the defendant demanding payment. The defendant did not deny that it issued the notes nor did defendant deny that payment was due. Defendant simply refused to make payment. With the courts permission I will approach the bench and show you the letters that were sent."* The judge granted his permission. I went to the bench and handed the judge the letters we had sent demanding payment and the one letter the defendant sent when they returned the 500-dollar note. I also presented the judge with a document from the Department of the Treasury that states *"Federal Reserve notes represent a first lien on all the assets of the Federal Reserve Banks and on the collateral specifically held against them.* I returned to our podium.

The judge then turned to Ms. Stierholz and asked her to present her side of the case. Ms. Stierholz agreed that we had sent the letters to the bank and demanded payment. She then said that Federal Reserve notes were legal tender and legal tender equaled lawful money. The Federal Reserve Banks do not have any obligation to redeem their notes except with other notes.

When Ms. Stierholz finished, I replied that the notes on their face state that they are payable in dollars. All we want is whatever the law declares are dollars. I told the judge, *"I have four coins that all declare on their face that they are dollars. With your permission, I will approach the bench and show you what I mean."* The judge granted his permission, and I went to the bench and laid out the four different coins. I pointed out to the judge that all four of the coins stated on their faces that they are one dollar. But that is very confusing, because each one is of a different weight and size and made from different metals of different values. How can they all be the statutorily defined **dollar**? I continued, saying, *"As far as the legal tender issue is concerned that is not an issue in this case. "You, your honor, could write a check to me, and I could give it to Greg. If Greg accepts it, I would have legally tendered him and would no longer have any obligation to him."* The Judge stated, *"That would only be true if the check was good."* I then stated, *"That is right and that is just exactly what this case is all about. Can they make their notes good? We want them to make final payment".* The judge's face turned very red.

I continued, *"The contract, (the note), states on its face that it is payable in dollars, and we want final payment in what the statutes declare are dollars. A liability or an obligation to pay cannot in-and-of itself be final payment for that obligation."*

The judge asked me, *"What do you say a dollar is?"* I replied *"The only place in law that I could find where it stated what a dollar is, is the 1792 coinage act. Where it states" Dollars each to be of the value of a Spanish milled dollar as the same is now current, and to contain three hundred and seventy-one grains and four sixteenth parts of a grain of pure, or four hundred and sixteen grains of standard silver. "I have searched the law for 18 years and cannot find where that part of the 1792 coinage act has been amended or repealed."*

The judge asked, *"You want silver then?"* I answered, *"No all we want is what the statute says a dollar is. If the law has been changed and I have somehow missed it in my research, we will take whatever the law says a dollar is".*

The judge turned to Ms. Stierholz and asked if she had anything else to add. All she said was that this case should be in federal court as they have exclusive jurisdiction.

I responded *"I don't believe that to be true. The Federal Reserve Bank of Minneapolis pays taxes to the city of Minneapolis. I doubt if they would pay taxes to someone that didn't have any jurisdiction to tax them. This court is the proper place for this case to be heard."*

The judge indicated that he had heard enough for him to make his decision.

I asked if I could make a final statement. The judge gave his permission. I stated, *"It is clear that we all work and get paid yet the debt collectively gets greater. The household debt is now $6.2 trillion. The business debt is over $5 trillion. The Federal government debt is $5.6 trillion. The only way that could be was if nobody was making final payment. All we want is final payment."* That made the judge really uncomfortable. The hearing was closed.

Two days later we got the courts ruling. It read: the parties are hereby notified that the Court has ordered that: PLAINTIFFS CLAIM IS DISMISSED WITH PREJUDICE SO THAT NO NEW ACTION CAN BE STARTED

Greg and I didn't want to start a new action so we just moved for the case to be transferred to the District Court of Hennepin County for trial by jury. The District Court accepted the case gave it a file number and assigned it to judge Bruce Hartigan. Judge Hartigan issued a SCHEDULING ORDER which read:

> Based on all the files, records and proceedings herein,
> IT IS HEREBY ORDERED THAT:
> 1. The deadline for bringing non-dispositive motions shall be June 1 2000.
> 2. The deadline for bringing dispositive motions shall be June 1 2000.
> 3. The deadline for completing discovery shall be June 1 2000.
> 4. A Pre-Trial Settlement Conference is set for August 1, 2000 at 9:15 a.m., Courtroom #653, Hennepin County Government Center, Minneapolis, Minnesota, at which time a trial date will be scheduled.
> 5. A Joint Statement of the Case shall be submitted to this Court one week prior to the Pre-Trial Settlement conference.
> 6. That this matter is referred to Hennepin County Arbitration for arbitration services upon completion of discovery, or prior to completion of discovery if all parties agree.

We immediately started the discovery process by sending a Request of Admissions to the Defendant which read: You are hereby requested, according to the provisions of Rule 36, to admit or deny the truth of the following statements of opinion, fact, or the application of law to fact, and the genuineness of any documents attached hereto. The request for admissions contained 37 requests. At about the same time, Kristina Stierholz, Attorney for the Federal Reserve Bank, filed the notice of removal of action to Federal Court.

As soon at Ms. Stierholz received our request for admissions, she filed a motion to stay discovery and to dismiss the action from Federal Court for failure to state a claim. She also filed a motion for sanctions against me for using the legal system to harass the Federal Reserve Bank. In essence, she stated that it was not plausible for us to believe that the Federal Reserve Bank should be expected to honor their contract and make payment of its notes, and it was unreasonable for us to believe their notes could be both proof of their liability and payment of that liability.

MARK B. DAYTON
STATE AUDITOR

STATE OF MINNESOTA
OFFICE OF THE STATE AUDITOR

SUITE 400
525 PARK STREET
SAINT PAUL 55103

(612) 296-2551

October 10, 1994

Mr. Gregory K. Soderberg
2410 Fourth Drive S.W.
Austin, Minnesota 55912

Dear Mr. Soderberg:

Thank you for taking the time to contact me with your inquiry about the property tax status of the Federal Reserve Bank in downtown Minneapolis. I asked the Research and Information Division of our office to respond to your request.

According to the Hennepin County Property Taxation Department, the Federal Reserve Bank, located at 250 Marquette Avenue, paid the following property taxes between 1991 and 1994:

Year	Property Taxes Paid
1994	$675,660
1993	$746,705
1992	$846,173
1991	$962,906

The Federal Reserve System is an independent agency, it is not part of the federal government. For these reasons, the Federal Reserve System's property is subject to property taxation in Minnesota.

If you would like more information, I would urge you to contact Mr. Patrick O'Connor, the Hennepin County Treasurer, at 8603 Government Center, 300 South Sixth Street, Minneapolis, Minnesota 55487-0063. Mr. O'Connor's telephone number is (612) 348-4084.

Again, Mr. Soderberg, thank you for taking the time to contact me. I trust you will find this information helpful.

With best regards.

Sincerely,

Mark B. Dayton
State Auditor

Ms. Stierholz stated in her motion for sanctions that it would be ineffective to sanction plaintiffs monetarily because we would just want to know how and with what final payment should be made with. To make a long story short, the United States District Court denied the Federal Reserve Bank's request for sanctions and granted its motion to dismiss for failure to state a claim for which relief could be granted. The ninth circuit Court of Appeals upheld the District Court's finding.

The Federal Reserve Banks and the United States Government told us Federal Reserve Notes have no value in-and-of themselves. Their only value is what they will buy. You can go down to the store and the store will pay you in goods what the bank owed you. The bank now owes the store instead of you. The banks and the government simply will not pay their obligations.

I don't have any problem with the fact that the money the banks issues doesn't have any value in-and-of it self. <u>But if it doesn't have any value why are we forced to pay interest for the use of it?</u>

Modern Money Secrets hiding in plain sight:

One can only pay interest by capturing someone else's borrowed Principal!

Chapter 11

The Creation of Money and Money Flow Under the Federal Reserve Monetary System.

Today the only creator of money is the banking system. The bank creates the money when an individual, a business, a corporation or government goes to the bank and gets an interest-bearing loan.

To create or manufacture the money, the bank simply makes a book-entry for the amount of the loan to a new or existing checking account. The promissory note signed by the borrower increased the bank's assets; the book-entry to the checking account increases the bank's liabilities. *"A bank lends by adding the borrower's promise to repay to its loan assets and adding the amount of the loan to its deposit liabilities."* Source: Money: master or servant? Federal Reserve Bank of New York as so source for chart.

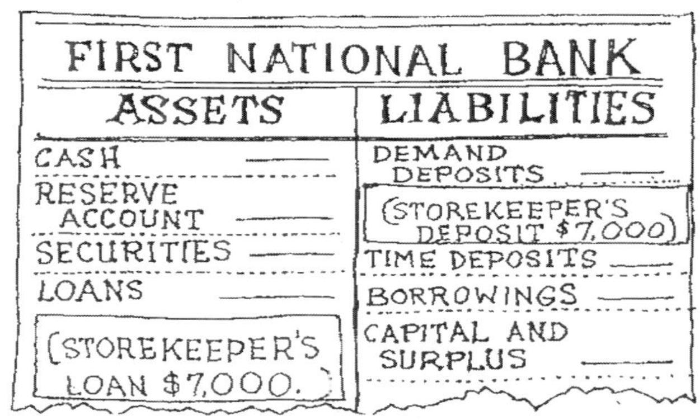

The money goes into circulation when the borrower writes a check, uses a credit card or in some other way draws upon his loan account. In most cases, the borrower puts up real tangible property that he owns as collateral for the loan. If the borrower can't repay the loan with interest, the banking system takes the collateral. The bank doesn't loan any tangible property, it doesn't loan anything it had before the loan was made. The bank only loans a promise to pay. The bank's books show that the bank has increased its liabilities.

In the court case United States vs Dale, Assistant U.S. Attorney LeAnn Larson LaFave, *admitted that all one receives through a loan is an extension of credit, that extension of credit does not consist of a known natural chemical substance nor does it consist of known chemical substances. The credit received is the correlative of a debt – that which is due as repayment of loans.* Black's Law Dictionary states—correlative-Having a mutual or reciprocal relation, in such sense that the existence of one necessarily implies the existence of the other.

In other words, the bank only records what they claim the borrower owes (the borrowers promissory note) and the existence of that signed promissory note implies the existence of a loan. The bank makes it a court enforceable claim by introducing to the court the borrower's signed promissory note, promising to pay the money back to the bank and requests the court to use its power to force the borrower to pay. As there is no way for the borrowers to create any money except through borrowing from the banking system, sooner or later the bank gets someone's real property for nothing and in time gets everyone's real property for nothing. The banks get everything for nothing and they are the one's who scream the loudest that there is no free lunch!

The saddest part of all this, is the fact that although it is all fraud, smoke and mirrors, we do get purchasing power when we get a loan from a bank and the people have faith in the banking system even though the people don't know or understand anything about how the banking system works.

I have had bankers tell me that they only loan money that a depositor had deposited in their bank. How many of you have ever seen on a bank statement where the bank has taken the numbers out of your checking or saving account and loaned them to someone else? However we all clearly see that when we write a check, and spend, give or loan those numbers in our checking account to someone else, those numbers are deducted from our checkbook balance.

When pressed to explain just how they can loan the depositor's money to someone else when the depositor still has the money recorded in his checking account, they told me that they put the depositor's money in the vault and make the loan as a promise to pay the borrower. The fallacy there is that checkbook money can't be put in the vault.

The Federal Reserve System Board of Governors in 1939 stated: *"Almost all bank deposits owe their origin to bank loans. It may seem it ought to be the other way around – that bank loans would owe their origin to banks deposits. But this is not so."* Many people believe that there are actual Federal Reserve Notes printed up dollar for dollar for every checkbook dollar (the numbers) that we have in our checking accounts. **However, that is not true**.

BOARD OF GOVERNORS
OF THE
FEDERAL RESERVE SYSTEM
WASHINGTON, D. C. 20551

September 28, 1999

The Honorable Rod Grams
United States Senator
2013 2nd Avenue North
Anoka, Minnesota 55303

Dear Senator:

Thank you for your letter of August 18, which was forwarded to the Board by the Office of the Comptroller of the Currency, enclosing correspondence from your constituent, Byron Dale. Mr. Dale is inquiring about the value of currency and coin in circulation and "checkbook money."

While we do not know the origin of the 1983 data that Mr. Dale requested we update, we took the liberty of providing 1983 and 1999 data for all three items. The 1983 data will provide Mr. Dale with an accurate point of reference. The table below lists the three data items that Mr. Dale requested:

	1983 (billions)	1999 (billions)
Total coin in circulation[1]	$14	$26
Total currency in circulation[2]	$148	$506
Checkbook money[3]	$350	$607

Mr. Dale also requested an update of a 1993 statement by Barry Goldwater, but we have been unable to determine the origin of the quotation. We

[1] U.S. Currency and Coin Outstanding and in Circulation, Treasury Bulletin, Financial Management Service, U.S. Treasury Department.

[2] Federal Reserve Board staff estimate that two-thirds of all currency in circulation is held outside the United States.

[3] Demand deposits at all commercial banks other than those due to depository institutions, the U.S. government, and foreign banks and official institutions, less cash items in the process of collection and Federal Reserve float, and other checkable deposits, consisting of negotiable order of withdrawal and automatic transfer service accounts at depository institutions, credit union share draft accounts, and demand deposits at thrift institutions.

The Honorable Rod Grams
Page Two

can tell Mr. Dale that the replacement value of structures and durable equipment owned by individuals and businesses in the U.S. is estimated by the Department of Commerce to have been $21.2 trillion at the end of 1997.[4] That figure excludes land and assets held by federal, state, and local governments.

The wealth (net worth) of households and nonprofit organizations (usually referred to as the household sector) was $37.0 trillion dollars at the end of 1998. That is, households had assets, such as homes (including land), deposits, equities, and pension reserves, of $43.2 trillion and liabilities, mortgages, consumer credit and other debts of $6.2 trillion. The source is the Flow of Funds Accounts, published by the Federal Reserve Board.

I hope this information is helpful. Please let me know if I can be of further assistance.

Sincerely,

Donald J. Winn
Assistant to the Board

Above is a letter I received from Donald J. Winn, Assistant to the Board of governors of the Federal Reserve System, sent to me through the office of Rod Grams United States Senator. In the letter, Mr. Winn stated: *"In 1999 the total currency (Federal Reserve Notes) in circulation was $506 Billion. The Federal Reserve Board staff estimates that two-thirds of all currency (FRNs) in circulation is held outside of the United States. At the same time there was $607 Billion in checkbook money."* FRN are printed by the United States Bureau of Engraving and Printing at a cost of about 4.2 cents per note. It makes no difference if the bill is a one dollar note or a hundred dollar note.

DEPARTMENT OF THE TREASURY
BUREAU OF ENGRAVING AND PRINTING
WASHINGTON, D.C. 20228

March 27, 1987

Mr. Byron C. Dale
Secretary, Treasurer
Commercial Trust of South Dakota
Post Office Box 53
Mobridge, South Dakota 57601

Dear Mr. Dale:

Your personal check #020 for $412 00 is herewith returned.

The Bureau of Engraving and Printing is not authorized to print or issue United States paper currency for direct delivery to the public. Currency notes are placed into circulation by your local financial organizations and can only be obtained from that source.

We can be of no further assistance to you in this matter.

Sincerely,

Linda W. Coleman
External Affairs Staff

Enclosure:

We can see clearly from the above letter that The Bureau of Engraving and Printing is not authorized to print or issue United States paper currency for direct delivery to the public. If you want more Federal Reserve notes you have to go to a bank and buy them at face value dollar-for-dollar with checkbook money that was borrowed from a private commercial bank.

The borrowers from the banking system, **as a whole**, simply cannot pay their indebtedness to the banking system. The interest on the newly created money makes the indebtedness to the banking system grow but it doesn't increase the money supply. Therefore time increases the indebtedness, but time doesn't increase the money supply. Sooner or later someone must default on his or her loan and by simple deception of the mind the bank ends up the owner of the real tangible property that someone else produced. These are the simple facts and the reasons why the people produce untold wealth yet collectively get deeper into debt.

We suffer under this debt not because we use paper money, nor because our paper money is not redeemable in precious metals. We suffer under this debt because past bank and governmental leaders switched our money from an evidence of wealth to an evidence of debt, because money is loaned into circulation not exchanged into circulation. The only way out of this debt is to have and to use debt free money. This only be done by making money an evidence of wealth and exchange it into circulation.

To further explain how the system works, under the federally charted banking system we will start at the point where the government wants to spend $100 more money than they brought in through taxes. The Congress authorizes the Treasury to sell a bond (*issues a promise to pay at interest*) through the auctions held at the Federal Reserve Bank of New York. A Primary Bond Dealer buys the bond from the treasury (*agrees to accept the Treasury promise to pay at interest)*, the bond goes on the books of the Treasury as a liability and it goes on the books of the Primary Bond Dealer as an asset. To pay for the bond, the Primary Bond Dealer (usually a bank) creates new checkbook money on its books by adding a new liability to its books for one $100. The Primary Bond dealer then transfers the checkbook money to the United States Treasury where the new checkbook money goes on the books of the Treasury as an asset. The chart below shows the transaction that happens with the flow of checkbook money from the Primary Bond Dealer to the United States Treasury.

From the Third Edition of the Federal Reserve System Purposes and Functions we learned that checkbook 'money' is what we have when we have monetized numbers in our checking account at a bank. They are also called bank deposits. Page 6 states: *"All bank deposits are a form of credit. Basically, they represent amounts owed by banks to depositors. They come into existence by an exchange of bank promises to pay customers for the various assets which banks acquire—currency, promissory notes of business, consumer and other customers, mortgages on real estate, and Government and other securities."* Treasury bonds are Government securities.

MONEY FLOW

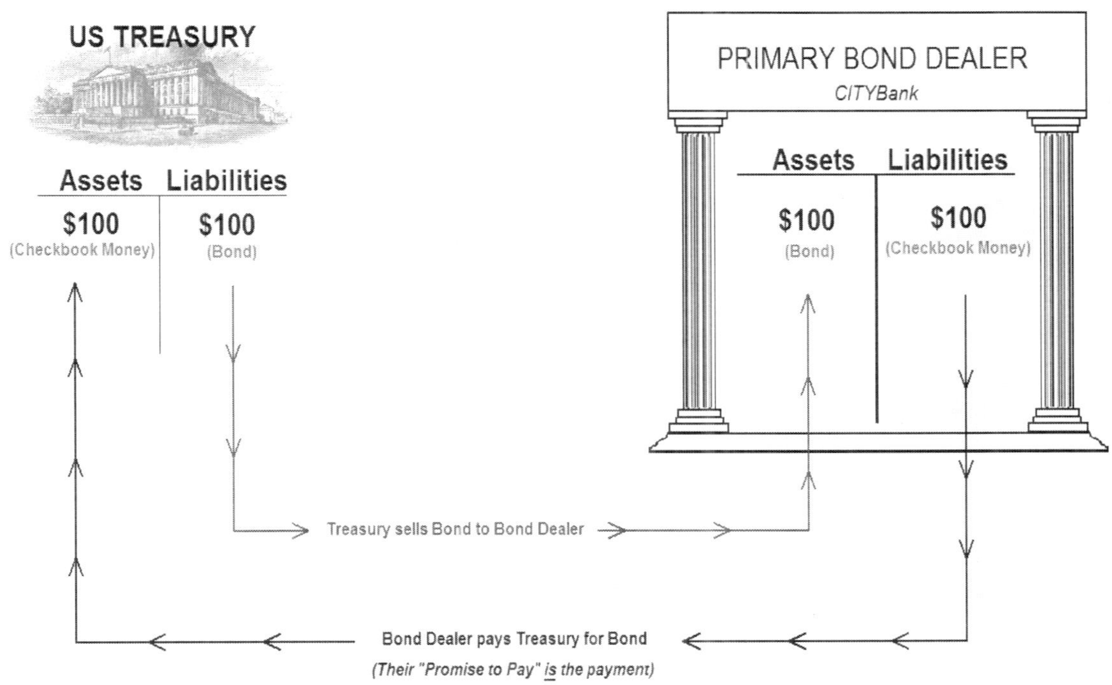

At first glance, the above chart looks like both the U.S. Treasury and the Primary Bond Dealer made a straight-up exchange of promises to pay; the Treasury's bond (*a promise to pay*) for the Bond Dealers credit (*a promise to pay)* placed in a checking account. Each one gained a new liability and a new asset.

However we know from experience that quick glances do not always tell the whole story. Let's take a closer look at what really happened. The Treasury issued a bond for $100 with interest (for this writing we will compute all interest at

10%). With this promise to pay $100 plus 10% in interest, the Treasury's debt will start out as $100 but will grow to $110.00 that must be paid when the bond matures. The Treasury's debt is a debt upon the people. However, when the Primary Bond Dealer issues its promise to pay to the Treasury (*in the form of checkbook credit*), that is considered new money. That new money will increase the money supply by $100. The liability of the bank does not need to be paid, because through deception upon the mind, it is accepted as payment.

The whole process and concept of the creation of money by the banking system is based on mystical magic, deception and out-right bold-faced lies that force us all into interest-bearing debts; debt that can be passed from person to person and on down to the next generation but can't be paid with debt money!

MONEY FLOW

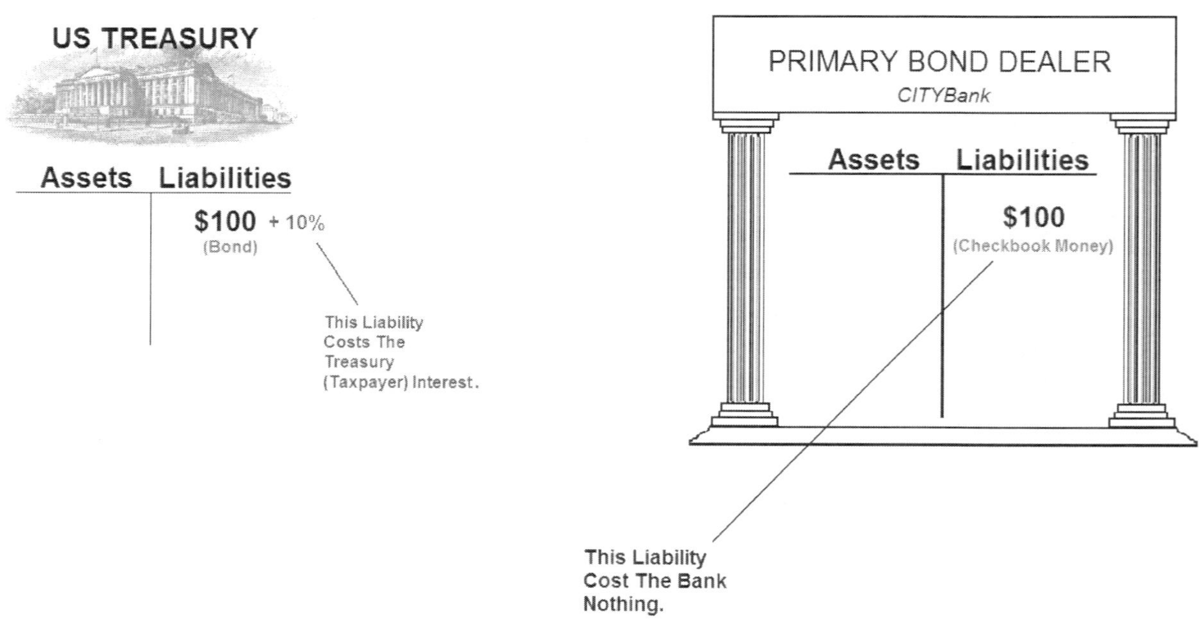

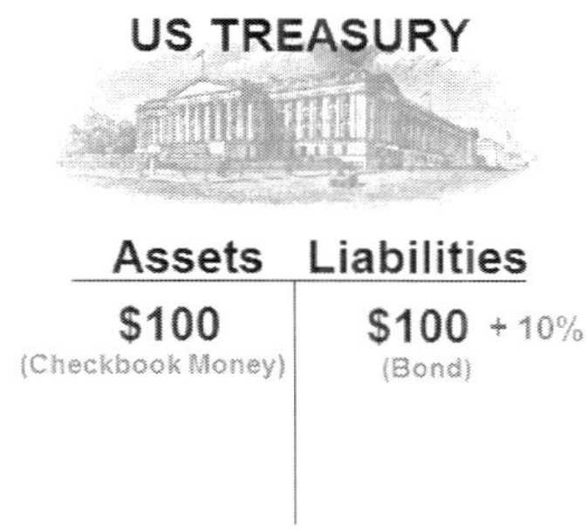

When the Federal Reserve System decides it needs more collateral in order to have more Federal Reserve Notes printed or when it wants to increase the money supply. The Federal Reserve System through its trading desk at the Federal Reserve Bank of New York goes into the open market and buys a bond from a Primary Bond Dealer. The Federal Reserve Bank pays for the bond with a check issued on itself, signed by one of its officers. This check is paid for by creating a liability on itself. Source: Modern Money Mechanics. The fed can also do this to buy any asset it wants. This is a nice way of saying that the Fed pays for the bond by writing a check upon an account that does not have any funds in it. Of course, we all know that in reality it is impossible to draw water out of a dry well.

This action creates a new liability on the books of a Federal Reserve Bank, (a promise to pay) that goes on the books of the Primary Bond Dealer as asset to the bond dealer.

The Federal Reserve Bank has gained a new asset, by creating a new liability. The Primary Bond Dealer loses one asset, the bond, and gains another asset (the promise to pay) from the Federal Reserve Bank.

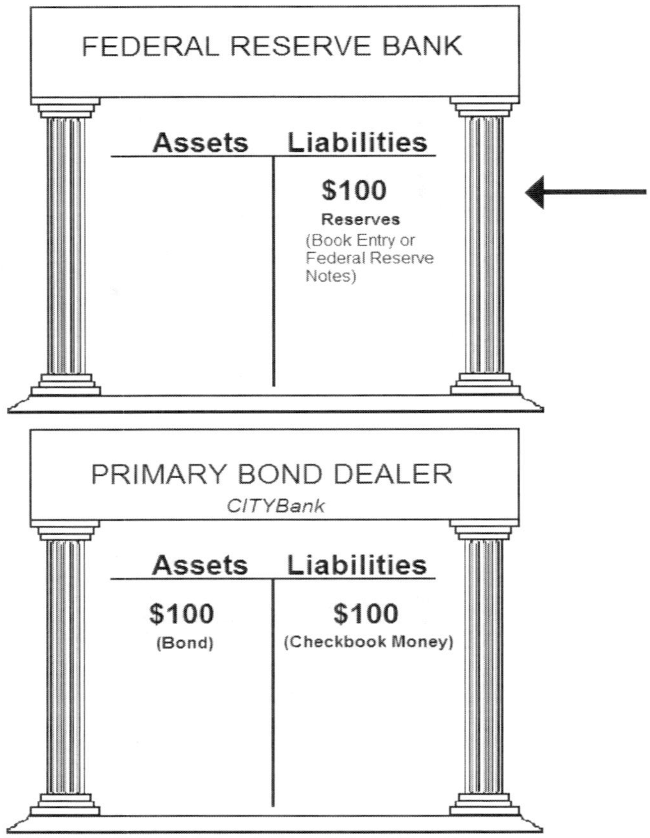

The Primary Bond Dealer, having a bank account at a Federal Reserve Bank, receives an increase in that account for the amount of the bond. Therefore, a member bank's reserve account and the seller of the checking account both increase by the amount of the check written by the Federal Reserve Bank. Source: Federal Reserve System Purposes and Functions Third Edition pages 100 and 101.

Two very magical and deceptive things have happened. First, a promise to pay has become the actual payment. Second, one hundred dollars has become two hundred dollars. One hundred dollars in the checking account of the bond dealer and one hundred dollars into the reserve account of a bank. Those of us that live in reality know these things are impossible and can only seem possible by deceiving the mind.

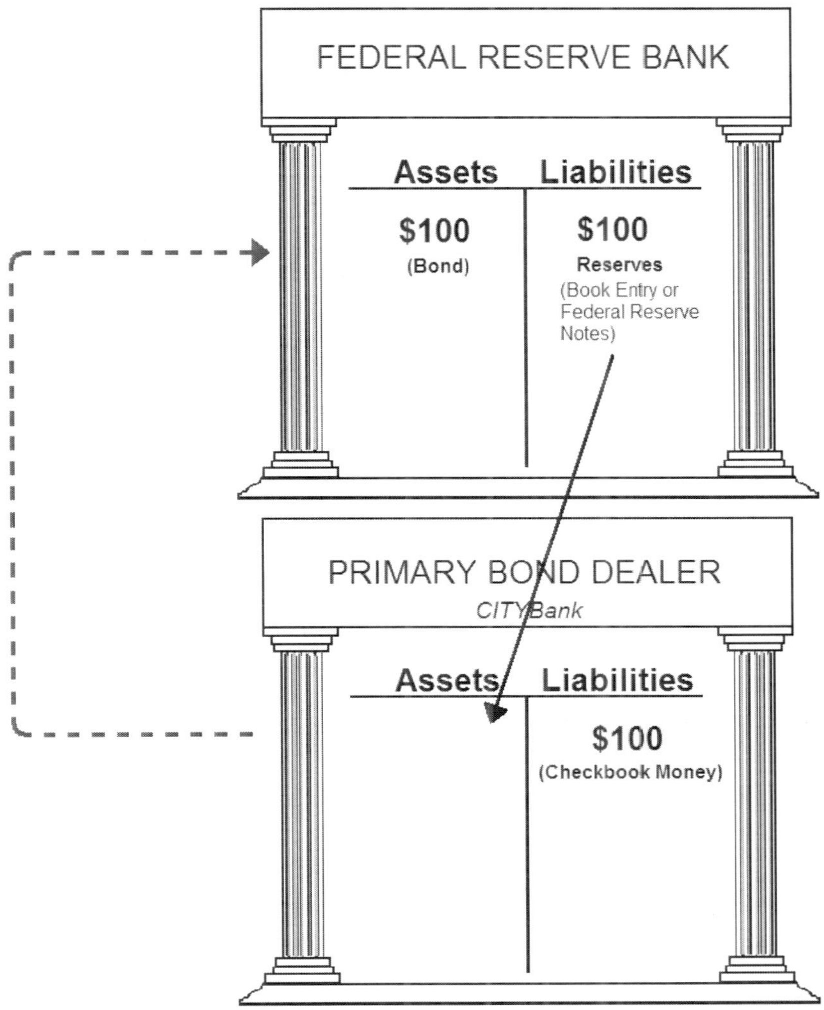

The Bond Dealer now has the funds to buy another bond from the US Treasury, or spend it in other ways. A commercial bank has new reserves. *"This deposit is likely to be transferred in part to other banks and quickly loses its identity amid the huge interbank flow of deposits"* Source: Modern Money Mechanics To make a loan a commercial bank must have a deposit which it can call reserves. At this point things get confusing. In a personal letter to me Russell L. Munk states that *"A private commercial bank which has just received extra reserves from the Fed can make roughly six dollars in loans for every one dollar in reserves it obtains from the Fed."* Other bank sources say that bank can only loan a percentage of a bank deposit. However, both Russell L. Munk and the other sources agree that the actual process of money creation takes place in the commercial banks. For this example, we will work with a 10% reserve and 10% interest. Most times, the Primary Bond Dealer and the commercial bank are one and the same entity. In this example, the Bond Dealer is CityBank and CityBank is a commercial bank with new reserves to make an interest-bearing loan to man 1. We will now follow the credit, the "bank's promise to pay" that we use for our medium-of-exchange as it flows out to the people. Collectively, we must borrow and pay interest to the banks in order to have a medium of exchange.

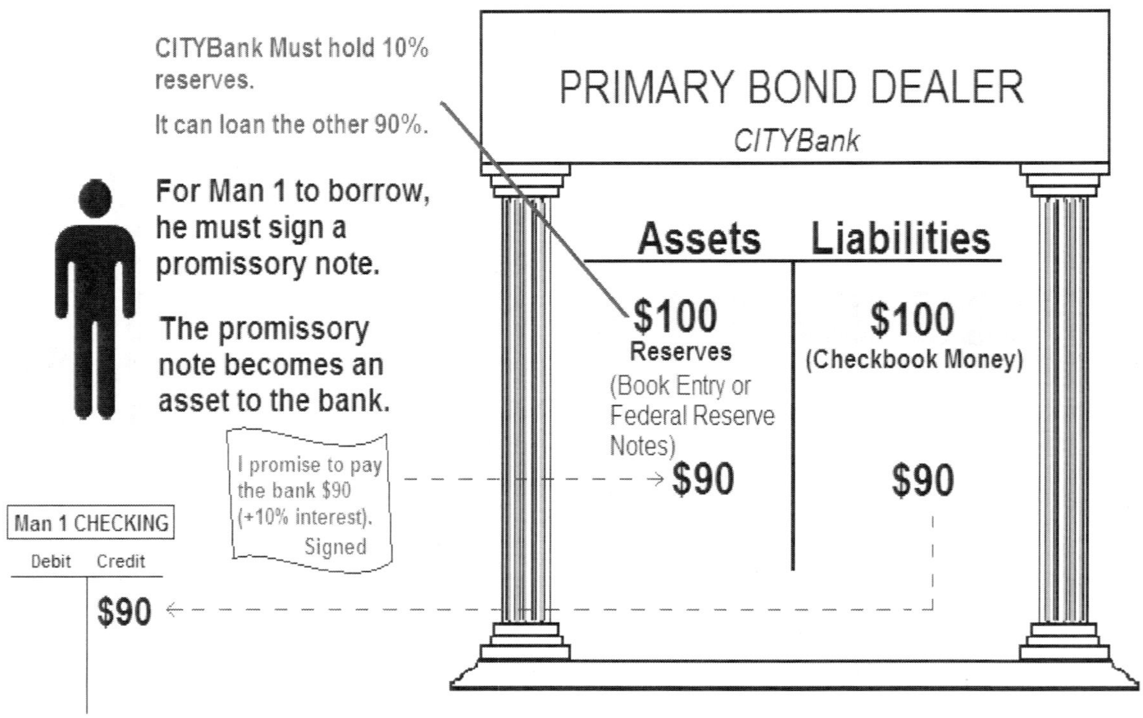

To get the loan from CityBank, Man 1 must sign a court-enforceable promissory note, promising to pay the bank back the principle of the loan plus the interest. Man 1's promissory note becomes a new asset on the financial books of CityBank. CityBank's loan to Man 1 goes on the books as a new liability of the bank because the bank is only loaning Man 1 a promise to pay. The bank's promise to pay is not enforceable by court action or any other way and is in fact never paid. The numerical accounting of the bank's promise to pay goes into

Man 1's checking account and becomes checkbook 'money'.

Man 1 can then spend the checkbook 'money' by writing a check. Man 1 writes a check to Woman 1 for ninety dollars. At this point Man 1 has spent all of his borrowed money. Man 1 has no Money but he still has a debt to Citybank for ninety dollars which will become $99 when the interest becomes due. Woman 1 deposits her check from Man 1 in her account at Commercial Bank 1.

We are told that now Commercial Bank one will present the check Woman 1 deposited to CityBank 1 for payment. CityBank 1 will transfer $90 in reserves to Commercial Bank 1 as payment on the check. Therefore, CityBank is left with only ten dollars in it reserve account and Commercial Bank 1 will have $90 dollars in its reserve account.

At that time, CityBank 1 reduces its deposit liability because it no longer has a liability to Man 1. Commercial Bank 1 now has a $90 liability to Woman 1 and $90 of new reserves. Source: personal letter from Brian F. Madigan Assistant. Dir. Board of Governors Federal Reserve System

Woman 1 has ninety dollars in her checking account that is considered as an asset that she can spend at any time. She does not owe any money.

With the new reserves Commercial Bank 1 can now make a loan to Man 2 for $81. To get the loan, Man 2 will have to sign a court enforceable promissory note for the $81 plus ten percent interest payable to Commercial Bank 1. Man 2's promissory note becomes a new asset to Commercial Bank 1.

Now at this point in time, if you walked into Commercial Bank 1 and asked where they got the money that they loaned to Man 2, they would tell you they got the money from Woman 1's deposit. Those of us that live in the world of reality know from personal experience that is not true. If it was true Commercial Bank 1 would have had to debit Woman 1's checking account for eighty-one dollars and that doesn't happen. If Commercial Bank 1 had really loaned Woman 1's money to someone else, she would not be able to spend her money. But, she can and will before Man 2 pays back his loan.

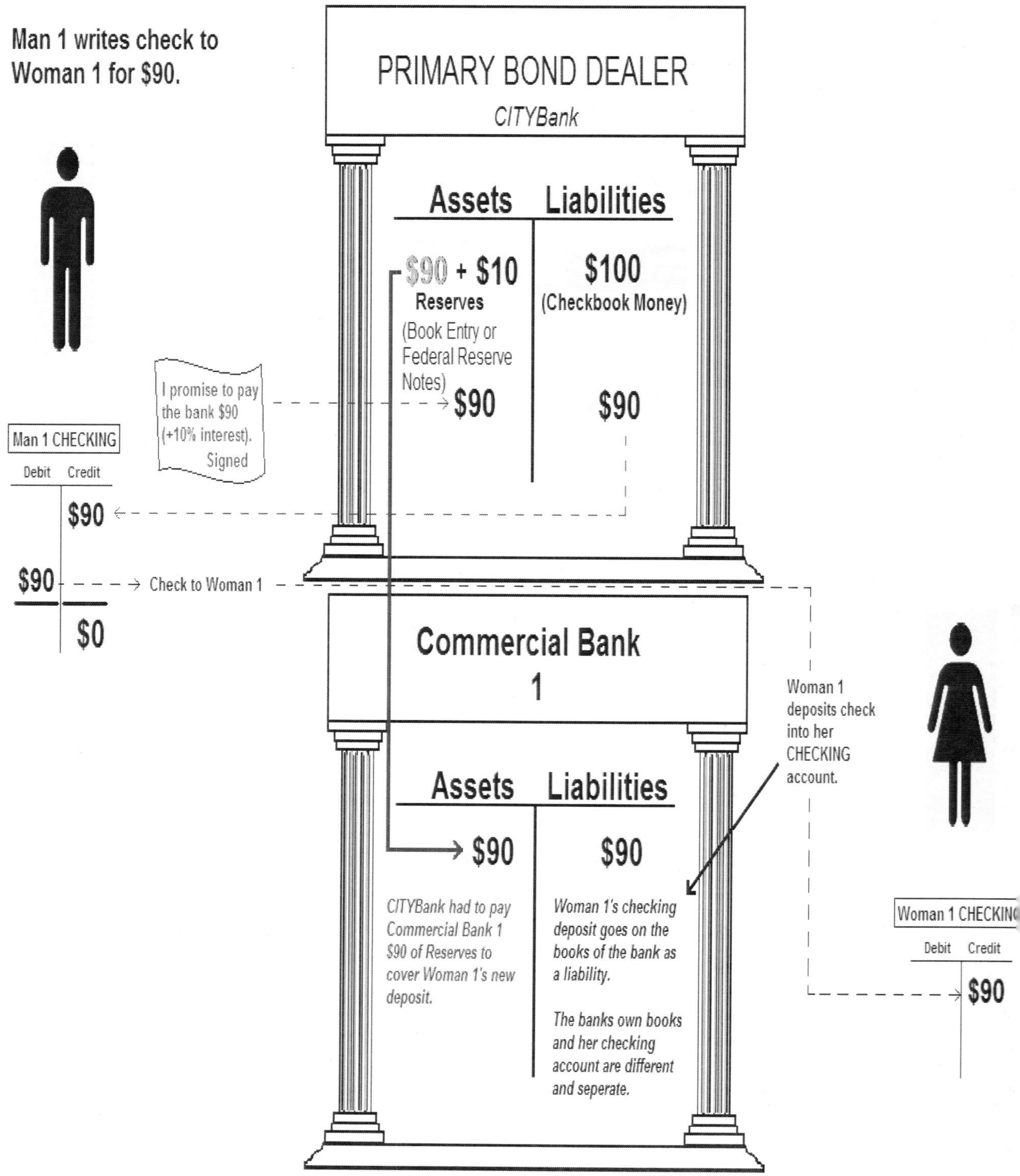

At the same time, the bank system speaking out of the other side of their mouth will tell you that the loan to Man 2 increased the money supply. We know that if Commercial Bank had loaned Woman 1's money to Man 2, there would have been no increase in the money supply. We also know that there was an increase in the money supply because now Woman 1 still has $90 in her checking account that she can spend at any time. Man 2 has $81 in his checking account that he can spend at any time. Those of us that keep thinking, looking and studying also know that banks do not really make loans out of the money they receive as deposits. If they did this, they would be acting just like financial intermediaries, and no additional money would be created. What they do when they make loans is to accept promissory notes in exchange for credits to the borrowers deposit accounts. Loans (bank assets) and deposits (bank liabilities) both rise. Reserves are unchanged by loan transactions. The deposit credits constitute a new addition to the total deposits of the banking system. Source: Modern Money Mechanics

We also know that all one receives through a loan is an extension of credit, this extension of credit does not consist of a known natural or man made chemical substance. The credit received is the correlative of a debt - that which is due as repayment of loans. Source: Assistant U.S. Attorney LeAnn Larson LaFave Black's Law Dictionary states-correlative-Having a mutual or reciprocal relation, in such sense that the existence of one necessarily implies the existence of the other. In other words, the existence of the borrowers signed promissory implies that something was loaned.

In a few hours, Man 2 writes a check to Woman 2 for $81. Woman 2 now has $81 and no debt. Man 2 is still in debt to Commercial Bank 1 for $81 that will soon be $88.10 when the interest comes due and he will have no money. Clearly, the interest is making the debt grow faster than the money supply. For anyone to have money, someone somewhere has to obtain an interest-bearing loan from a private for-profit commercial bank.

Woman 2 deposits the check she got from Man 2 into her checking account at Commercial Bank 2. Commercial Bank 2 sends Man 2's check to Commercial Bank 1 for payment. Commercial Bank 1 reduces its deposit liabilities and Commercial Bank 2 increases its deposit liabilities. Commercial Bank 2 now has $81in deposit liability to Woman 1 and $81of new reserves.

If we follow this all the way, we will end up with $100 of reserves in different banks and $900.00 of new checkbook money in the hands of the people and $990.00 of debt owned to the banking system. A couple of questions arise:

1. How can the banks pay all of the $900.00 worth of checks with only one hundred dollars worth of reserves?
2. How can the borrowers pay the total debt of with $990.00 owed to the banking system with only $900.00 worth of checkbook money especially when a lot of that money is in the hands of people who did not borrow any money?

Now let us take this a step farther. Woman 1 spends the $90 she has in her checking account by writing a check to Store 1. Now Woman 1 has no money as all her money has been transferred to Store 1. Store 1 takes the check and deposits it into Commercial Bank 3. This is where things get really sticky. When Commercial Bank 3 sends Woman 1's check to Commercial Bank 1 for payment, how does Commercial Bank 1 make final payment on Woman 1's $90 check? It can't do it by transferring reserves to Commercial Bank 3, because Commercial Bank 1 only has ten dollars in its reserve account? It appears that Commercial Bank 1 must borrow $90 in reserves from a Federal Reserve Bank and the Federal Reserve Bank must loan it before Commercial Bank 1 could move $90 in reserves to Commercial Bank 3.

If that is true, then the banking system is creating a lot more reserves than we have been led to believe. We know that can't be totally true. If it was true that the banks pay every check with reserves, then there would not have been any fractionalizing. There would not be any high powered money (*money that will support 9 times or of its value or more in checkbook money*).

The banking system and our educational system only teaches us about the first expansion of money, but we know that the checkbook money that was borrowed will not stop with one or two transactions. It will keep moving from one checking account to another as long as people buy and sell or until someone capturers back the money he borrowed and repays his loan principal. When the principal of a loan is repaid that money in extinguished. That same borrower must also capture some money that someone else has borrowed to enable him to pay the interest on the loan. The interest will go to the bank as profit and will not be extinguished.

Each time money is deposited in a bank, that bank will have a new deposit and therefore will be able to make a new loan. Stop and think. How many times that money will move into different banks and how many loans could have been made if the first loan was a loan for 30 years. Think about how much interest would be generated from all the loans that would have been generated from a big thirty year loan before the loan was paid and the money extinguished.

A bank liability (debt) is shifted to someone else every time money is moved into a different checking account. You can create money by using a credit card after you sign the forms sent to you, by the credit card company, promising to pay the credit back in the future with interest. The bank then uses that promise to pay as an asset on their books and then puts the credit you are going to use as a liability. The minute you use your credit card to buy something the 'money' moves into circulation. The seller of the goods has been paid in check-book money; but the buyer of the goods has not paid for them yet.

Let me use a specific example to further explain interest. Let's say that there is a total money supply of ten thousand dollars all created as a 10% interest-bearing loan by a private commercial bank.

One man borrowed it all and invests it all in a shoe factory and the materials to produce shoes. It takes one year to get all the materials together, make and sell one thousand pairs of shoes at ten dollars a pair. The total money supply is only ten thousand so when he has been paid for the shoes he will have captured back all the money in circulation.

Ten thousand dollars is all the owner of the shoe factory can return to the bank. If the man that owned the shoe factory raised the price of his shoes to twenty dollars. He could only sell five hundred shoes before he would capture back all the money in circulation. He could not even sell the rest of his shoes unless more money is created. No matter what he does, he can't pay the borrowed money, plus the interest, unless the money supply is increased.

If the owner of the shoe factory is going to return the original borrowed ten thousand plus one thousand in interest, the money supply must be increased by at least one thousand and more if the shoe factory is going to have a profit. To increase the money supply, under the present system, someone must borrow from a bank. Therefore, the bank must make another loan before it even gets paid the interest on the first loan. There are those who like to argue that if the factory owner sold some of his shoes to the banker he could pay his interest but that is not true. The money he would get from the banker would only be part of his borrowed principal. The interest the banker receives and spends does not increase the money supply it only circulates some of the borrowed money. This argument does not consider the fact that borrowed money in circulation goes into the hand of people who don't borrow. As soon as the money is paid back to the banker, the money is extinguished. No more shoes can be produced until more money is created and loaned at interest.

These are the principles under which the money system functions and the facts of how every dollar is created and how all businesses are run. Now, multiply that by the millions of loans that are made every day and then add compound interest to many of those loans. It should be easy to understand why we have over forty-eight trillion dollars of debt drawing interest. (Grandfather economic report 2007) Now in 2008 it is over fifty-three trillion.

These facts are not clearly seen because there are such vast numbers of loans being made and extinguished daily. Banks do spend a large part of the interest back into circulation. However, this spending of interest does not increase the money supply. It simply puts someone's loan principal money back into circulation. In addition, vast amounts of principal debt is not repaid, the loans are repudiated through business losses, repossessions and bankruptcies. Money borrowed and not repaid stays in circulation until it is used by someone to pay their loan principal. The same is true of the interest money that is received by the banks and spent back into circulation. How can we borrow $100 put ten in saving for a rainy day or for old age and at the same time pay $110 back to the bank? It is clearly impossible unless someone borrows more money.

Demand deposits (checkbook money) make up the bulk of the United States money supply. The rest is Federal Reserve Notes and coins which in reality only give a physical form to demand deposits. They move into circulation when someone buys them from a bank by drawing down the face value amount of the bills or coins from a checking account. This process destroys the checkbook money and moves the Federal Reserve Notes and coins into circulation.

Some writers say coins and the Federal Reserve Notes printed by the Bureau of Printing and Engraving are debt free money. One such writer stated: *The significant point about coins and notes money created by the government is that this money is created debt-free and spent into the economy by the government. Of course, government has no particular need of these coins and notes; banks are the institutions requiring a supply of cash, the government therefore sells the coins and notes that it creates. The government acquires the face value of those coins and notes in number money which is then spent into the economy as debt-free money. The 3% created by the State is the notes and coins, and the only cost to the taxpayer is the relatively insignificant cost of minting. However, taxpayers benefit directly because an amount equivalent to the face value of those notes and coins is spent by the State, into the economy, as a direct, debt-free input.*

Let's take a close look at that misleading and false statement starting with, *"the government has no need of the coins and the currency money that it can create at little cost and spend directly into circulation." ... the government therefore sells the coins and notes that it creates. The government acquires the face value of those coins and notes in number money which is then spent into the economy as debt-free money.* Source: a post put on Ellen Brown's Web of Debt web-site

It is obvious that a government that is ten trillion dollars in debt would have a very great need for money that it does not have to borrow. It is true that the government sells the notes that they print and the coins that they mint for number money. It is true that the government sells the coins for face value. The government does not sell the notes they print for face value, they sell the notes for the just the cost of printing. The number money is not debt-free. All number money is created as interest-bearing money. Only a total idiot would borrow money if he could create and spend his own money free of debt and at a fraction of its face value. In the U.S.A., the Bureau of Engraving and Printing produces the Nation's paper currency and sells it to the Federal Reserve System for 4.2 cents per note whether the note is a one dollar note or a one hundred dollar note. However the notes are not considered money until they are monetized and issued by a Federal Reserve Bank. Source: A personal letter from M. M. Schneider, Acting Executive Assistant, Bureau of Engraving and Printing

To obtain notes, a Federal Reserve Bank must pledge collateral equal to the face value of the note. Collateral must consist of the following assets, alone or in any combination: 1) gold certificates, 2) special Drawing Right certificates, 3) U.S. Government securities, and 4) "eligible paper," as described by Statute.

Federal Reserve Notes are obligations of the United States, and the United States has a first lien on the assets of the issuing Federal Reserve Bank. Source: A personal letter from M.M. Schneider Dept of the U.S. Treasury

A Federal Reserve Bank obtains currency notes from the Bureau of Engraving and Printing. It pays the Bureau the cost of producing the notes. The Federal Reserve notes then become liabilities of the Federal Reserve Banks. The issuing Bank records both a liability and an asset when it receives the notes form the Bureau and therefore does not show any earnings as a result of the transaction. A commercial bank which belongs to the Federal Reserve System can obtain FRNs from the Federal Reserve Bank in its district whenever it wishes, but the commercial bank must pay face value for the notes. *Source a personal letter from Russell L. Munk Assistant General Counsel US Treasury.*

The coins we use in the U.S.A. are created by the United States Mints. The cost of the coins varies with the cost of the metal and the technique used. The United States Mint purchases coinage metals under sealed bidding procedures on an average monthly basis. A special fund named the Treasury Coinage Metal Fund is used to make payment for the metals. 1980, it cost $.0078 to mint a one cent coin. It cost $.0192 to mint a five cent coin. It cost $.0095 to mint a ten cent coin. It cost $.0217 to mint a twenty-five cent coin. It cost $.0404 to mint a fifty cent coin. It cost $.0310 to mint a dollar coin. Mint coinage stocks are sold to and shipped directly to the Federal Reserve banks at face value, which, in turn, sells them to the commercial banks for the face value of the coins, the profit the government makes is called Seigniorage. Source: A personal letter from Jerry A. Yelling Chief Assayer U.S. Mint. It costs approximately twelve cents to mint the Golden dollar coins. Source: A personal letter from Bradford E. Cooper United State Mint

The commercial banks then sell them to the general public which pays for the coins with checkbook money that has been borrowed from the banks. It is true that the US Government makes a profit on the coins. However, the way they are put into circulation does not give the people any debt-free money.

If the commercial banks operated on a fifteen percent reserve, they could expand a one thousand dollar government debt up to about six thousand dollars of private debt. You can read about money expansion in most college economic textbook. The Federal Reserve Bank of New York illustrated it very well with the following cartoon. If the commercial banks operated on a 10 percent reserve, they could expand a one thousand dollar government debt into nine thousand dollar private debt.

However, fractional banking has a destructive side that the college textbooks never tell you about.

Now that you have seen what the bank says, let's go back through the loan process one more time. When the bank creates the money as a book-entry and loans it to Jake the plumber, only the principle is created and the principle of $850.00 is all that Jake receives. But Jake has to pay back the principle plus the interest on the debt. At 10 percent simple interest on a one year loan the interest would be $85.00 so the loan to Jake of $850.00, creates a total indebtedness of $935.00. It is the same with Helen's loan of $722.50. It would create an indebtedness of $794.75. As the process continues, the money supply will have been expanded to more than $6000.00. But the total indebtedness of the people would have expanded to more than $6600.00.

Source of cartoon: The story of banks the Federal Reserve New York

When the expansion of the money supply is accomplished though interest-bearing loans, the usury on the loans always causes the total indebtedness of the people to grow faster than the money supply. As Thomas Woodward, Specialist in Macroeconomics writing for the Economic Division Congressional Research Service of the Library of Congress stated: *"There is no such thing as "debt-free" money under US law."* That makes it impossible for **all** the borrowers to repay the loans. In addition, when a loan is paid back to the bank, the principal amount of the loan is extinguished and the money supply is then reduced by the amount paid back.

This leaves a dark picture of expanding debts, rising bankruptcies and an increasing cost of living plus all the mental stress and hidden social problems that come with extreme money shortages. Nobody wants to suffer through bankruptcies so they attempt to pass their interest cost onto someone else through higher prices while raising the cost of living for everyone. The banking people call it price inflation.

Many people suffering from a shortage of money begin to engage in all sorts schemes, some legal some not, to get someone else's borrowed money so they can pay the interest on their loans or to have money and be free of debt themselves.

Mr. Robert H. Hemphill, credit manager of the Federal Reserve Bank of Atlanta, put it this way,

"If all the bank loans were paid, no one would have a bank deposit and there would not be a dollar of coin or currency in circulation. This is a staggering thought. We are completely dependent on the commercial banks. Someone has to borrow every dollar we have in circulation whether its cash or credit. If the banks create ample synthetic money, we are prosperous; if not, we starve. We are absolutely without a permanent money system. When one gets a complete grasp of the picture, the tragic absurdity of our hopeless position is almost incredible, but there it is. It (<u>the banking problem</u>) <u>is the most important subject intelligent persons can investigate and reflect upon.</u> It is so important that our present civilization may collapse unless it becomes widely understood and the defects remedied very soon." (emphasis added)

The banker doesn't like me. I can't get the money I need to engage in commerce.

The banker likes me and will loan me all the money I need.

The defect Mr. Hemphill talked about is not about what is used as money. The defect is about how money is put into circulation. When money is loaned into circulation, it makes financial slaves out of the people. Then when money is removed from circulation when the loan is repaid, it always leaves the people at the mercy of the lender. It creates total financial enslavement to the masters of money.

It does indeed take money to engage in commerce. If the lender does not loan to you, you are shut out of commerce to a very large degree. If the lender loans to you, you now have an obligation to perform for him. Add interest to the loans and the total debt is unpayable in money. It is very important to fully explain what I mean by "unpayable in money". An individual can pay the interest he owns on his loan in bank credit money, however, he must use money that someone else has borrowed to pay the interest on his loan. Therefore, he does not truly pay the interest debt. He only shifts the debt to someone else. I think it is very important to explain that it is true that one can borrow and then use that money to do things that will enable the borrower to capture lots of other people's borrowed money to the point one might not have any personal debt and have a lot of money. However, to do so someone somewhere must have the debt and no money.

The interest obligation to the lender can't be paid in money unless and until someone else becomes obligated to the lender for that much money. Therefore the interest just keeps growing on someone else's debt.

Robert L. Rewald economist Flow of Funds Section Board of Governors of the Federal Reserve System) told me in a personal conversation *"In our financial system an individual can get out of debt, but **collectively** we cannot get out of debt".* Once the people have been deceived and their minds tricked into accepting 'obligations to pay' as payment and therefore money, they become economic slaves to the issuer of the fraudulent obligations. The privately controlled banking system gets everything by issuing promissory notes that they never have to pay, and the people become enslaved by unpayable interest-bearing debt.

Over time, as interest constantly increases the obligations to the lenders, all freedoms and all property rights except for the lenders are destroyed. Liberty is lost. The people become debtor slaves to the lenders. Unless our money system is changed, people will remain economic slaves to the creators of the money (lenders) forever. The preamble of the United States Constitution states: "*We the People of the United States, in Order to form a more perfect Union, establish Justice, insure domestic Tranquility, provide for the common defense, promote the general Welfare, and secure the Blessings of Liberty to ourselves and our Posterity, do ordain and establish this Constitution for the United States of America.*"

If we read Article 1, Section 8) in the light and spirit and of the preamble, clearly the new Congress was given the duty and the authority to monetize the peoples' production as wealth to the people. If money is created in any other way, there can be no general Welfare, only general enslavement. Hamilton took the Congress down the road to general and overall enslavement. Congress started in the right direction but used the wrong process with passage of the 1792 Coinage Act, wherein they set forth the principles for an honest liberty and prosperity-producing money system. Where the people's production was monetized for the benefit of the producers, where everyone receives the sole right to benefit from their own production. Under the 1792 Coinage Act, Congress "monetized" the people's production FREE TO, AND FOR THE BENEFIT OF, THE PRODUCER through the process of coining raw resources of the earth into money.

Under the 1792 Coinage Act, any person could mine gold and silver bullion and take it to the U.S. Mint which would "monetize" that bullion by assaying, weighing and stamping it into coins. The person would leave the mint with his production "monetized" in the form of coins that passed from hand to hand as the medium-of- exchange, as they were traded for other goods and services. Said money represented the production of the people as a wealth to the people with no debt to anyone. What they forgot to take into account was, at that time, there was no gold or silver mined in the United States.

The first gold found in the new United States was in 1799 by John Reed's son Conrad. He found a large yellow rock in a creek. The Reed family didn't know it was gold; they used it for a doorstop until 1802 when a jeweler happened by and identified it as gold.

Our "brilliant" founding fathers passed a monetary bill that couldn't possibly work because they had to depend on imported gold and silver and the gold and silver flowed back out of the country as fast as it flowed in. The right principles were employed; money must represent the production of the people without any debt to the people and that is the principle on which gold functioned. If the founding fathers had only understood how to use paper money in a way that would have monetized the people's production as a wealth to the people instead of interest-bearing debts, today we would be living in a wealthy debt-free nation with few taxes.

Modern Money Secrets hiding in plain sight:

People are deceived into believing that money and credit are interchangeable, but there are not. Money is what one uses to make final payment with. Credit is always what someone's owes!

Chapter 12
AMERICA'S MONETARY FUTURE

I do not know what America's monetary future will be. I believe that I do know what it could be and what it should be. I believe that everything works under a designed plan. We all know that cars are designed. We all know engineers are employed to design our roads and bridges. Everyone that has ever done research or studied our Federal Reserve money system knows that it was designed by bankers to work for their benefit.

I know that most people have never given much thought to money with the exception that most us would like to have more of it. Most people think that money is just out there. We have been led to believe and taught that we only need to be highly motivated to work hard and efficiently or, be better educated and we can earn lots of it. However, that doesn't seem to work for most people. A good ponzi scheme works well for some people until they get caught.

Hopefully, most of the people will soon learn and understand that money is 'not just out there'. Money is not a thing of nature. Money is a man-made concept, mostly of law and from commonly accepted practices. Someone must produce what is used as money. How money is used and moved into circulation is much more important than what is physically used for money. Our biggest problem is that few people have taken the time to try to design a money system that would work equally for the benefit of the people.

The few who will take the time to try and design an honest, moral, workable and sustainable money system do not seem to be willing to put in enough time, thought and research to understand all the aspects of what the banker's money system really does to most of the people. Therefore, they don't seem to be able or willing to work with others who are trying to do the same thing.

There are some goods things about our present money system. It is uniform throughout the nation and it is very convenient to use in the exchange good and services. The problem is that it steals from the masses for the benefit of the few.

While attempting to design a money system, let us quickly review history to see if we can find any principles to guide us. The first thing we find is what we have used for money has been constantly changing. Throughout history, money has been some commodity (a form of wealth) ranging from pretty rocks and shells to plants and animals that most anyone could produce and traded between the buyer and the seller. The principle here is that money should be replenishable wealth and it should be transferrable without incurring debt. The disadvantages have been that there was little uniformity. Most commodities were not, and are not convenient to use, and it was hard to make change.

Various metals have been used including iron, copper, zinc, silver and gold. These metals, when traded into circulation, were still wealth. As the refining process became more advanced, the coins became uniform and were produced in multiple denominations. They more useful in making transactions.

The disadvantage with most metal money was that there were too many other uses for the metals and they are heavy to carry. The additional disadvantage with silver and gold is that there has never been enough of it to consummate all the transactions of goods and services. Immoral people soon saw that scarcity could be a positive thing, at least for those had the gold. They declared gold and silver's scarcity was a good thing because it gave greater value to the metals. People eventually decided because it was so scarce and so valuable it would be wise and more convenient to leave the gold in a safe vault and use the receipt as their medium-of-exchange. It didn't take too long for immoral men to see that could make a great profit by counterfeiting the receipts and loaning them at interest.

The concept of money started as a simple agreement or understanding but it was soon codified in law. Once any form or kind of money is codified into law, it becomes fiat money.

The principles that we have leaned so far are that money should:

- Represent wealth
- Have uniformity
- Be convenient to use
- Be plentiful enough to be a general medium-of-exchange for everyone
- Be traded or spent in to circulation in a way that benefits the entire population

How money moves into circulation is one of the most important factors in designing a money system. It must move into circulation in a way that will provide economic freedom and prosperity for all the people who will be using it to make honest and fair exchanges.

Enclosed is an article entitled, "The Technological Role of Fiat Money" by Narayana R. Kockerlakota, Senior Economist Research Department, Federal Reserve published in the Federal Reserve Bank of Minneapolis' Quarterly Review summer 1998 with a few comments that I have added in parenthesis and italicized and underlined. In that article he said:

> "Fiat money unlike all other things people use has no intrinsically usefulness" *(<u>He should have said: Today our money does not consist of any known chemical substance and therefore cannot be used to produce anything</u>.)*
>
> "Thus, monetary economics can be viewed as merely large interlocking networks of gifts (*<u>transactions</u>*). If agents in the economy know the history of all gifts, (*<u>transactions</u>*) then any allocation of resources achievable in the economy with money is achievable without it. This analysis leads to a simple conclusion. If the function performed by money can be superseded by a perfect historical record of transactions, then money's only technological role must be to provide that record." "In other words, money is a form of record keeping, societal memory." "I conclude that the only technological role of money is to provide a limited form of societal memory of transactions." <u>Narayana R. Kockerlakota The Technological Role of Fiat Money</u>

Mr. Kocherlakota left out several important facts in his theory. He did not address the fact that the money we now use only gets into circulation through the process of interest-bearing *loans* from private commercial banks. This means when two parties engage in transactions using money, there is always a silent third party not engaged in the transaction, receives a benefit and *the interest on the money.*

That silent third party is the banking system that is getting paid an interest

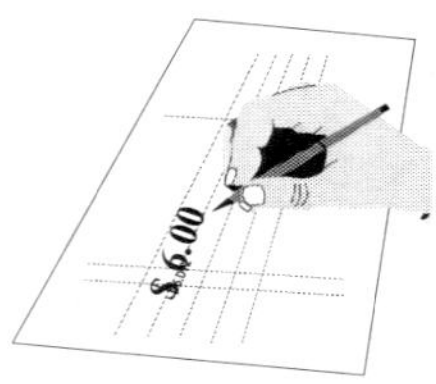

fee, for the use of the money. This interest fee gives the banking system something for nothing, a free lunch because the cost of creating money

for the banking system is nothing but a little ink or electricity.

If Mr. Kocherlakota has come to his above conclusion honestly, he could not possibly condone the perpetual interest payments the banking system receives on societal memory. Mr. Kocherlakota's article clearly points out a deficiency of economists. They mostly deal in theories that are not grounded in facts or reality and form conclusions that are not grounded on fact. With that said, I think that Mr. Kocherlakota did point out that a sufficiently accurate record keeping system, without loans and interest could replace coin and paper money entirely The whole concept of money is to make the trading of goods and labor, buying and selling, simple and efficient.

Many of our founders wanted the creation of money to be in the hands of the United States Congress. This should mean, "in the hands of the people for the benefit of the people." My research has led me to conclude that the main reason that they wanted the creation of money in the hands of the Federal Congress was to have uniform money throughout the nation. Because of all the confusion that came when every colony, some churches, some individuals and many different banks all issued differing forms, colors and sizes of currency. I

I believe that many of the founding fathers did not like bills of Credit. I also believe that the most of them, like most people today, did not truly understand the principles that money should function under or did they understand the principles that the banking system functioned under. There were led, by

Hamilton, to copy the existing European banking system.

There are only three ways newly created money can be moved into circulation. It makes no difference if that money is shells, gold, tobacco, silver, or just numbers in an accounting system. It makes no difference if it is done by a private banking system or the government or by individuals. The creation of money should never be done for a profit, only as a service to aid the people in commerce. We must never lose sight of the fact that money was invented to enhance **buying and selling.** Every money transfer and almost all commerce is transacted by the process of spending and receiving money.

Gifting, Loaning, and Spending

Creation of a stable, uniform, national monetary system is almost impossible for the people to do individually. It is however, the most beneficial thing that people can do collectively working through their government. To **gift** money into circulation, there must be a benefactor and a recipient. To **loan** money into circulation, there must be a lender and a borrower. To **spend** money into circulation, there must be a seller and a buyer. Each way produces totally different results. This is true whether the creator of the money is a private banking system or the government. We will try, as best we can, to examine the results achieved using each of the three ways.

'Gifting'

If money is created and then selectively given to a just a few people, it gives those people a huge advantage over everyone else. This is what is occurring now. The private banking system gets to create all the money as a promise to pay, that they never have to pay. The bankers get everything as a free gift to themselves.

Most people would see no need to work or to produce very much if they got paid regardless whether they **produced or not. T**his principle would hold true for almost everything. People would probably still do many things for personal pleasure.

With people not working or producing anything, just sitting around waiting for the next payday, practically all commerce would stop. We simply would not have most of the goods and services that make life livable and enjoyable. For an example: Would you want go to a café everyday and be the cook, waitress or the dishwasher, or would you rather go to the café everyday and just sit down and be served if you got the same paycheck either way?

Gifting all money into circulation equally to everyone would also destroy the very concept of money which is to make buying and selling (trading of goods and services) more convenient and more efficient. It is clear to me that gifting all money into circulation would not be the best way.

'LOANING'

Loaning new money into circulation at interest obligates the borrower to the lender for the principal and the accrued interest as long as the money is in circulation. Time and interest on loans makes the debt grow; but time and interest does not make the money supply grow. This is what results when the banking system gets to create all the money as a free gift to itself. The Bible states: *"The borrower is the servant to the lender",* and that is so true. When one gives something away, he has no control over the recipient of the gift. The same holds true of the spender of money. Once the money is spent, the spender loses all control over the money. However, that does not hold true for the lender. When a lender loans on a written promise to pay back, the lender has an element of power and control over the borrower until the loan is repaid. That is why the banking system has the power it has over the people.

In spite of the volumes of books that have been written on the subject, there is only one way to produce real wealth; that is through a combination of ideas, labor and raw resources. There are several ways to acquire wealth, or maybe we should say to transfer wealth from the producers to the non-producers. The best way to transfer wealth from the producers of the wealth to you is to gain the power to issue money as a free gift to yourself. Then loan that money into circulation for everyone else to use as an interest accruing debt to you. It is the best way because, for the most part, the people never seem to be able to understand what is happening. The next best way is to obtain the power to force an involuntary tax on the people. It is the second best way because it seems to be much easier for the people to realize that they are being over-taxed.

Some of America's founders were honest and believed in the principles set forth in the Bible. "*Thou shall love thy neighbor as thyself,*" that *"thou shall earn your bread with the sweat of your brow"* and *"thou shall not steal"*. It is clear that others were greedy men and lovers of power and practitioners of corruption.

Once, the Constitution was adopted, the more practical ones fought and succeeded in having the Bill of Rights added to protect the people from improper activities by men in government.

Government's duty is to secure rights, not to transfer wealth!

"All men are born equally free and independent, and have certain inherent rights, among which are those of enjoying and defending life and liberty, of acquiring and protecting property and the pursuit of happiness. To secure these rights governments are instituted among men, deriving their just powers from the consent of the governed." BILL OF RIGHTS SOUTH DAKOTA CONSTITUTION.

Ownership of property and receiving the benefit of one's own labor, production and management should lead to financial success. This is the foundation that supports all freedoms and rights. In order to have property ownership and receive the benefit of one's own production, there must be honest contracts and an honest court system for the protection of those contracts. I am sorry to say, we no longer have these.

It is self-evident that commerce, the standard of living and quality of life, can be enhanced by the proper use of money. Think how much better it would be for most everyone if our medium of exchange, was just a medium-of-exchange and not also a medium-of-theft for the benefit of the elite.

There is simply no question that for a nation to grow and prosper there has to be an increase in the money supply to match the increase in the production of goods and services. Like everything else, there is an honest, moral way to increase the supply of money as well as a dishonest, immoral way. The most immoral and deceptive way is to increase the money supply is through interest-bearing loans.

Whether we choose to admit it or not, there are higher laws than man-made laws. Man can pass all the laws he wants which violate higher laws, but he cannot change the higher laws of gravity, the laws of math, the laws of energy and the laws of physics. Often, it seems there is no consequence for violations of the higher law. But the fat lady has not finished singing yet!!

Hamilton understood that creating 'money' and loaning that 'money' into circulation drawing usury is the greatest tool there is for transferring wealth from the producers to the non-producers. Interest-bearing debt is the best tool there is for stealing the peoples right to the benefit of their own production by controlling the issue of money one gains not only economic power, but also political control.

The power to create and issue money as an interest-bearing debt owed to the creator and the lender is the greatest tool on the face of the earth to produce a super-rich elite and keep them in power.

There is an old saying that, *"It takes money to make money."* If one man or a group of men are allowed to have a monopoly over the creation of money for their own personal profit, they will have an advantage over all other men that is impossible to overcome until that monopoly is revoked and that privilege is destroyed. That's why we have laws against other monopolies.

There is no subtler, no surer way to destroy a nation than to DEBAUCH the currency (create money as loans). The laws of compounding usury will always strip all wealth from the producers and give it to the issuers of the loans.

When talking about compound usury, we are seldom if ever told about its dark side. We are told often of the wonderful power of compound usury (earning interest on both principal and the accumulated interest). We are told how compound usury can make a modest investment grow into an enormous amount. For example: If you invested $10,000 at seven percent compound usury for thirty years you would expect your investment to grow to $76,122.55.

Sounds great! Compound usury must truly make money grow! Now just for a moment, let's step out of the dream world hype of banking, financial planners and Wall Street: and ask **Just how does Money grow**? From where does the interest money come? When you put money into an interest-bearing account, does it turn into something like rabbits that mate and quickly reproduce? What

happens? The increasing money added to your account has to come from someplace. I assure you it does not come from the natural reproduction of money. To understand financial planning, economics, growing public and private debts, ever-increasing taxes and prices etc., we must always remember that **all** new money is created and put into circulation as interest-bearing debt obligations. Today, someone somewhere must go into debt in order for money to exist. If your bank account is increased without you personally borrowing, someone else's borrowed funds had to have been transferred into your account. "*There is no such thing as "debt-free" money under U.S. Law.*" Thomas Woodward Specialist in Macroeconomics, Congressional Research Service * The Library of Congress June 13, 1994

As a population grows and the increasing population produces and consumes more goods and services, the money supply must grow if the amount (volume not value) of money held by each person is to stay steady. The money supply must increase if the growing population is to have profit and savings. Example: if a population of ten people each had two chairs and the population grew to twenty people then the volume of chairs would have to increase to forty chairs if all twenty people were to have two chairs. If the increase less the 40 chairs someone would have to go without two chairs (a drop in their standard of living) If you doubled the value of the twenty chairs the twenty people still could have two chairs. In other words, when the economy grows more money is needed, but never forget that under the present system *"the actual creation of money always involves the extension of credit by private commercial banks."* Russell Munk, United Stated Treasury. That must change if we are to enjoy peace, prosperity and freedom in this nation!

If governments don't borrow, the private sector must or today's money cannot exist. If you invest $10,000 at seven percent compounded annually and thirty years later get $76,122.55; someone, somewhere had to borrow $66,122.55 at interest before it could exist and be put into your checking account!

If you have money and don't have any debt, someone somewhere must have the debt and not the money! If the amount of money you borrowed plus the amount needed to pay the interest owed is not in your account but is in someone else's checking account when your loan comes due, you will clearly have a problem.

We must never lose sight of the fact that when money is created and loaned into circulation, only the principal of the loan can be placed into circulation. Interest and time makes the debt grow, but not the money supply. When someone repays a loan, the principal is extinguished, but the money used to pay interest lives on as someone else's debt.

When money is created through the lending, at interest process, there is simply no way to create the money to pay the interest on the loans-except for more borrowing at interest. Therefore if money is to stay in circulation the debt must constantly grow.

Many people claim that the interest money comes from increased production (worker productivity). But, when was the last time your personal production (goods and services) turned into money? Did you ever wave a magic wand over a shoe, a shirt, a bushel of corn, a new car or an hour of labor and see it turn into money? If that could be done why would you or anyone need to borrow in the first place? Why would you work for anyone just to get paid money?

Others seem to think jobs create money. There is no question that in America today jobs are important. Most education is geared toward preparing one to enter the work force to working for someone and earn a wage. Only corporations and the rich are expected to own the businesses and create the jobs. We are told over and over that the more schooling one has the higher income one can expect to earn.

We have come to believe that the true benefit of jobs is the money income. However, shouldn't the real benefit of the job be the production of goods and services that makes life more enjoyable? Money is the tool that has made division of labor possible. The division of labor is what has made modern mass production possible. The jobholder's earnings should flow from the monetization of production, not from the monetization of debt, thereby providing the way for the worker to obtain his share of the production without debt to anyone. His fair share is not one millionth of what the CEO receives.

If a community is suffering an economic downturn, the first reaction is to look for ways to bring new jobs into the community. The belief is that those jobs will some-how create the money the community needs to prosper. The community leaders look for investors to invest in something that will create new jobs. However, if jobs themselves created money, why are the investors needed?

Does your job really create new money? No, your job does not create new money unless your job is a loan officer for a private commercial bank whose loans create the credit that we use for money. Remember what Russell L. Munk, United States Treasury said ***"the actual creation of money always involves the extension of credit by private commercial banks***." ***"Money is created when loans are issued and debts incurred; money is extinguished when loans are repaid."*** John B. Henderson, Senior Specialist in Price Economics Congressional Research Service Library of Congress

Money, like toys, cars, shoes, houses, etc. must be manufactured. Money does not come from natural reproduction like people, plants, and animals and doesn't naturally grow like young people, plants and animals.

Creating more jobs and putting more people to work does not increase the money supply nor grow the economy--it simply redistributes the money that has already been manufactured and is available. Without money, there can be no division of labor and jobs, and the economy simply dries up. If you want to heat up the economy, the money must be increased. This can be verified by a brief look at history. In 1918, 32,000 banks in the United States were borrowing new reserves from the newly created Federal Reserve Banks. They put up the promissory notes from farmers and merchants as collateral. They expanded on those reserves by making more loans. At one time the banks in Iowa had fifty-two dollars loaned out for every dollar they had in reserves. The farmers and merchants spent the funds. The country was flush with capital. Economic times were booming, probably not for the farmers who were getting deeper into debt, but for the rest of the country who was getting the benefit of the money the farmers had borrowed and spent. The roaring twenties 'roared' on borrowed money. The trap had been set. How did they spring the trap? Here are the facts as given by Mr. John A Simpson, President of the First National Bank of Watherford, Oklahoma, from first-hand information. *"In January of 1920, while in Washington on business for the Oklahoma Farmers' Union of which I was state President, I visited with John Skelton Williams, Comptroller of the Currency. We had the following conversation.*

Mr. Simpson: *"When is deflation going to begin?"*

Mr. Williams: *"The other members of the Federal Reserve Board voted a few days ago to have it begin in May."*

Mr. Simpson: *"Don't you know that this will be a calamity to this country?"*

Mr. Williams: *"I told the other members of the board that it would break lot of little banks, and they cold bloodedly replied to me, that they ought to break, there are too many of them. I told the other members of the board that such a policy would ruin lots of farmers, and they just as cold bloodedly answered, they ought to be ruined, they are getting so prosperous they will not work."*

In the early part of May 1920, the powerful big bankers, working through the Federal Reserve Board began a policy of pulling the currency out of circulation and restricting bank credit. To make the money supply shrink, the Federal Reserve Banks notified the 32,000 banks that were doing business in the United States and had borrowed credit from them to repay the funds that they had borrowed. In order for the banks to pay back the funds they had borrowed from the Federal Reserve Banks, they had to demand that the farmers and merchants to whom they had made loans that they had to pay their loans. As the loans of credit were repaid, the credit money was extinguished. As the commercial bank paid their loans to the Federal Reserve Banks, currency was taken out of circulation.

Mr. Simpson went on to say that in the 1930's he went to the Washington and personally saw the bales of currency that had been taken out of circulation.

On October 24, 1929, the stock market crashed. Through the repayment of the loans nearly $3,000,000,000 was removed from circulation. This recall of the money supply forced the closing of 20,000 banks ending competition for the big banks. Two million farmers lost their farms and their homes through foreclosures and tax sales. Thousands of small businesses were put out of business by bankruptcy courts and the big banks picked up the choice properties for pennies on the dollar.

Thousands of jobs dried up and breadlines appeared. Shacks made of packing boxes, scrap iron and materials picked out of dumps sprang up on the outskirts of towns. Whole families lived out of their cars and small trucks and warmed themselves before fires in barrels. Commerce for much of America slowed to a crawl. The great depression had been <u>created</u>.

All the calamities from fires, floods, tornadoes and all the pestilence of disease combined does not equal the misery and suffering that American citizens have endured at the hands of the bankers through the manipulation of the money and the wars the banker has financed.

In the 1940's, we had war and the money poured forth and the economy improved greatly. Lots of young men went off to be killed and injured. Where did the money come from? It came from interest-bearing bank loans, of course. When the bankers increase the money supply through interest-bearing loans, the economy gets a boost and grows. When the

bankers pull back the money by calling loans or raising interest rates or refusing to renew loans when loans come due, the economy really slows down and the people suffer. The bankers and their cronies have names for it; they call it the business cycle. They also call it periods of inflation and periods of recession.

Source of pictures: The Story of Money Federal Reserve Bank of New York

Imagine a small nation with a population of 100 people and a total money supply of $100 all created as interest-bearing loans by the bank. Let's say that 75 people have jobs and 25 do not. The 75 people produce 75 widgets with a retail price of one dollar. (One widget equals the total monthly goods and service produced per person). If each employed person is paid one dollar a month, 75% of the money supply is needed each month to meet the payroll. 75% of the money supply must move completely through the economy to the wage earner, back to the wage payer then back to the wage earner each month. That leaves $25 or 25% of the total money supply available to be held out of circulation (the monthly cycle) in short or long term saving.

We create 25 new jobs that produce 25 more widgets. Now we have 100 people producing 100 widgets. No money has been created by creating more jobs and producing more widgets. The only thing that has been created is more widgets. 100% of the money supply is now needed to meet the monthly payroll and to pay for all the goods produced services each month. Therefore all money must come out of saving and move into circulation (the monthly cycle). The money has to be redistributed from one purpose to another, or more money must be created.

The people want and need to have some savings for a rainy day and for retirement. If 50% of the people reduce their spending so that they can save ten cents monthly out of their pay and put it in saving $5.00 or 5% of the money, supply a month would move from circulation into savings. Without an increase in the money supply this savings creates a real problem. The nation can't meet its $100 monthly payroll with only a circulating money supply of $95. To meet the monthly payroll either jobs must be eliminated or wages reduced. Or more money must be created.

The same problem surfaces if instead of increasing the total number of jobs we give half the population a wage increase. 50 people continue to work at $1 per month and 50 receive a raise to $1.50 per month. It would now require $125.00 to meet the monthly payroll. Even if all the money must came out of saving and moved into circulation it would be impossible to meet the monthly payroll unless the money supply was increased.

To have 'savings', more jobs, more production or higher wages for some, without lowering someone else's standard of living, the money supply must be increased. **The money supply is the fuel that runs the 'economic engine' not** more **jobs** and more **production**.

Jobs do not create money. Jobs create goods and services. Goods and services do not create money. Only loans create money. It should not be that way! There is a better way to create money.

In making the complete monthly cycle from wage payer to wage earner and back to wage payer the money may pass through a few or many hands. The more hands it passes through in a given time span, the greater the velocity. The greater the hustle and bustle, the faster society must move and the larger the GDP will be. To Illustrate: A wage earner working in a store gets his monthly paycheck. Before leaving the store he cashes his check and buys something for 10 cents from that store. He would have increased the GDP by 10 cents. Those 10 pennies made the complete cycle from the wager payer to the wage earner and back to the wage payer in one transaction.

If the wage earner takes his pay and puts gas in his car, that transaction will increase the GDP. If the gas station owner uses that same money to pay the phone bill, that transaction again increases the GDP but it does not increase the money supply. If the wager earner's money passes through ten hands, or makes ten transactions, before it finds it way back to the wage payer, the velocity of money is greater. The GDP has grown by a factor of ten but the money supply has not grown. Many people mistakenly state, money is created by the velocity of money. Velocity of money can grow the Gross Domestic Production (GDP) but it does not and cannot increase the money supply.

People have a natural tendency to multiply. If the population of our example nation grows to 200 people and 150 people are to be in the work force at one dollar per month a money supply of $150 in circulation is required to meet the monthly payroll cycle. This, of course, is impossible if the total money supply is only $100.

How do we increase the money supply to enable 150 people to have paying jobs without lowering the pay of those working before the increase? To have a sustainable economy, it must be through monetized production, not monetized debt.

In America today, all new money is created by private commercial banks making interest-bearing loans to customers. Therefore, at this time **the only way to monetize one's production is to use it as collateral for an interest bearing loan from a private commercial bank.**

Again quote Russell L. Munk, the *"actual creation of money always involves the extension of credit by private commercial banks."* This means that before there can be an increase in the money supply, someone must go to a bank and borrow something that the bank does not have. The bank creates the money when the borrower signs the promissory note and numbers are entered into his checking account. The bank only loans credit -- *the credit the borrower receives does not consist of any known chemical substance.* LeAnn Larson LaFave Asst. U.S. Attorney Credit from a bank only deceives the borrower's mind into believing that he received something other than a number in his checking account. Because most people never question what really happens when they get a loan from a bank, they are all very willing to your credit as their medium-of-exchange. That fact alone gives the bank credit purchasing power. The borrowers can then go forth and purchase goods and services in the market place. This gives the borrower user rights but not ownership rights. Upon obtaining the mortgage from the borrower the bank gets the ownership rights on everything that the borrower had before the loan, but also a mortgage on everything the borrower purchased and all the increase thereof, including the borrower's labor. In our court system, the bank's equity means everything. The borrower's equity means nothing.

Under the present monetary system production is monetized as a debt to the producer and a wealth asset to the banking system. Think about it! Take a good honest look! Banks don't produce anything from raw resources. They don't work with anything that has reproduction capabilities. Banks just shuffle numbers. Yet bankers have become some of the wealthiest (in land, building and real goods) people in the world.

Banks should not be the creators of the money as a profit for the owners. Banks should be nothing more than accounting and account transfer companies that charge a fee for service rendered. Just like the World Wide Web's on-line servers are information transfer centers or companies. They do not create the information, they simply make the transfer of the information other people create or generate much faster and easier.

Sadly, banks are not just accounting and account transfer companies, nor are they lenders of other people's money, as many people including bankers would have you believe. Banks are the creators of all the money we use *as loans to the borrowers and as a profit to the banks,* through deception.

There can never be an interest charge on money if a nation is to have a sustainable monetary system. People should not be forced to have debt before they can have a medium-of-exchange. To have a sustainable monetary system, money can only be a tool to make exchanges easier.

Interest and time makes the debt grow. Time and interest does not make the money supply grow. With each interest bearing loan, we are creating a debt greater than the money supply. Interest causes the spread between the debt and the money supply to grow greater with each passing day. Interest is a cost of doing business. The greater the interest load, the harder it is to generate a profit after paying the interest. The harder it is to generate a profit, the harder it is to pay the interest. The harder it is to pay the interest, the greater the pressure to cut both labor and raw resource costs. The more you cut wages, the harder it is for the wage earners to buy the things they need like food, housing, transportation and heath care. Wage earners receiving lower wages may also need help with childcare because lower wages forces both parents (not all but most) to work outside the home to earn the income needed.

It is the unpayable cost of interest that causes the loss purchasing power. It is the unpayable cost of interest that adds to the cost of living. It is the unpayable cost of interest that forces more members of families to work more jobs and longer hours to try to maintain the same standard of living. It is the unpayable cost of interest that causes large companies to move their production lines to countries where laborers are paid less. This leads to trade deficits where more money flows out of the country to buy imports, than flows back to pay for exports. This unpayable cost of interest causes the lose of many factory and other jobs, slowly forcing us to loss the ability to produce the things we need in our own country. The ever-growing cost of unpayable interest causes ever-growing money shortages. Spending more and more bank credit money on an education system that doesn't teach our children about the evils of debt-money and the unpayable cost of interest will never help our children.

When people find that they simply cannot earn enough to pay for all the things they need, they cry to government for help. Many politicians will gladly start new social programs. Very few politicians have been willing to address the problems with our money system.

To fund these social programs taxes must be increased or the government must borrow more. This simply leads to another round of greater interest costs and higher taxes. This leads to an even greater shortage of money for nearly everyone, until finally the interest load and the tax load become greater than the people can bear.

The imminent concern of a very knowledgeable salesman *is that collectively we have borrowed so much money that soon the interest on the debt will be greater than the total consumer income! That will be the day when almost everyone will be forced to stop buying.*

My concern is based in letters to me from the U.S. Treasury that state, "The actual creation of money always involves the extension of credit by private commercial banks." "When the principal is repaid it is uncreated." "Money for paying interest on the borrowed money comes from the same place other money comes from." *That means we must borrow the money to pay the interest too!*

When money is created as a loan, ***only the principal can be created. It's impossible to create the money to pay the interest****. The 'interest' we believe we pay is only another person's loan principal captured in the process of commerce. Until it gets too big, the unpayable interest debt is simply transferred to another party causing our collective debt to constantly grow. The unpayable interest or 'cost of money' must be added to the costs of goods and services resulting in a constantly growing 'spread' between the prices of raw products and the prices of finished products, causing ever growing pressures to cut labor costs and raise taxes and producing growing shortages of money in most all economic sectors. To meet these 'shortages' we try to trade more things produced with more borrowing. The result is an 'over-stored' America, too many giant stores trying to selling the same stuff to too few customers. Our debt and the interest on it forces us to seek foreign labor who will work for less.*

The root cause of our evolving 'dog-eat-dog' environment happened when we stopped putting new money into circulation debt free and started loaning it into circulation as unpayable interest-bearing debts. More and more, we are told, "If you are to get an increase in your share of business, you must take it away from someone else." The more we hear it, and repeat it the more palatable it becomes.

This salesman's nightmare should be an imminent concern for all of us. When the year's total interest debt exceeds the nation's total yearly income, our Nation's financial system will likely fail. **The buying will likely stop**, or at least it will slow down a lot. Today (2008) all you have to do is listen to the news, and you will hear how a slowdown of consumer income will start to slide us into recession. A slowdown of consumer income causes a slowdown in sales, a slowdown in sales causes many people to get their work hours cut. A decline in wages, always lead to a decline in the standard of living.

America has lost most of its production base to outsourcing and off shoring. Those jobs have been replaced with lower paying jobs in the service sector. Now these large businesses are pushing for more and more immigration, both legal and illegal, to drive down wages in the service sector. These businesses seem not to understand that they are slowly killing their own markets. It's a spiral stairway going down a circular path to national destruction unless we start spending all new money into circulation debt-free and in the way it will benefit everyone and not just make a few very rich.

John Maynard Keynes said: "There is no subtler, no surer means of overturning the existing basis of society than to DEBAUCH the currency. The process engages all the hidden forces of economic law on the side of destruction, and does it in a manner which only one man in a million is able to diagnose."

The only way to DEBAUCH money is to change it from a representation of wealth to an evidence of debt! Every nation that has used a DEBAUCHED monetary system has been forced to march towards destruction by debt.

'Spending'

The only way to stop this headlong rush to destruction by debt is to reform our money system to where money represents wealth the people produce. A system in which the people will collectively, create their own money working through their government. The government acting as an agent of the people will create the money and spend it (debt-free, interest-free, fee-free, and tax-free) into circulation in a matter that is most beneficial to all the people. In order for anyone to spend, they must buy and pay for something. When anyone buys something he becomes the owner of that thing. This is true whether the buyer is an individual, a private business or the government. One needs to give a lot a thought to what the government should own and hold in trust for the people compared to what the people should own personally.

There is a group that promotes the concept that government should monetize the production of raw farm production. This sounds like a good idea if you are a producer (a farmer) of raw farm production and very short of money. However, this group has never really stopped to think through the entire process. If one just monetized raw farm products there would not be enough money to move the added value products at the retail level because the production would be monetized at the raw material value not the retail value. To illustrate: if the government created the money, to buy the wheat from the farmers for one dollar per bushel. The farmers would have to spend the money for things they needed for the money to get into general circulation.

This is the time honored way money has been used, to buy and sell. Once the government buys the wheat it becomes the owner of the wheat. The government could sell the wheat to the millers to be made into bread. This is where the problems start. If the government sold the wheat to the millers at the same price it paid the farmers, one dollar a bushel the millers would have to obtain most all the money in the system (from the people who received it from the farmers who spent) to pay the government for the wheat minus the spoilage. Realistically this could never happen.

After the mill operator buys the wheat from the government he will add value to the wheat by processing it into loaves of bread. Let say 20 loaves of bread to a bushel of wheat. He sells a loaf of bread for ten cents. The money supply would have to double before the bread could be moved to the consumer. However, at this point in time there would be no money in circulation, not twice as would be needed to move the bread to the consumer. Because the money would all have had to go back to the government before the wheat could move to the miller, clearly an unworkable system.

If the government loaned the farmers the money, with the wheat being the collateral for the loan the farmer would have to spend the money before any one else would have the money to buy the wheat. If interest was charged on the loan, the interest on the loan would make the farmers debt to the government would grow, but it would not make the money supply grow. Soon the farmers would be in bankruptcy. As before there would not be enough money in circulation to enable all the value added in making of the bread to be bought by the consumers. This illustration points out that when production is monetized at the raw resource level there is no way to create the money needed to sell product at retail prices. For a monetary system to work production must be monetized at the retail level.

There are only two ways to monetize anything. One way is to take the physical thing you want to monetize and process it in such a way that it can be printed into bills or stamped into coins that are declared money by the law of the land or common agreement. (If the law is not the common agreement of the people, then honest informed juries should not uphold it.)

For this illustration we will use wheat. To monetize the wheat, one would have to process the wheat in a way that it could pass from hand to hand as the circulating medium-of-exchange. If all the wheat was monetized in this manner, there would be no wheat available to be used for food. The other way to monetize the wheat would be to make a token of some kind (a bill or a coin or an accounting system) that represented the value of the wheat. That was the principle of gold, silver and tobacco certificates. One can use that principle on anything.

That is what we now do with paper money and our coins. We call it paper money, but it is not made out of paper. Our paper money is made out of cotton and linen that is processed in a way that enables it to be used in the printing process. However it doesn't monetize cotton or any other fiber. It only monetizes debt. The most important thing is that money must represent wealth and be spent or traded into circulation, not loaned.

This could easily be accomplished by having the people create their own money working collectively through the government that they created to serve their needs. Governments only propose should be to do collectively the things that are very hard to do individually such as creating money and building and upgrading the nations' transportation systems. The United States Constitution gave the federal government the power and authority to create the nation's money and to build post offices and post roads. That is what federal government should do. The government should combine the two by creating the money and spending it into circulation to build and upgrade the transportation systems. It is a money system that would work for every nation on the face of the earth. Roads are one of the few things that government should build and hold in trust for the people to use. Government for the most part does that now. If done correctly, this could be done free of taxes, tolls and fees and at the same time provide the people with a debt free medium-of-exchange. If this was done correctly it would take the cost of interest and most taxes out of the cost of doing business. The cost of living would go down and the standard of living would go up for most people.

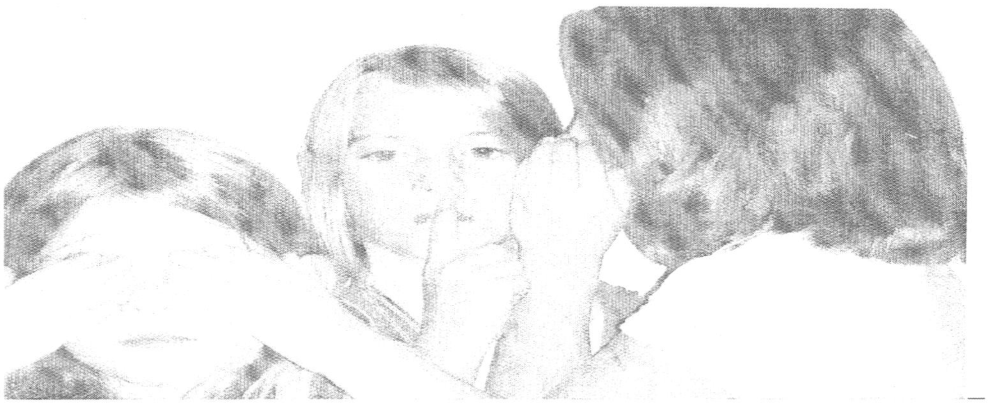

Modern Money Secrets hiding in plain sight:

You cannot pay off debt through inflation with cheaper dollars, as those dollars are also borrowed dollars.

Chapter 13
A Summary

Twenty-seven years ago I began to sense that something was wrong. I began to ponder why when most people work most of their lives producing wealth, and providing for their families and on the surface, it looked like most of them were succeeding. Yet when one looked a little deeper, it was clear that collectively the people were getting deeper into debt with each passing year. How could it be that collectively each year the people produce more wealth, yet at the same time these same people are collectively getting deeper into debt? The more I thought on this troubling phenomenon, the more I came to realize that the answers could only be found by examining just how our monetary system works.

I started researching with these questions in mind. How is our money created and how is it moved into circulation? To get answers, I wrote letters to the U.S. treasury and others. The answer received from Russell L. Munk, assistant general counsel for the United States Treasury, was: *"the actual creation of money always involves the extension of credit from private commercial banks."* This means interest-bearing loans. Mr. Munk then went on to say, *"You may want to know whether the bank is the one getting the benefit of the new money, since the bank owns the new money while the customer has merely borrowed the money. The bank does indeed get the benefit of the new money".* The banking system creates all the money and only lets the people use it when they borrow and pay interest on it. **Money is only created when someone goes to the banking system and gets an interest-bearing loan.**

My next question was, *"If all money is created as interest-bearing loans, how is the money created to pay interest on the loans?"*

The answer received from Mr. Munk was, *"The money to pay the interest on loans comes from the same source as all other money."* In other words, it also has to be borrowed from a commercial bank. John M. Yetter, answering for the United States Treasury, stated in his answer: *"The money that one borrower uses to pay interest on a loan has been created somewhere else in the economy by another loan".* John B Henderson, Senior Specialist in Price Economics Congressional Research Service, the Library of Congress stated: *"Money is created when loans are issued and debts incurred, money is extinguished when loans are repaid".*

"If all the bank loans were paid, no one would have a bank deposit and there would not be a dollar of coin or currency in circulation". Robert H. Hemphill, credit manager of the Federal Reserve in Atlanta

My next question was, *"Just what kind of credit do banks extend to us?"* I found the answer to that question in the Third Edition of the Federal Reserve System Purposes and Functions, page 6. *"All bank deposits are a form of credit. Basically, they represent amounts owed by banks to depositors. They come into existence by an exchange of bank promises to pay customers for the various assets which banks acquire—currency, promissory notes of business, consumer and other customers, mortgages on real estate, and Government and other securities."*

Black's Law Dictionary defines credit as: *"Time allowed to the buyer of goods by the seller, in which to make payment for them".* In other words, consent is given from one person to a second person to obtain goods from the first person and pay for them at a later time. <u>The banks however, don't part with any goods or anything physical.</u> How can the bank give the borrower the right not to pay the producer of goods for the goods?

Credit is also defined in Black's Law Dictionary as: "*an entry on the right hand side of an account".* This is in fact what banks do; they pay the seller of the goods with their promise to pay and record it in their book as a loan to the credit card holder, and call it checkbook money. The loan to the credit card holder goes on the books as an asset to the banks. The credit card holder pays the bank for the goods plus interest, if not paid within thirty days. The seller of the goods must also pay the bank a fee for allowing the customer to pay the bank instead of the seller of the goods. The seller of the goods can use the bank's promise to pay (also called check-book money) to buy anything he wants, including coins or paper currency. If only a few people try to do it at the same time. *"When individuals or businesses want currency or coins to spend, they write a check, exchanging one form of money (checkbook money) for another (cash) both are a liability of a bank."* Source Department of the Treasury Office of Public Correspondence Fact sheet OPC-5. One really needs to ask, *"just how can a promise to pay ever become **the payment.**"*

When someone exchanges the checkbook money for the currency, the liability of a commercial bank is in effect shifted to a Federal Reserve Bank, as Federal Reserve Notes move into circulation. If one individual or business writes a check to another individual or business, the bank's liability just shifts to the other individual or business.

The currency is a liability of the issuing Federal Reserve banks and an obligation of the government (what they owe to the people). Source personal letter from M. M. Schneider Acting Executive Assistant Bureau of Engraving and Printing. The net effect is that the banking system creates and loans a promise to pay to the government and receives an interest profit for itself. The government then uses its power to tax the people to guarantee the bank's promise to pay. The government receives nothing except what it first takes from the people. So the government's guarantee of the currency is based on a mortgage on all homes and other property of all the people in the nation. This fact is well articulated in the Congressional Record, March 9, 1933 on H. R. 1491, pg. 83 talking about the Federal Reserve Act: *"Under the new law, the money is issued to the banks in return for government obligations, bills of exchange, drafts, notes, trade acceptances, and bankers' acceptances. The money will be worth 100 cents on the dollar because it is backed by the credit of the nation. It will represent a mortgage on all homes and other property of all the people in the nation."*

The banking system therefore gets the benefit of a fraudulent system where the banks create our currency as a promise to pay. The people must borrow the bank's promise to pay and pay interest to have a medium-of-exchange. The banks owe, the government owes, and the people owe and **nothing** was loaned to anyone. Yet the banks can go to the courts and force the people to give up all their real physical property to pay the loan that was never made. The debt is one of deception, just a trick played on the minds of the people. The net long-term effect is that the people doing the work (the producers) lose their rights to gain the full benefit of their production. The men running the banking system and the corporations that grow up around it gain control over everything.

You need to really think about the above statements. When you go to a bank to get a loan, you must sign a promissory note promising to pay back to the bank the amount you are borrowing plus the interest on that amount. To fund your loan, the bank simply puts numbers into a checking account (a deposit), representing the amount that the bank *owes* you (the banks promise to pay), an amount that the banking system will not pay. I hope the only reason this fraud is allowed is because the people simply do not understand what is happening.

If you can't repay the loan plus the accrued interest, the bank can take your home, your cars, your business and anything else it can get its hands on. You must never forget the fact that the money needed to pay the interest is never created. You can't pay the accrued interest, in money form, unless and until someone else goes into debt and you have done something to transfer the number in their checking to your checking account. This leaves the other person with the interest-bearing debt but not the money.

Think about the legacy of all the debt our parents have left to us and about how much more debt and misery (loss of purchasing power, more taxes, a lower standard of living or suffer living through a total money collapse) we are going to leave to our children, if we don't wake up and demand that the monetary system be changed and it must be changed that all new money be put in circulation be free of debt.

Until we wake up and change our money system to a system where all

money is spent or exchanged into circulation debt-free, **each generation must go deeper into debt than the generation before it if the system is to keep functioning, or they must suffer a monetary collapse**. If we simply open our eyes and our minds, we can see all around us the consequences of this debt money system. Lou Dobbs talks a lot about *the consequences* of the debt money system on his show on CNN. He calls it the war on the middle class. Even David Walker, Comptroller General of the United States, is starting to talk about the consequences of a debt money system. He, like Lou Dobbs, simply do not seem to understand the real root of the problems they so clearly see, or for what ever reason they have chosen not to talk about it.

Under this system, without debt, we have no dollars. If you have money in your pocket, in a checking account or in a savings account, that money could not possibly exist unless someone, either individually or collectively, has an equal amount of debt.

We need to really start thinking about the consequences of all this **fraudulent** debt we are leaving for our children. We don't have much time left. At the rate at which our total debt is growing, it will not be long before the total interest bill will be greater than the total income of the American people. The following chart shows the cost of servicing just the interest on the debt is increasing much faster than family income (wages).

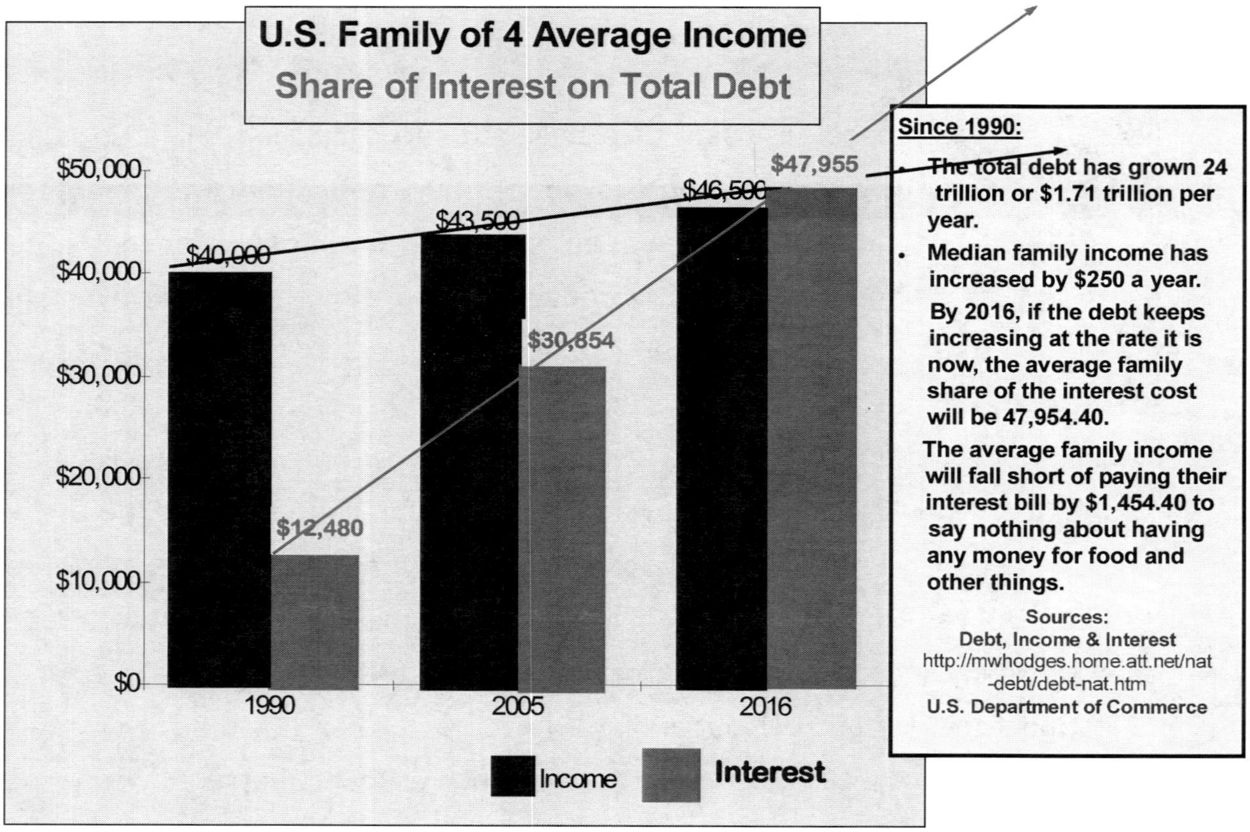

Rob Grunnewald of the Federal Reserve Bank of Minneapolis has confirmed that the figures of this chart seem to be accurate.

The Grandfather Economic Report found at http://mwhodges.home.att.net/nat-debt/debt-nat.htm, was endorsed by Dr. Milton Friedman when he stated, *"I certainly commend you for the Grandfather Report".* It has also been endorsed by Gerald P. Dwyer, Vice Present of the Federal Reserve Bank of Atlanta.

According to this report, the total debt, in 1990, was $13 trillion. This includes the household (consumer) debt, the business debt and the federal, state and local government debt. This doesn't include the huge unfunded government liabilities that David Walker talks about. This amounts to $52,000 per person or $208,000 for a family of four. That family's share of servicing the interest load on that debt at 6% would have been $12,480 per year. In 1990, the median family's income was $40,000.

In 2004, America's total debt was $37 trillion or $128,560 for every man woman and child. This comes to $514,240 for a family of four. A family's share of servicing the interest load on this debt at 6 percent would be $30,854.40 per year. According the U.S. Dept. of Commerce the median family income was $43,500.

The total debt has grown $24 trillion, or $1.71 trillion per year since 1990. The additional interest load has grown by $102,600 billion a year since 1990. This means that the interest load for a family of four has increased by an average of $1,425 a year since 1990. If the debt keeps increasing at the same rate, by 2016 the median family's share of servicing the interest cost will be $47,954.40.

The median family income has increased by $250 a year since 1990. If their income increases at the same rate their annual income, by 2016 will be $46,500. This means the Median family's income will fall short of paying their share of the interest bill by $1,454.40 to say nothing about having any money for food and other things.

In 2006, America's total debt was $44 trillion dollars, or $147,312 per man woman and child. This comes to $589,248 for a family of four. The family's share of servicing the interest load on this debt, at 6 percent, would be $35,355 per year. The total debt has grown $31trillion, or $1.94 trillion per year since 1990. The additional interest load has grown by $116.4 billion a year since 1990. This means that the interest load for a family of four has increased by an average of $1,560 a year since 1990. It is clear that the debt is growing faster with each passing year.

It has become very clear that collectively, as a nation, we can't borrow our way to prosperity. In 2008, the total collective debt is over $53 trillion. The debt is now growing at over four trillion, not just the 1.7 trillion a year that the chart was based on.

As you have just read, the answer to why we have all this unpayable debt is that under our present monetary system, to have money, **we must have** interest-bearing debt.

The growing spread between wages paid and the prices of raw materials and price charged for most retail sales is why more members of families must work more jobs and longer hours to try to maintain the same standard of living.

This is why you see large companies moving their production lines to countries where laborers are paid less. This leads to trades deficits where more money flows out of the country to buy imports than flows back to buy exports. This causes the loss of most of our factories and our ability to produce the thing we need and want in our own country.

America has lost most of its production base to outsourcing and off-shoring. Those jobs have been replaced with lower paying jobs in the service sector. Illegal immigrants who will work for less are taking many of these jobs. The more you cut wages, the harder it is for the wage earners to buy the things they need and want without borrowing more.

The more raw resource prices are held down, the harder it is for the raw resource producers like the farmers, ranchers, lumberjacks and miners to make ends meet. They are forced into more debt or forced out of business. All this leads to excess debt and a shortage of money for nearly everyone until finally the interest load becomes greater than the total income of the nation. Interest on large debts, high taxes and low wages slowly kills the retail market, the housing market and other markets. There is less money after paying taxes and interest for the consumer to use for purchases. We are on a spiral stairway to national destruction unless we start putting all new money into circulation debt-free.

As John Maynard Keynes said; *"There is no subtler, no surer means of overturning the existing basis of society than to DEBAUCH the currency. The process engages all the hidden forces of economic law on the side of destruction, and does it in a manner which only one man in a million is able to diagnose."* The only way to DEBAUCH money is to change it from a representation of wealth to an evidence of debt!

The only way to stop this headlong rush to destruction by debt is to reform our money system so our money is a representation of the wealth the people produce and not an evidence of debt! Creating the money and spending it into circulation in lieu of taxation or borrowing to rebuild the nation's transportation system could easily do this.

The United States Congress has failed to properly serve the people they were elected to represent, serve and whose rights they swore to protect! Instead they have followed Hamilton's lead and served the bankers and their system. Congress has failed to "monetize" the people's production as an asset to the producers instead Congress has aided the **bankers in monetizing the people's production as assets to the banking system and unpayable interest-bearing debts to the people!**

For the people to get their production monetized, they now must sign promissory notes payable to the banking system secured by mortgages. The bank then enters numbers in a checking account saying *"you have a deposit with us."* They then draw interest as unearned profit from the producers. **The people have been forced to incur interest-bearing debt in order to have a medium-of-exchange to enhance buying and selling**!

The debt may be owed directly to the bank by personal loans or indirectly to the bank through school, county, city, state and federal governments' debt. Loans to local, state and the federal government help to mask the effects of the growing debt because people do not feel the interest pinch in their personal lives. Most of the people who receive money that local, state and federal governments have borrowed and spent don't perceive it as debt because they get to capture that money without increasing their personal debt. This leads them to believe that all money is not created as debt, because some have money and they don't have any debt. This is akin to saying that it can't be true that bananas are grown on trees; because I have bananas and I don't have any banana trees.

Just because most of people have not understood how our money was changed from a representation of wealth to a representation of debt does not change the fact that all new money is created as interest-bearing loans. It doesn't change the fact that when all new money is loaned into circulation accruing interest, the interest is unpayable in money because only the principal of a loan can be put into circulation. There is no procedure to create the money required to repay the loan principal plus the accrued interest! The money needed to pay the interest can only be acquired by shifting the debt to someone else, that someone maybe a government body, a business or another person.

Every loan would end in default if each loan had to stand on its own. However, in the world of commerce, loans simply don't stand alone, everyday millions of borrowers engage in commerce. Money is constantly moving from borrowers to non-borrowers and back again to borrowers. Many borrowers, like governmental bodies never really attempt to pay down their debts. They just tax enough to pay the interest and then borrow more. If that was not true, their total indebtedness would not constantly grow. The profit that people believe they have earned simply comes from someone else's borrowed principal. Therefore, the ever growing interest costs and taxes keep driving the cost of living higher and higher, finally destroying our prosperity and liberty.

I have had people tell me that fractional banking is a good thing, that we could not have a money system without a banking system that creates money. There is no other way we could have the money to go to stores and buy all the food and goods we want. There is no other way that we could acquire the money to buy a home, a car or build a business if we couldn't borrow. On the surface there is no question that it looks like the money system is working. The people can get quicker and easier loans. More capital is available to engage in commerce. We have used it for years, why change it?

These people refuse to look at the effects of the interest. The interest on money always drives up cost of doing business until most people will not be able to make their loan payments. A largely unseen by-product of the fractional banking system is that it makes some people very rich and leaves most people poor. *"Almost all the benefits of economic growth since [the 1970s] have gone to a small number of people at the very top."* Robert Reich, Financial Times Jan, 29, 2008. *"Since the mid – 1970s, however, income growth has been confined almost entirely to the top earners."* Robert H. Frank NY Times, March 9, 2008. "*The modern American economy distributes the fruits of its growth to a relatively narrow slice of the population."* David Leonhardt, NY Times, April 9, 2008. This leaves most people living from paycheck to paycheck or living on government assistance. As long as fractional banking continues, it will create compounding unpayable public and private debt.

There is no question that the Federal Reserve System is a fraud. It is an indisputable fact that our money system is based on debt and that it arose from and functions using fraudulent practices. In times past it appeared on its face to be working. However, now in 2008, with all the bailouts and the Federal Reserve having to create new entities like the Commercial Paper Funding Facility (CPFF), the Asset Backed Commercial Paper Money Market Mutual Fund Liquidity Facility (AMLF), and the Money Market Investor Funding Facility (MMIFF) to purchase billions of dollars of short-term debt from money market mutual funds to shore up a key pillar of the US financial system. It is clear the system has not been working. The AMLF, CPFF and MMIFF are all intended to improve liquidity in short-term debt markets and thereby increase the availability of credit. Source Financial Times

Credit is debt. Our financial crises started because people already had so much debt they couldn't make their house payments. How can more debt be the answer? One only has to pay a little attention and then look under the surface and examine our bank controlled money system more closely to clearly see that it is not working as a good general medium-of- exchange for all the people.

Let's look at the average person's return on labor. By that I mean how many hours the average person must labor to buy universally needed household items. My close friend and co-author, Greg Soderberg, works in sales for a radio

station. One day in 1993, he was at Martz Furniture in Leroy, Minnesota and happened to see an old furniture store sales flyer. According to the original store ledger, in 1870, Martz Furniture sold a new wooden chair for thirty 30 cents. *"WOW".* Greg exclaimed. *"Look at that!" A new wooden kitchen chair like that would cost $100.00 dollars today!"* The store manager responded, *"Yes, but we earn a lot more money per hour now than they did back then."*

On the way back to the radio station Greg thought about what the store manager said. On the surface, the manager's comment seemed to make sense.

The people earned less for their labor, so things should have cost less. Today, they earn more for their labor, so it is not so bad that things cost more. Greg is quite a thinker and began to question, in terms of real purchasing power, if we really do get paid more for our labor than we used to. The real consideration is not how much I get paid for an hour of labor, but how many hours I need to work to pay for each purchase.

Greg headed to the library to do some research. From the U.S. Dept. of Commerce Historical Data, he learned, that between 1860-1870, an average laborer earned $1.50 daily or 18.75 cents per hour. Remember then no Income nor social security taxes were taken from the check.

In 1870, it took the average laborer 1.6 hours of labor to purchase a new wooden kitchen chair.

In 1993, the average laborer earned $8.23 an hour. The same kind of wooden chair costs $100.00. The average worker had to work 12.2 hours to purchase the chair, clearly receiving much less purchasing power for his hours of labor. Take the income and social security taxes out of the $8.23, and the worker worked more than the 12.2 hours to purchase the chair.

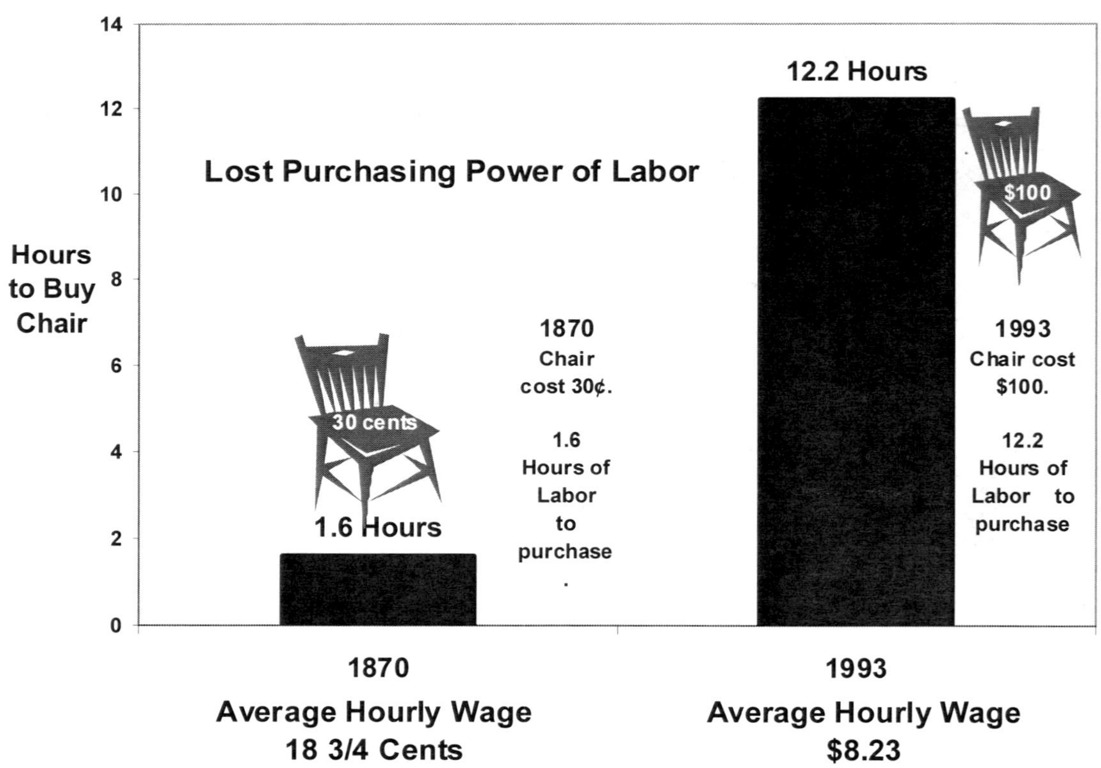

To understand how a person can get paid more dollars and receive less purchasing power for each hour of labor, you must understand the effect of charging interest on the total money supply. When all money is loaned to the people at interest, the money supply is increased but the debt load is also increased. When the debt load is increased, so is the interest expense. When the interest expense is increased, both the cost of doing business and the cost of living increase. When the cost of doing business increases, the price of the finished product must also increase or the cost of raw materials, labor and/or profit must go down.

We must never forget that in a money system where all new money is created and put into circulation as interest-bearing loans, only the principal of each loan can be created and moved into circulation. There is simply no procedure to create the extra money required by this system to pay the interest. **Money does not grow naturally!!** Money can't reproduce itself.

"The money that one borrower uses to pay interest on a loan has been created somewhere else in the economy by another loan."

John M. Yetter, Attorney-advisor Department of the Treasury

This fact can be hidden for a long time if our governments borrow from the banking system and spend that money into the economy. The people in the private sector can acquire that money and use it to engage in commerce without incurring any private debt. But in time, when the money supply is increased by government debt instead of private debt, the government will need to increase taxes to pay its interest! When taxes increase, the cost of the taxes must be added into the selling price of the finished product, or someone must suffer a cut in profits, in living standards or both! This increase in not nearly as noticeable in the early years when the total debt is relatively smaller than it is when the debt money system is nearing the end of its life cycle. All debt money systems will fail in the long term. Most people misstate that truth by stating that all fait or paper money systems will fail. This is not true.

All businesses, except financial institutions, take labor, ideas and some raw resource of the earth and do something to it to add value. Then, they try to sell the value-added product to someone at the value added price. From the added value, they hope to gain enough to pay their operating costs. These costs include interest and taxes. Hopefully they will have enough left over to provide for their cost of living, saving and expansion.

Let's consider a small hamburger stand as an example of what is happening in all businesses. In our hamburger stand, the raw products will be labor, raw hamburger and flour. We combine our labor with flour to make buns, form the raw hamburger into patties, cook them and sell hamburger sandwiches as the finished product. It takes money to engage in business. When all money is created through the lending process, someone will have to borrow to access the money. The owner of the hamburger stand must borrow the first 50 cents to buy the raw hamburger and the flour. The customer comes in and buys the hamburger for a $1.50 with a credit card this increases the money by more borrowing. The total money supply has increased to $2.00.

If the cost of the raw hamburger and flour is 50 cents and the finished hamburgers sells for $1.50, the $1.00 of added value could be used to pay the interest, taxes, other operating costs and the cost of living for the owner of the hamburger stand. When the economy grows and business grows, more money is needed to buy more raw hamburger and flour to make more hamburgers. As the hamburgers are sold, even more money is needed and the money supply must be increased.

An increase in the money supply is called inflation. When the money supply grows, it enables the total economy to grow. Therefore money inflation is a very good and necessary thing. However, when money is increased as interest-bearing debt, an increase in the money supply also increases the interest-bearing debt. As the total debt grows, the total interest bill grows and must be added to the cost of doing business.

To illustrate, let's say the cost of interest forces the cost to the hamburger stand to go up 25 cents per hamburger. If the other costs, profit and standard of living stay the same the increased interest cost must be added to the selling price of the hamburger. This drives the selling price up from $1.50 to $1.75. This price increase requires another increase in the money supply if the same number of hamburgers is going to be sold at the higher price. This leads to price inflation. This is destructive inflation. It is not the constructive monetary inflation that you must have to enable people to have saving and a monetary gain from production of good. This is monetary inflation that has not added to or aided in the production of more goods. It is monetary inflation for the sole function of making one wealthy from a profit of money on money. This is the only inflation that could be called a hidden tax upon the total economy. A tax collected by the banking system, not by the government.

Two things cause government to grow:

1. Lack of money by people who do not get the full monetary benefit of their labor and production. People who can't earn enough by their labor and production turn to government for programs to help them.
2. Colossal greed by a few. The enormously greedy like the big bankers and big corporate executives who demand millions of dollars in salaries and the lobbyists that are paid huge salaries to get people working in government to give their employer a great gain through the government's power to tax.

As government grows taxes increase. Taxes, like interest, are a cost of doing business. When taxes to a business increase, business must pass that cost on to the consumer in the form of higher prices. If they don't, their profit is cut. To illustrate, let's say the tax increase to the Hamburger Stand amounts to 25 cents per hamburger. This tax, just like the interest, cost causes the price of the hamburger to go up. Now we have a $2.00 hamburger. This price increase again requires another increase in the money supply if the same number of hamburgers is going to be sold at the higher price; more price inflation. Taxes transfer money from the producers to the non-producers who work for government. These workers may or may not be needed, but most of them do not add to the production of a nation.

In time, higher prices meet with price resistance. Therefore, businesses look for ways to cut costs. If people can't or won't control their politicians, governments will not cut taxes. Cutting taxes always cuts into someone's paycheck or power base. Politicians talk a lot about the need to cut taxes. But seldom really do cut taxes, without soon raising taxes or fees somewhere else.

Up to this time, not enough people have understood the destructive side effects of creating and putting money into circulation as debt. They have not in large enough groups, demanded a change in the money system. Many changes in our society have come through the court system. Up to this time, the courts have not allowed anyone who has understood the destructive side of our present money system to address the issue. The combination of these facts have made the two greatest and totally unnecessary costs, interest and taxes, of engaging in commerce untouchable, so business must look elsewhere to cut costs.

Profits are the name of the game for corporations. Gaining profit by cutting the price of raw material makes the spread between the prices of raw material and finished goods greater. This makes it harder for the producers of raw material to stay in business. We have already seen thousands of producers of raw materials and small businesses forced out or taken over by bigger companies, who are then taken over by even bigger corporations.

That leaves labor as the only place left to cut. Hardly a month goes by without hearing about some company downsizing, merging, reorganizing or moving overseas, to cut labor costs.

The following companies have announced job cuts since the start of 2009.

Note: Some figures are approximations from percentages of labor force, with total labor force estimations obtained from recent 10K filings.

Company	Number of cuts	Date	Industry
NEC Corp.	20,000	1/30/2009	**Computer Hardware**
Dexia	900	1/30/2009	**Financial**
Chicos	180	1/30/2009	**Retail**
Caterpillar	2,110	1/30/2009	**Manufacturing**
Cessna	2,000	1/29/2009	**Aerospace & Defense**
Bon-Ton Stores	1,150	1/29/2009	**Retail**

Company	Number of cuts	Date	Industry
Charles Schwab	600	1/29/2009	Financial
Walt Disney ABC	200	1/29/2009	Media & Entertainment
Kodak	3,000[7]	1/29/2009	Consumer Products
Oshkosh	1,050	1/29/2009	Automotive
AstraZeneca	6,000	1/29/2009	Health care
Jabil Circuit	3,000	1/28/2009	Manufacturing
Nissan	110	1/28/2009	Automotive
Ford Motor Co. Credit	1,200	1/28/2009	Financial
Allstate Financial	1,000	1/28/2009	Financial
Boeing	5,500	1/28/2009	Aerospace & Defense
AOL	700	1/28/2009	Technology
Abbott	200	1/28/2009	Health care
Dell	unspecified	1/28/2009	Computer Hardware
Starbucks	6,700	1/28/2009	Food & Beverages
Panasonic	650	1/28/2009	Consumer Products
Avery Dennison	3,600	1/27/2009	Chemicals
Best Buy	unspecified	1/27/2009	Retail
Quiksilver	200	1/27/2009	Retail
Corning	4,900[6]	1/27/2009	Materials
Weyerhaeuser	220	1/27/2009	Materials
Baker Hughes	1,500	1/27/2009	Energy
Navistar International	700	1/27/2009	Automotive
Target	unspecified	1/27/2009	Retail
Volvo	650	1/27/2009	Automotive
ING Group	7,000	1/26/2009	Financial
John Deere	700	1/26/2009	Manufacturing
Sprint Nextel	8,000	1/26/2009	Telecommunications
Home Depot	7,000	1/26/2009	Retail
Caterpillar	20,000	1/26/2009	Manufacturing
Pfizer	20,000[3]	1/26/2009	Health care
Corus Group	3,500	1/26/2009	Metals
Texas Instrument	3,400	1/26/2009	Computer Hardware
Harley-Davidson	1,100	1/23/2009	Automotive
Polaris Industries	460	1/23/2009	Automotive

Company	Number of cuts	Date	Industry
American Greetings	200	1/23/2009	**Consumer Products**
Compass Bank	1,200	1/23/2009	**Financial**
Schlumberger	5,000	1/23/2009	**Energy**
Microsoft	5,000	1/22/2009	**Computer Software**
Hunstman Corporation	1,175	1/22/2009	**Chemicals**
Ericsson	5,000	1/21/2009	**Telecommunications**
BHP Billiton	6,000	1/21/2009	**Metals**
Clear Channel Communications	1,850	1/21/2009	**Media & Entertainment**
Eaton	5,200	1/21/2009	**Automotive**
UAL Corp	1,000	1/21/2009	**Transportation**
Intel	6,000[4]	1/21/2009	**Computer Hardware**
GM	339[5]	1/21/2009	**Automotive**
Williams-Sonoma	1,400	1/21/2009	**Retail**
Rohm and Haas	900	1/20/2009	**Chemicals**
Warner Bros.	800	1/20/2009	**Media & Entertainment**
Honda	3,100	1/16/2009	**Automotive**
WellPoint	1,500	1/16/2009	**Health care**
Circuit City	30,000	1/16/2009	**Retail**
Hertz	4,000	1/16/2009	**Transportation**
Blue Cross Blue Shield of Michigan	1,000	1/16/2009	**Health care**
Advanced Micro Devices	1,100	1/16/2009	**Computer Hardware**
ConocoPhillips	1,300	1/16/2009	**Energy**
Google	100	1/15/2009	**Technology**
Autodesk	750	1/15/2009	**Technology**
MeadWestvaco Corporation	2,000	1/15/2009	**Materials**
Saks Fifth Avenue	1,100	1/15/2009	**Retail**
Barclay's	2,100	1/14/2009	**Financial**
Cummins	800	1/14/2009	**Manufacturing**
Motorola	4,000	1/14/2009	**Telecommunications**
Barnes and Noble	100	1/14/2009	**Retail**
Pfizer	700	1/13/2009	**Health care**
ING Group	950	1/13/2009	**Financial**
Neiman Marcus Group	375	1/13/2009	**Retail**
World Wrestling Entertainment	60[2]	1/9/2009	**Media & Entertainment**

Company	Number of cuts	Date	Industry
Boeing	4,500	1/9/2009	Aerospace & Defense
Cessna	2,000	1/9/2009	Aerospace & Defense
Dell	1,900	1/8/2009	Computer Hardware
TDK Corp.	8,000	1/8/2009	Materials
Walgreens	1,000	1/8/2009	Retail
Haliburton	unspecified	1/8/2009	Aerospace & Defense
Schlumberger	1,000	1/8/2009	Energy
EMC Corp.	2,400	1/7/2009	Computer Hardware
Ethan Allen	350	1/7/2009	Retail
New York & Co.	350	1/7/2009	Retail
Macy's	900	1/7/2009	Retail
Logitech	500[1]	1/6/2009	Computer Hardware
Alcoa	13,500	1/6/2009	Metals & Mining
Cigna	1,100	1/5/2009	Health care

As of February 6, 2009 more than 600,000 people were unemployed in America.

In a debt money system, economic and social power and control will constantly flow to fewer and fewer people until there is only one lender. The result is that it takes more and more hours for the average worker to buy the necessities. The hours in a day are limited! Now it takes two 'income-earners' in most families to have a decent standard of living and it's getting tougher all the time.

Economists never address the effects the cost of interest has on prices. Economists never address the fact that all this debt to the banking system is forced debt. It is forced debt because when the financial system has a monopoly on the creation of money there is no other way to create and put other money into circulation. Economists never address the fact that all this interest on the debt is unpayable in money. Economists always address the debt as simply people wanting to spend future income now instead of waiting till the income has been earned.

It seems strange that when the price of many things like gas, stocks and housing go up in price it is not called inflation. It seems that only when the cost of wages goes up that economists get excited about price inflation. Price inflation comes, they tell us, because *"there is too much money chasing too few goods".* However from my personal observations, there are a lot more goods in the economy than there is money to buy them. If that is not true, why are there so many stores advertising their goods for sale with no money down and no interest for one year or more? It appears they know they are trying to sell to people that don't have enough money.

When was the last time you went into a store and tried to pay the store clerk more for the goods or services than the stated selling price because you just had too much money?

When was the last time you didn't take a trip or didn't buy something because you simply had too much money?

When was the last time you knew of someone who didn't make their house payment because they just had too much money?

There never can be too much money chasing too few goods if the production of money is based on the production of goods. The only way to have too much money chasing too few goods is when money is loaned into circulation on the promise of future production which may or may not get produced. Even then the real problem is too much debt, not too much money.

The 1978 Eighth Edition of Money: master or servant published by the Federal Reserve Bank of New York states: *"If the flow of money payment increased when we couldn't increase the flow of goods and services, we would see symptoms of inflation – but if the flow of money payments didn't keep pace with production and distribution, we would see symptoms of recession"... Only when changes in money encourage or enable greater production and consumption can money be an effective economic servant ... creating additional money can only raise prices, unless we increase production."* The language here is not too clear but what it says in layman words are, "*creating additional money can only raise prices if there is no increase in production." ... "We've seen that money's principal job is helping provide a smooth flow of goods and services from production to consumption." ... "the flow of money payments should be balanced with the flow of goods and services."*

According to what the Federal Reserve Bank of New York said above the 700 plus billion dollar bailout should be the most inflationary thing the banking system could do.

Economists also tell us that inflation is a general price increase. However, what we see is not a general price increase but a growing S P R E A D between the price paid for the raw materials and labor and the price demanded for the finished products. This spread will continue to grow as long as we suffer under a debt based money system or until the weight of the interest load causes the monetary system to break down. That may be what we are seeing in 2008. As I write this book I heard on the news that millions of Americans now owe more on their houses than the house is worth. Governments will also continue to grow in size and become more socialistic as long as we have a debt-based money system. In time, all private ownership and most freedom will be lost.

On Wednesday, August 4, 1999, President Clinton stated *"smaller debts bring less interest costs"*. This is true. So clearly the answer to lower costs and lower taxes for everyone is to monetize wealth instead of interest-bearing debt.

My hope is that by this time you agree with me that it is time for all Americans to ask, how did we collectively get over 53 trillion dollars in debt when all we do is produce wealth? We must demand that our governments be limited to their only true function. That function is to secure to the people their rights to Life, Liberty, the Pursuit of Happiness, the right to own property including owning their own money free of debt.

This cannot and will not happen unless we have monetary reform. Money is the power that drives all things; the oil that keeps all things running. If the money system is based on a false, corrupt and unsound foundation that benefits only a few, then most will suffer. If the money system is based on a sound, moral, honest foundation everyone will benefit.

The only sound, moral, honest foundation on which a money system can rest upon is when the people's production is monetized as wealth to the producer without debt or interest*!*

Many people agree on the need for money reform. Unfortunately, most people seem only able to think about what is used for money and whether the government or a private entity should issue the money. What they should think about is what money represents and how the money is moved into circulation and how that affects our lives? A money system can exist without a banking system, but a banking system cannot exist without a monetary system. The Bible says, In the beginning God applied energy and created everything and saw that it was good. God did all this and incurred no debt. That is the principle we need to apply to the total economic system.

Everything we need exists. It comes from the earth and the sun. When we apply our physical and mental energies to these natural resources, we can and do create all kinds of things to better serve our needs and wants. We can also recycle old products to create new products that better serve our needs. There is no debt in this process. Debt only comes when we foolishly monetize the wealth we produce as debt to ourselves.

Before there was a banking system, people had the ability to work, produce and exchange things among themselves. No debt is required to make trades of goods and services. The concept of money arose from the desire to make the process of trading goods and services easier and more efficient. The concept of money did not arise because people wanted or needed to be in debt. Our present banking system arose from the desire of a few to gain great benefits without working and producing anything. Now if we use money to engage in buying, selling and trading, someone must be in debt to the banking system allowing the banking system to get a huge benefit without any production. The banking system cannot get those benefits until a producer loses most of the benefit of his production.

If someone is allowed to write bad checks, he gets everything for free. That is what we are allowing the banks to do when we allow them to create the money as a promise to pay knowing that they have nothing to pay their promise with.

Economists have told me that creating money as a promise to pay is the only kind of money system that will work and that creating money as a payment for work performed, simply cannot be done and will not work, it would create uncontrollable inflation. **What utter nonsense that is.**

The truth is that creating money as loans (based on a promise to pay by the lender and a promise to perform in the future) is the only way that the money supply can increase without increasing the goods. It is a money system that will always fail. If money is created based on the production of wealth at the retail level, there would be no monetary inflation. It is the only money system that is sustainable.

Freedom, justice, fairness and liberty demand that the money system functions independently of the banking system. These principles would make Americans economically free. There can be no real freedom without economic freedom.

It should be clear to any thinking person that if the founding fathers had believed that the government could just create money, there would have been no reason to give congress the power to borrow. If government could create money without any production there would be no need to borrow or any reason for anyone to work. There also would be nothing to buy.

Don't confuse creating money with monetizing production. That is what you do when you monetize gold and/or silver. However, there is a better way to do it than using gold and/silver.

Ask yourself, if Americans worked under the principles of free coinage set forth in the 1792 Coinage Act, did they get the money before the metal bullion was dug out of the ground or before the metal was stamped into money? No of course not! The idea of doing the work before one is paid is a principle that most everyone believes in, except when they go to the bank for a loan. Then they forget the principle of work before receiving money.

The Constitution of the United States says, *"We, the People of the United States, in Order to form a more perfect Union, establish Justice, insure domestic Tranquility, and to provide for ourselves and our Posterity, do ordain and establish this Constitution for the United States of America."* Do you really believe that we can have any of the above when we all owe our souls to the company store (the banking system)? **The answer is clearly NO!**

There can be no liberty when we are slaves to anything, including debt. There can be no liberty when a person must get permission from the government before they can earn an honest living. There can be no liberty when a man must have a license from anyone for every occupation in which he wants to engage to earn an honest living.

Modern Money Secrets hiding in plain sight

Bankers own all the money all the time. The public simply borrows it and pays interest to use it.

Chapter 14

Where do we go from here?

Let's begin with solutions that other people who write about 'the money problem' have proposed and why, in my opinion, they would not address the underlying problems of the current debt-credit based monetary system.

Go to gold-backed currency?

People who support this concept don't see that there is **no** difference between a gold-backed currency loaned to you and non gold-backed currency loaned to you. Either way society must be in debt to have money in circulation. The facts are that we have never had a gold-backed currency in America. Even before the Constitution was adopted, we had bank issued money. The first principle of bank issued money is to loan many times more of face value currency than there is gold (or anything else) to back it. This in and of it self, would create a shortage of gold. Soon after the goldsmiths turned into bankers by starting fractional reserve lending, the banker soon gained control or owned most of the gold and thereby control over the money system through the mathematics of interest. Gold-backed currency proponents also refuse to address the fact that there has never been enough gold to work as a total general medium-of-exchange.

Reintroduce gold and/or silver as the money?

There are people who say they would like to reintroduce gold and/or silver coins as money with the free coinage of gold and silver. This would be a good concept if one was starting a new nation with many producing gold and silver mines. The principles of free coinage are good as they are the principles of monetizing production.

However, when asked where would the gold and silver would come from and how much gold and silver would be needed, they don't seem to have reasonable answers. Some writers say that there can be no shortage of gold or silver money as any amount of money will always serve all needs of society. They only think in terms of the value of money, they do not consider the volume of money. The following illustration proves that kind of thinking is flawed. If the total number of cows in the world was 25, and the total number of people was 25 each person could have a cow. If the total number of cows in the world was 25, and the total number of people was 100, it would be impossible for each person to own one cow. The value of the cows would have nothing to do with the volume of cows. The same principles apply to gold and silver. If whatever is used for money is so limited it would be impossible for most people to hold any of it; it cannot serve as a general medium of exchange.

A point that is never discussed by people who want to go back to gold and silver coins is how would we keep the gold and silver coins in this country? With the huge trade deficit that we have now it would only be a few years before the gold and silver would all leave the country.

Another point about silver or gold coins that people never talk about is that there is a constant wearing down of circulating gold and silver coins. If gold coins were circulating as the only money, the coins would become lighter with each passing year. At some time, the coins would need to be melted and re-coined back to full weight. Sooner or later, someone will need to have three worn coins melted down and re-coined into two full weight coins or melted down and have newly mined gold added to the coins to bring them back up to full weight. Who is going to have to take that loss, the holder of the coins or the government? No one should have to suffer loss for simply taking the coin.

Some of these people suggest that we use gold and silver coins along with fractional banking and let the people decide which kind of money they wanted to use. That could be done but history proves that when that is done, a secondary market for the metals develops because it allows people to buy and sell silver and gold without using silver or gold coins as payment.

The price of silver and gold in the coin can now vary from the face value of the coins. The coins could be melted down and bought and sold as bullion. The metals can be used to make jewelry or other things that can be sold for a higher price in bank created money, than in the face value of the coined money. The gold and silver could be hoarded and taken out of general circulation thereby forcing the people to use the other kind of money. To keep your savings in gold and silver might not be a bad thing to do as a sound saving plan but that could be called hoarding and it too would take money out of circulation and force others to use something else as money.

If we implemented gold and silver coinage and allowed the banks to retain their loans, they could simply call in their loans and take all the coinage from the people as payment on the loans. The people, still needing a medium-of-exchange (money) would have to go to the banks and borrow the coins back. The banks would still control the money supply as interest bearing loans. That is truly what the problem is, it is not that we don't use gold and silver for our money.

Reintroducing gold and/or silver as money would not provide the people with many real benefits. It would not reduce the tax load. It would not reduce the interest drag on society. Nothing would change.

There are some who advocates that we re-monetize gold and silver by having the government buy up all the gold and silver with government obligations (debt) and then mint the gold and silver into lawful money coins. The government would then pay off their obligations with the newly minted coins. That would put the coins into circulation. We would still have to face all the problems of how to deal with the debts we already have plus the trade deficit that we have.

If we did re-monetize silver and gold, people with no gold or silver would have no money. If the people who had excess gold and silver were permitted to loan it, at interest, to the people who did have gold and silver those people would still have interest-bearing debts with a very small chance of paying it back, nothing much would have changed. If the average person used their silver and gold coins as their medium of exchange while the very rich lent theirs out at interest, it would only take around 25 years until the very rich would gain the ownership of all the coins through though the math of compound interest. For an example: If one loaned 10% of the total money supply of $7,700,000,000,000 @ 10% = $770,000,000,000 compounded once a year for 25 years, earnings due the lender would be $8,342,000,000,000.

In 1995, Murray N. Rothbard stated that a return to the gold standard would require gold valued at near $7,500 an ounce. Common sense tells us that gold valued at $7,500 an ounce could not be coined into coins that could circulate as money. At $7,500 an ounce, gold would be $15.63 per grain. At that value, one could not coin a gold dollar. It would be so small it could not be seen. Take a dime from your pocket. It weighs 35 grains. The $15.63 per grain gold coin would be 35 times smaller than the dime in your hand. A coin the size of a dime would be worth $547.00. The most that could be done would be to have coins made of less valuable metals with a speck of gold in the coin or have a paper representation of the gold. If you are going to do that, there is no reason to fool around with the gold.

I was talking with a college economics teacher about money. A few minutes into the conversation, he looked at me and asked, *"Are you one of those gold nuts? You gold nuts would starve all of us to death."* I answered, "*No, book entry money is fine with me. It's that I don't like high taxes and huge debts."* His reply was, *"Oh, then you must be okay".* We ended up having quite a lengthy discussion about the flaws of our present monetary system and ways to correct them.

If we went to only gold and silver coins and the supply of the metals were not large enough for all of the people to have some money, we would still have a money disaster.

Go to interest free loans?

Others propose that congress should create the money and put the money into circulation as loans, but not charge interest. That would slow the growth of the debts. It would not provide a way to pay off any of the already huge existing debt and still have money in circulation. Interest free loans are only a different version of debt money. Under any version of a debt money system, when a loan is repaid the money is destroyed. Someone would still have to borrow and have debt for a medium- of-exchange to exist. The interest on the already huge existing debt would keep on growing. This holds true if we used United States notes.

Just cancel all the debt

This proposal never seems to consider that to write off all the debts, would also wipe out most people's assets or jobs because they are tied to somebody else's debts. Everyone recognizes debt when it's owed personally. However, few people realize that most of the financial assets that they worked so hard to accumulate are actually the debts of someone else (person, business or government). Stocks, bonds, currency, social security, all bank deposits, (checking and saving accounts) notes, mortgages on land and buildings, and accounts payable are all **debts or claims against the income and assets of someone else (person or business).** Canceling all debts would wipe out all checking and saving accounts, social security, pensions, retirement funds, the stock and bond industry, all insurance companies, etc. Most people I know would like to get rid of their debts. I don't know anyone who wants to lose all their assets. It's important to realize that, in a debt-money system, when the liability is destroyed, so is an asset. Accountants tell me that under our current system everything must be put on the books as both a liability and an asset.

Writing off all the debts would leave most of the older people now living on invested funds, pensions, and social security or government programs out in the streets with nothing. This is what makes all 'debt repudiation' a very undesirable option as a solution. Even if we would just wipe all debt off the books, (we might be able to do that if we did it the right way) that still leaves us with two problems:

1. How to change our money system so that we can have money without incurring debt.
2. How to get that new money into circulation.

Change the origination of money

I have heard people argue that Congress should create the money and make the loans instead of the Federal Reserve banking system. They think that changing the origination of the loans is some kind of a solution, a solution to what? It's true that if Congress created all the money as interest-bearing loans the Government, not the banks, would get the interest. But the people would still have to be in debt before there could be any money in circulation. There would be no way to create the money needed to pay the interest without someone else going deeper into debt. It is impossible to pay debt with borrowed "debt" dollars. All we can do is shift the debts from person to person or from a person to a business or from one business to a different business or from a business back to a person and then on to the next generation. Interest always increases the debt but it never increases the money supply.

Chapter 15
What is the best overall solution for Money Reform?

Before a solution can be found, we must truly understand what the problem or problems are. My studies and my research have convinced me that the love of money and the lust for power are the taproot of all the problems of America and probably the whole world. This taproot is fed from the roots of ignorance and apathy. This ignorance and apathy only exist because of the complete lawlessness of the men and women serving in our governments and our courts. This lawlessness is enabled and aided by our education systems, our media and our main line churches which are all controlled by the need for money and their almost total ignorance about how the monetary system really works.

The men and women serving in our governments and in our courts have turned this nation from a nation ruled by law into a nation ruled by the whims and greed of men. They refuse to honor and uphold the basic laws of our nation the constitutions of the States and of the States united, viewed in the light of the preamble of the Constitution of the United States:

> *"We the People of the United States, in Order to form a more perfect Union, establish Justice, insure domestic Tranquility, provide for the common defense, promote the general Welfare, and secure the Blessings of Liberty to ourselves and our Posterity, do ordain and establish this Constitution for the United States of America."*

What does it mean to establish Justice and insure domestic Tranquility? According to Webster's New World Dictionary *justice* is defined as *the quality of being righteous, fair and having sound reasoning. Tranquility* is defined as *being free from the state of being emotionally worried, troubled or anxious.*

Please take your nose off the grind stone and your feet off the treadmill and take a really good look around you. Do you honestly believe that our government's federal, state, or local officials are really working to make this a more perfect place to live? Do you really believe that our court system is really working to establish fairness and honesty and to insure that we live in a state of tranquility? Do you really think governments are working to secure our right to own property, when they tax people out of their homes, when they get too old to work, (especially after they have paid taxes for 45 years)?

Do you really think that they are working to insure our right to earn a good living for our families while working in the occupation of our choice?

How can we have any of these things in a nation where the people are getting deeper into debt every hour of their lives?

I have found that before a person can be convinced that changes are needed, it is necessary to get that person to honestly understand that there is a problem.

As Americans, we have became so accustomed to living under the strain of huge debts and oppressive taxes and being deceived by our educational system into believing that huge public and private debts are needed for our capitalistic system to function. It has become an accepted part of life to believe that huge, oppressive taxes are needed to fund government.

We are told over and over, that because we have so many new modern inventions that life is better than it has ever been. In some ways that is true. Most people have never stopped to think about how illogical it is to be working to produce all these new inventions and new forms of wealth that are supposed to make life easier, yet a large percentage of the people have ended up working longer hours, maybe two jobs and end up having little to show for it except greater and ever-increasing public and private debts. If we do think about it we are told not to worry because some how the next generation will pay it for us.

The information for the chart below was taken from a speech by David Walker, America's Total Debt Report, and from the website of the Federal Reserve Bank of New York. After Greg made this chart, I took it and went to visit with the president of the Minnesota State Senate, James P. Metzen, who is a banker in South St. Paul.

I ran into Senator Metzen as I got into the elevator to go up to his office.

I said "I would like to get a loan from you". I could see that he didn't quite know what to say. So I said that *"I really didn't want to get a loan. I just want to give you my financial statement and see what you think".* I then told him that my total worth was 38 thousand dollars. My total outstanding debts were 53 thousand dollars. I had bills coming due that totaled 51 thousand dollars. My cash on hand was 6.8 thousand dollars. "Is there any chance I could get a loan to pay my up coming obligations"? He looked at me and said *"Man, you are already broke".* At that point I gave him a copy of the chart below and said, *"if you change the thousands to trillions that is the financial statement of the United States."* Senator Metzen was still studying the chart

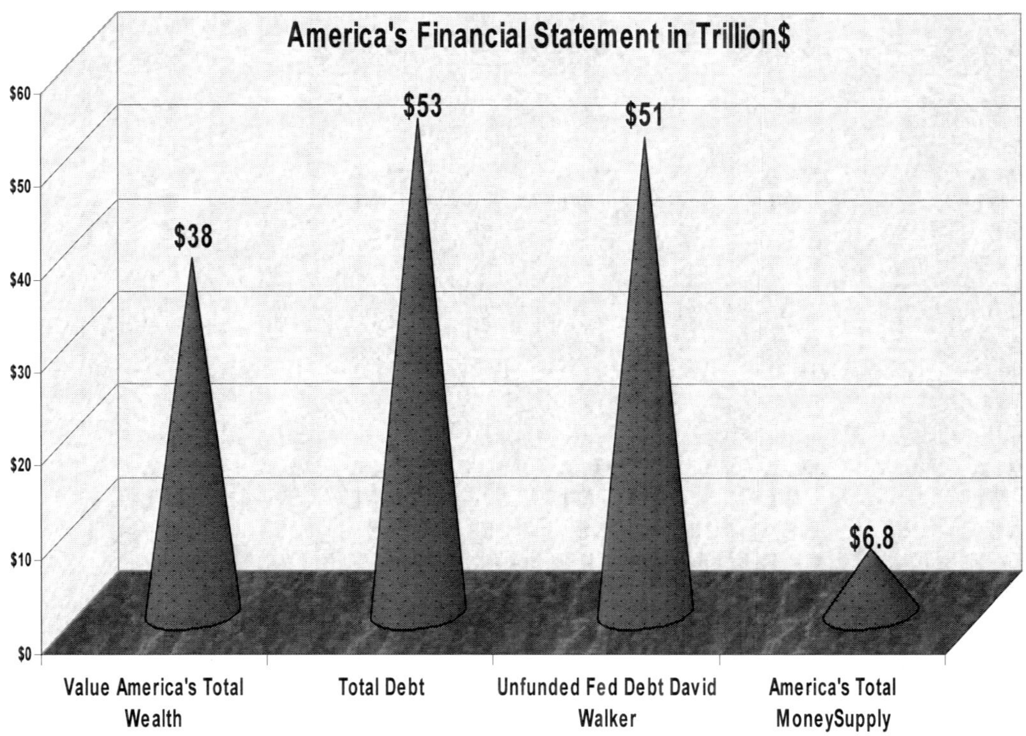

SOURCES:
($38) Speeches given by David Walker, *U.S. Comptroller General* & "Campaign Warns of Fiscal Doom", *St.Paul Pioneer Press*, 10/30/06
($53) America's Total Debt Report-*Michael Hodges*
($51) Speeches given by David Walker, U.S. Comptroller General
($6.8) *Federal Reserve Bank New York.*

as I walked away.

I don't think there are many charts that show more clearly what the United States Congress and the state governments have done to this nation by allowing the banks to control the money system and by allowing them to loan all the money to us at interest. There is no way we can have justice, tranquility, prosperity and the blessing of liberty with a debt/credit based money system!

We must find an effective way to educate ordinary Americans about our fraudulent, deceitful, and inequitable **DEBT MONEY SYSTEM.** We must find a way to get the people to stop and **think**. People must understand how unreasonable, unjust, immoral and destructive our debt money system is and that it steals from the people every day of their lives. They must realize that the real reason for huge debts, high taxes, cash flow problems, bankruptcies, inflation, recessions, lack of the ability to pay for health care, need for child care, and the other social and financial troubles we have, stems from the fact that **EVERY** dollar we use **must** first **be borrowed** into existence at interest. Hopefully this book will help you to understand these things and will enable you to get others to understand.

The banking interests keep telling us that inflation is bad and that it is caused by *"too much money chasing too few goods".* However, every business and almost every person I know produces goods or services and uses them to chase after money they cannot produce. If too much money is so bad, why do so many people buy lottery tickets hoping to win *"too much" money?* Why do even the richest of people always want more of it? I challenge you, to ask everyone you see which problem they would rather deal with: too much money or too much debt and the inability to pay their bills.

Most people are happy with the convenience of our current money system. Very few have ever stopped to question just how the money system works. They just know they seldom have enough money or that they just simply can't get enough money by working at the average job. They see that it is easy to get the buying power of money by using a credit card or by getting a loan. A credit card is just a loan without speaking face to face with a loan officer.

If debt, and the growth of debt, is not a problem, there is no reason to ever foreclose on anyone. If the growth of debt is so desirable, why not just rewrite the loans for everyone and let the debt grow, just like they do for the federal government and the financial system? If it is morally and financially OK for the people to have ever growing debt collectively through their government, it should be morally and financially OK for the people to have ever growing debt individually.

The concept of monetized debt is a deception upon the mind and a lie upon its face. If the concept of the promise to pay, is considered payment, was extended to the general population and not limited to just the banking system, there would not be any debt. As soon as you gave your promise to pay you would have also paid your debt. Hopefully at this point, we all agree that mandatory debt and interest on that debt are the biggest problems America and the world face. They need to be eliminated. There are only two ways to eliminate debt. **Repudiate it or pay it**.

In a debt money system, most everyone's assets are someone else's liabilities. Keep in mind that repudiation of someone's debt means destruction of someone else's assets. Most people I know would gladly have their *debts* wiped off the books. I have not met anyone who thinks it's a good idea to have their *assets* wiped off the books. We need to see if there is a way that the debts can be wiped off the books of the banks without the assets of the working people and the nations money supply being destroyed.

WEALTH is created by the combination of knowledge, labor and raw resources. Let's monetize our wealth instead of our debts! We must change our money system from a system based on DEBT to a money system based on production of WEALTH. That is the only way America can have a productive, prosperous, sound, and sustainable economy.

Wealth was the principle of the free coinage of gold and silver money. People worked to extract gold and silver, raw resources of the earth. They could take it to the mint and have it weighed, assayed and stamped into coined money. They then could take that monetized wealth home and spend/trade it into circulation debt-free to obtain other things made by other people.

This process created new wealth and new wealth money. It created money without debt or interest to anyone. It embodied the true concept of money which is simply a tool to enhance the trading of goods and services. The true concept of money is not to control people or to give power to a few at the expense of the many.

The trouble with gold and silver is not that the principles were wrong. Its deficiency is in the fact that there is not, nor has there ever been enough of it to make a good general medium-of-exchange!

There can be no true liberty unless mankind can live off of its own production without being forced to pay, in any form, tribute to anyone! We must introduce into commerce a medium-of-exchange that does not increase debt. This money must be an evidence of wealth production, and enter into circulation as payment for that production.

According to Webster's New World Dictionary, there are only two ways that production can be 'monetized:

(1) coin into money; To coin (using the word as a noun) money, one must take a piece of something that is produced such as gold, silver, platinum, copper, tobacco leaves, beads etc. process it and stamp it into uniform units and call it money through common consent or by the passage of law.

(2) coin (using as a verb) legalize as money. This can be accomplished by printing up a document that represents some type of production, or establishing an accounting system that will give the people a way to account for their production in a manner that can be used as their medium-of-exchange by common practice or the passage of law.

While considering how best to reform our money system, we must remember that we can't turn back the clock and pretend that we don't have all the debt and excess taxation that we have now. We have to start at this point in time. The first thing we need to do is forget about the concept of using gold and silver coins as our money. In America, we have never used gold and silver coins as our total general medium-of-exchange. Gold or silver coins have never even been the largest part of the total money supply.

I once thought the change to a wealth money system could be implemented gradually. As new wealth money was moved into circulation, the government, by law, would raise the reserve rate of the banking system two percent a month until the banking system would no longer be able to create any money. To prevent the banks from continuing to get unjust gains from the interest on outstanding loans, most of the interest income should be taxed from the banking system through an excess and fraudulent profits tax. The excess profits tax could be used to help fund the social security program and maybe pension funds until they are no longer needed. The banks could still provide checking and saving accounts, clear checks and provide other services as they do now as a 'fee for service' business.

The concept of having the government monetize production through the transportation system has been put into bill form, that we call The Money Reform Act. It was hand delivered to all members of Congress in 1991 and 1992. In 1993, nearly two million petition signatures were taken to Washington, D.C. by about 4,400 people requesting that Congress abolish the Federal Reserve and the income tax, and replace them with monetized production as set forth in The Money Reform Act. On May 9, 1995, Congressman Jon D. Fox, in a letter to Robert Power said that he had requested a hearing on the bill in the House Banking Committee. To my knowledge that was as far as the bill progressed.

I no longer believe that a slow transition is the best option. We have a continuously growing debt of over $53 trillion, not counting the $54 trillion of unfunded obligations (reported by David Walker, former Comptroller General of the United States and head of the United States Government Accountability Office). This does not include the big bailouts that are happening right now (late 2008 and early 2009). It is clear that the debt is now so huge and growing so rapidly that it would be impossible to ever produce enough to pay it. If the debt can't be paid, then we have no other option but to take a serious look at how to repudiate the debt and extinguish the debt dollars created by the issuance of credit, without causing a depression. As most taxes and all interest costs are eliminated, prices would come down. This will lead to positive and productive deflation.

We need to make a decision. Do we really want to be a nation of peace, justice, prosperity and liberty run under the rule of law, or do we want to remain a nation run by unbridled greedy men with great profits for only the few? We hope the people of this nation will join us in choosing to live in a nation of peace, justice, prosperity and liberty, run under the rule of law. If so, the first thing we need to do is to start changing our money from an evidence of debt to an evidence of wealth. We need to put money into circulation as **payment** for the peoples' productivity, not as any form of credit, debt or a promise to pay.

It has been my quest to find a way to reform our monetary system in the way that would be the most beneficial to the American people. I studied everything about money I could get my hands on. The U.S. Constitution states that Congress shall have the power to coin money and establish post offices and post roads. Using the word coin as a verb and combining these two Congressional duties into one would provide the perfect means to reform our monetary system. At the same time, it would monetize the production of the people and spend the money into circulation directly to the people doing the work, work that would benefit all of the people.

Thomas Jefferson stated: *(*words underlined and in parenthesis were added by the author*) "If the American People ever allow the banks to control the issuance of their currency, first by inflation* (now called (bubbles) *and then by deflation*, (now called recessions) *the banks and the corporations that will grow up around them* (because the bankers will always find a way to loan, (fund) the corporations they control) *will deprive the people of all property until their children* (us) *will wake up homeless on the continent their fathers occupied. The issuing power of money should be* taken from the banks and restored to Congress and the people to whom it belongs." The authors add to the above, "*The right of corporations to own businesses should be taken from them and restored to real people where it belongs."* These are the principles on which I have based my comprehensive plan to revitalize America.

Stated simply, there would be two ways to accomplish this: Federal Level or State Level. The difference would on the Federal level, this would go through Congress who has the power to create money under the U.S. Constitution or you could work through the State Chartered banking system. Process would be exactly the same. You would create the money as a bookkeeping entry (just like they do now) and SPEND it into circulation as payment for the project at hand. This would provide the greatest benefit to the majority of the people and would base the production of money on the productivity of the people.

At the same time, it leaves the average man free to govern himself. At this time this may be the only way to work ourselves out of the terrible mess in which Hamiltonian thinkers, economists and the bankers have put us in.

If interest is not outlawed and most of the debt wiped off the books, the newly created wealth money would flow to the banks through interest payments on the fraudulently created loans the banks already have on their books.

Monetizing the **complete** transportation system would require the least amount of change to free us from the financial mess we are in and save our economy from certain financial destruction. The transportation system would be built under much the same process it is now. The people themselves at the local level, not congressmen, would decide how and where the transportation system needs to be built, repaired or upgraded to best serve their needs. This could be done by the people living in the jurisdiction of local governments based on petitions or votes by 60% of the people requesting the project to be completed.

The local government could do it themselves, or they could work with their state government to hire the engineers needed to design the projects and call for bids from private contractors, exactly the way it is done now. The contractor meeting the bid specifications with the lowest and best bid would get the job. After the bid is accepted by the local (township, city, county, state) governments, they would send a copy of the contract to the Comptroller of the Currency requesting that the bid amount in money be created and delivered to them for distribution. The only oversight the Comptroller would have would be to make sure the project and the contractor were real. The contractor would use the money to pay fair and honest labor costs, raw material cost, heavy equipment cost, fuel cost and all other expenses and provide for his own profit.

The money would spread throughout the economy as the laborers and the producers of the raw materials and heavy equipment spend the new debt-free money to pay their own expenses, living costs, etc. The local government should take whatever actions are needed to ensure honest and fair competition.

The only change would be that **money** would come from the monetization of **wealth produced by** the people, **not** as monetized **debts** to the people.

The production of new wealth money and the outlawing of fractional banking and interest will take the interest and therefore much of the tax expenses out of the cost of production. This will cause prices to go down and the purchasing power of money will go up. In 2007, the U.S. Treasury paid $38.707 billion to the Federal Reserve. Source an April 1, 2008 letter from the board of Governors of the Federal Reserve System to Congressman John Shimkus signed by Laricke Blanchard Asst. to the Board.

There is a great need for upgrading and maintaining our transportation system. The wealth money created to accomplish this will stay in circulation and not be constantly extinguished as is the debt money.

The changes needed to move us from a debt money system to a wealth money system could be accomplished with only a few changes in our laws.

This change in the monetary system would allow the working people to have an honest medium-of-exchange and eliminate the need for debt. When the average person can earn enough from his production to take care of all his living expenses, there is no need for all the social programs we have. In a few years, this would lead to their elimination and the need for the taxes that fund them.

The transportation infrastructure will include all highways, roads, bridges, rail systems, tunnels, mass transit systems, personalized mass transit systems and the basics infrastructure of air transportation and other public commerce and postal needs. It would include maintaining existing infrastructure and new construction.

Everyone knows, our highways and roads are in terrible shape. Metropolitan areas are greatly overcrowded and they all need modernization, expansion, maintenance and repair. Most metropolitan areas are in dire need of personalized mass transit systems. Monetizing public infrastructure would provide billions of dollars of debt-free money and eliminate the need for billions of dollars of taxes and bonding at all levels of government.

The fractional banking system and interest on money must be outlawed. The math of interest shows that no country that allows interest can have a sustainable economy.

A new debt-free money system, plus the lowering of taxes at all levels of government, will give the people the opportunity to learn to live without their present addiction and servitude to credit.

All securities, notes, bonds or other evidence of indebtedness of the federal government, all fifty states governments and of all local government bodies shall be delivered to the General Accounting office of the United States Government. Where they will be audited to determine who the real lenders are and where they got the money that was lent. If the money that was loaned was simply created on the books of a lender at the time the loan was made, those loans would be declared fraudulent transactions and the debts simply written off the books. If the lender actually loaned earned income, then those debts would be paid with Federal Reserve Notes by the federal government and the borrower would be left free of debt.

Federal Reserve Notes are liabilities of the Federal Reserve banks, and they are obligations of the United States Government. Federal Reserve Notes are a first lien on all the assets of the Federal Reserve Banks and on all the collateral held against them. Congress has specified that Federal Reserve Banks must hold collateral equal in value to the Federal Reserve Notes that the bank receives. The idea was that if the Federal Reserve System were ever dissolved, the United States would take over the notes and would also take over the assets of the 12 Federal Reserve Banks. Source: a personal letter to me from the United States Treasury. This should be done. Then all the Federal Reserve Notes should be taken out of circulation and replaced with United States currency

We need to exercise our right to repeal the entire Federal Reserve Act as set forth in section 31 of that act and take over all the assets of the 12 Federal Reserve Banks as the act sets forth.

We need to criminalize fractional banking and the charging of interest for being the fraud that it is and for being the moral and oppressive crime that it is.

We need to reorganize the 12 Federal Reserve Banks and all the rest of the state and nationally chartered banks, into employee owned, fee-for-service, deposit holding, check clearing and money transfer businesses.

In the process of reorganizing the banks, we need to shut down and outlaw the credit card industry for being the illegal Ponzi scheme that it is, and wipe the credit card debt off the books. All the stock exchanges and futures exchanges should be outlawed and shut down as being nothing more than extensions of unlawful corporate Ponzi schemes and rigged gambling houses. No one should be able to buy and sell things that have not been produced. We also need to criminalize the buying and selling of currency.

All corporations need to be broken up and reorganized as small, independent, employee-owned and operated businesses. That should eliminate the great and unjust over payment for corporate executives and the underpayment of the average employee. As an example, Wal-Mart stores should all be turned into independent employee-owned stores. The big three auto corporations should be put into bankruptcy and reorganized into smaller employee-owned businesses.

If we are going to restore our manufacturing base, we will need to build new factories. They should be built and owned as employee-owned businesses. The finances to fund these new start-up businesses should come from no-interest loans. These loans could be administrated by an agency of the federal government like the FHA loaning offices we now have.

We could also have the government create new debt-free money to pay some of its unfunded obligations for example: social security, pension funds etc. (some of the funds for pensions from the big corporations might be recovered from the overpayment of the corporate executives.) These things could be done until there is enough wealth money in circulation for the people to eliminate what debt they might still have and have the time to accumulate enough savings so that help from government is no longer needed. Then these programs must be ended.

Book-entry money could also help to eliminate some of the inconvenience of every transaction needing to be completed by the transfer of printed currency. Book-entry accounting, in fact, might be the best way to start monetizing production. As it is the most common type of money we now use.

There is no reason why there would be price inflation when production is monetized, because the supply of goods and the money supply would stay in balance. All the debt money will be taken out of circulation as the debt free money is put into circulation. As the interest and taxes are wrung out of the system price inflation will cease to be an issue.

Wealth money is necessary before we can even begin to think about getting our government back within the bounds of the Constitution.

We also need to stop the monopoly on the law by judges and lawyers. Judges should never be lawyers and no lawyer should ever be allowed to be a judge. Any person pleading his own case should have the same power and right as any attorney and be treated the same. This debt money system has been challenged many times in court and would have already been declared unconstitutional, unlawful and the fraud that it is, had it not been for our very corrupt lawyer judges.

As debt is eliminated from all levels of society, most taxes can be eliminated at all levels of government. With a wealth based money system, interest and most taxes will be eliminated from the cost of doing business and the cost of living will go down in all levels of society. As the cost of living goes down, the purchasing power of paychecks would go up. As the cost of interest and most taxes are removed from the cost of doing business companies could afford to give wages increases. The people would no longer need all of the social programs that we now have. The people would receive many immediate, direct and indirect, benefits:

- First and foremost, the people would receive money issued as monetized production (wealth money). This will give them the ability to pay their current monthly bills without being forced into debt or having to force anyone else into debt to have money in circulation. This would allow the extinguishing of the debt without destroying the money supply.

◆ Better transportation systems that benefit all the people, and reduce our reliance on foreign oil.

◆ Lower gas prices due to elimination of all state and federal fuel and transportation taxes thereby lower freight costs,

◆ Less debt and greater savings will lead to, less need for government programs because people living in a wealthy debt-free nation would not need government help to pay their health care, child care, etc. costs,

◆ Smaller government,

◆ Lower taxes,

◆ More personal ownership,

◆ Lower cost of living,

◆ Higher standard of living,

◆ More economic freedom,

◆ Reduce social stress; more vacation and family time.

Thousands of people who now are working two and three jobs to maintain a decent standard of living, would only need to work one job to have a decent standard of living. Wages would be high enough so that once more, only one parent in a family would need one job to support the family. There would be enough <u>well paying</u> jobs for everyone. Jobs should and would pay better than welfare. It would be beneficial for people to get off the welfare rolls. A person should not have to suffer a loss of income to move from welfare to work.

I recall the time my parents sold a trailer home to a woman living on welfare. This lady was going to school to acquire the skills to get off welfare. About eight months after buying the trailer home, she was able to make the move from welfare to the work force. After about four months of being in the work force, she came to my parents with tears in her eyes. She didn't know what to do. Her job didn't pay her enough to enable her to make her house payments. She was being forced to decide whether to give up her job and go back on welfare so she could continue to make the payments on the trailer home, or keep her job and lose her home.

There are only three practical ways to bring about the needed changes:

1. Get the needed laws passed.
2. Get the needed changes by case law through the courts.
3. An executive order by an honest President.

Each way requires an enormous education process of the American people.

The east side of the United States Supreme Court Building in Washington is decorated with an eighteen-foot high sculpture of Moses holding the Ten Commandments. James Madison, our fourth President, called the Architect of our Constitution, wrote in the Federalist Papers, *"We have staked the whole future of American civilization not upon the power of government, far from it. We have staked the future upon the capacity of each and all of us to govern ourselves, to sustain ourselves, according to the Ten Commandments of God."*

Our sixth President, John Quincy Adams said, *"The highest glory of the American Revolution was that it connected in one indissoluble bond the principles of civil government with the principles of Christianity."*

If the principles of the Christian faith were summed up in just a few words they would be, "You shall love your neighbor as yourself." ***In other words, you would not do to your neighbor things that you would not want your neighbor to do to you.*** If you don't want to be in debt, you should not want your neighbor to be in debt so that you can have money. If you would not want your neighbor to take advantage of you, then you should not take advantage of your neighbor.

If life in America under the Federal Reserve Money System was summed up in just a few words, they would be; ***Dog eat dog, every man for himself and it's OK to misuse everyone you can, just as long as you gain monetary profit and or power.***

This is the way it has to be under a debt money system. Under America's monetary system today, if a man gains monetary success, then at least one or more persons must go deeper into debt or go bankrupt, in order to provide the money for other men to gain financial success and for others to just pay their interest.

If we are ever going to guide America toward the principle that all men have inherent rights to life, liberty and property and an equal right to keep for their own use the benefits of their own production, we must first guide America to an honest, moral, monetary system.

You have come to a fork in the **"Road of Choices",** the time has come when you must make a choice! Which one will you choose for yourself, your family and America? Will you choose?

- ◆ A Deceptive Money System,
- ◆ Ever-Increasing Taxes,
- ◆ Ever-Increasing Debts both Public and Private, placed upon your children and grandchildren
- ◆ Uncertain Future Full of Debt, Poverty, Socialism, and Fascism,

or

- ◆ An Honest Money System,
- ◆ Much Lower Taxes,
- ◆ Security for You and your Family,
- ◆ Higher Standard of Living,
- ◆ Wealth and Prosperity

There are only two choices. You can do ***nothing*** and the debts will grow until America will collapse under the weight of the interest bearing debt. Or, you will choose to have true prosperity and wealth. This means **you must work** for monetary reform so that our money represents wealth and freedom, not debt bondage.

As a general rule, people resist change, even if that change is for the better. The changes must come in such a way that the production and distribution of goods and services will not be disrupted. If people are allowed to hear the facts and understand the situation, they will welcome the change. We can't rely on America's mainstream media to educate our fellow Americans. That job is up to you. You must tell everyone you know and most of the people you meet about our disruptive, destructive monetary system.

WE CAN AND MUST CHANGE OUR MONEY SYSTEM TO HAVE TRUE LIBERTY AND PROSPERITY IN AMERICA!!!

All we need to do is to get 210 Congressmen and 51 Senators to read, study and understand the problem and act on putting the solution into practice. If the current office holders will not do it, we need ***to Elect People Who Will.***

If you would like to enjoy LOWER TAXES, LOWER PRICES, GREATER SAVINGS, A SECURE RETIREMENT, MONEY WITH GREATER BUYING POWER, WIDESPREAD PROSPERITY and greater PEACE-OF-MIND for yourself and all Americans, please devote a portion of your energies to making it happen.

"If all the bank loans were paid no one would have a bank deposit and there would not be a dollar of coin or currency in circulation. This is a staggering thought. We are completely dependent on the commercial banks. Someone has to borrow every dollar we have in circulation, cash or credit. If the banks create ample synthetic money we are prosperous; if not, we starve. We are absolutely without a permanent money system. When one gets a complete grasp of the picture the tragic absurdity of our hopeless position is almost incredible, but there it is. It (the banking problem) is the most important subject intelligent persons can investigate and reflect upon." Robert H. Hemphill Credit Manager of the Federal Reserve Bank of Atlanta

Do you consider yourself an intelligent person? If so, it's time you demand an honest, permanent money system.

Modern Money Secrets hiding in plain sight:

You cannot borrow your way out of debt!
There could be a better life after debt!